Environment and the law

An introduction for environmental scientists and lawyers

John F. McEldowney
Sharron McEldowney

LONGMAN

Addison Wesley Longman
Addison Wesley Longman Limited,
Edinburgh Gate, Harlow,
Essex CM20 2JE, England
and associated companies throughout the world

First published 1996

British Library Cataloguing in Publication Data
A catalogue entry for this title is available from the British Library

ISBN 0-582-22712-7

Library of Congress Cataloging-in-Publication Data
A catalog entry for this title is available from the Library of Congress

Set by 7 in 10/12 baskerville
Printed in Great Britain
by Henry Ling Ltd., at the Dorset Press, Dorchester, Dorset

Contents

This book is intended to provide environmental scientists and lawyers with an explanation and understanding of the main areas of environmental law. Included within the scope of environmental law is an explanation of the various institutions, agencies and organisations that have a role in environmental law. The book is also intended to provide lawyers with an explanation of the scientific and economic developments that provide the context for an understanding of the law. In seeking to address both legal and scientific audiences, it is hoped that the book will fill a gap in the existing literature.

Environmental law is a fast changing and rapidly developing area of law. It is clear that environmental law has come of age, offering its own distinctive methodology and approach to problem solving through a combination of regulatory approaches that include licensing conditions, inspection procedures, the use of the courts and different modes of self-regulation. This is a period of widely different perceptions about the role of regulation and the state. Privatisation strategies entail the movement from public to private ownership. In the case of the main utilities such as water, gas, coal and electricity this has profound effects on how the environment is best protected. At the same time there is considerable pressure to provide deregulation strategies, thereby reducing government control over the industry. Environmental law seeks to provide in many instances a regulatory structure to prevent pollution and avoid excessive costs. Ensuring a balance is a challenge that faces the future development for environmental law.

Environmental law also offers its own distinctive conceptual framework found in developments such as environmental impact assessment and integrated pollution control and the adoption of new institutions and ideas such as the recently created Environment Agency under the Environment Act 1995 and the European Environment Agency. European Community law is increasingly an integral part of UK environmental law. Wherever relevant, an attempt is made to integrate an analysis of Community law into the explanation of environmental law. At the same time there are areas such as planning law where UK law maintains its own distinctiveness. It is also important to consider areas where the UK has not fully implemented Community law and the discord between the Community and the UK can have importance in the future development of the law.

Environmental science is in fact a composite of a number of different disciplines. Environmental chemists, ecologists, microbiologists, hydrologists, environmental technologists and ecotoxicologists all contribute basic understanding and techniques that make environmental science the umbrella covering many disciplines. The challenge is to ensure that these different areas work efficiently and constructively in defining environmental harm and risk and designing mechanisms to monitor the environment. The future development of environmental law should ideally not be reactive, following on from the recognition of a problem, but proactive, avoiding harm to the environment and health. This requires environmental science to be predictive and efficient in anticipating the future impact on the environment of pollutants. As the end of the twentieth century approaches it is appropriate to consider future directions facing environmental law and science as well as reflecting on what has been achieved to date. In writing this book it is hoped that the challenges facing the two disciplines of law and environmental science will be approached by an understanding of the value of both disciplines co-operating in tackling environmental problems.

We owe a great debt to the many people who kindly gave of their time and assisted us in different ways in the writing of this book. At the University of Warwick, Gavin Anderson, Hugh Beale, Roger Burridge, Wyn Grant, Mike McConville, Han Somsen, Ann Stewart, David Storey, David Ormandy and Geoffrey Wilson deserve particular mention. Han Somsen, David Ormandy and Roger Burridge read many of the chapters and provided welcome advice and materials. At the University of Westminster, Jenny George, Geoff Holt, Ann Rumpus and Brian Knights deserve mention and at the University of Brighton, Steve Waite for his help and encouragement. At the University of London, thanks are due to Patrick McAuslan.

The Library staff at the University of Warwick have proved, as always, unstinting in their support, in particular Jolyon Hall and Liz Anker have been responsive to our demands for information and official publications. Finally, we owe thanks to Longman, our publishers, and to the anonymous reviewers of the manuscript, and to Gavin Adams for help with proof reading.

John and Sharron McEldowney
Kenilworth
August 1995

Acknowledgement

We are grateful to Cambridge University Press for permission to reproduce Figs 2.1 and 2.2 from Figs 2 and 6 in Spencer, J.R. (1989) *Jackson's Machinery of Justice*.

Whilst every effort has been made to trace the owners of copyright material, in a few cases this has proved impossible and we take this opportunity to offer our apologies to any copyright holders whose rights we may have unwittingly infringed.

Table of Cases

European Court

Table of Legislation

Table of Statutory Instruments

European Legislation

EC Directives

PART I
Introduction

Part I provides a general introduction to law. Scientists and others interested in environmental law must have a basic understanding of the general principles of law. Familiarity with a wide range of sources and information is required before it is possible to understand the legal analysis of enviromental problems. Perhaps the greatest difficulty confronting the non-legal specialist is the question of whether an environmental problem has a legal dimension. At the end of each chapter there is a short bibliography for the purposes of further reading and discovering more detailed information about environmental law.

1 General introduction to law

▶ What is environmental law?

The starting point for the study of environmental law is to explain the meaning of the term 'environmental law'. We begin with the question: what is law? In everyday life ordinary people are aware of rules and agreements that are honoured and obeyed. Some rules are obeyed because there is a strong moral sanction. In family life rules may be informally based and any sanction may be derived from the social behaviour of the family. Other rules in society are obeyed because there is a fear of prosecution, fine or imprisonment. In society as a whole, law is more formally defined than in social relationships. The failure to obey a law carries with it a possible sanction or punishment. This may involve prosecution after the police have collected evidence and the Crown Prosecution Service agrees there should be a prosecution in the courts.

Law may be generally defined as a way of regulating human behaviour. *Environmental law* is a term that is used to include the various laws that are applied to the environment. Legal definitions of environmental law are more narrow. The Environmental Protection Act 1990 defines the environment as consisting of all, or any, of the following media, namely the air, water and land; and the medium of air includes the air within buildings and the air within other natural or man-made structures above or below the ground'. This describes the focus of most environmental law. More recently s. 4 of the Environment Act 1995 creates an Environment Agency for England and Wales and for Scotland the Scottish Environment Protection Agency. General environment and recreational duties, which are devolved on both Agencies, are provided under the 1995 Act. Responsibilities for the environment are defined in terms of pollution control and include a Code of Practice covering environmental and recreational duties. Ministers may give the new Agency guidance 'towards the objective of achieving sustainable development' (see s. 4(3) of the Environment Act 1995).

Another way to describe environmental law is to concentrate on the harm caused to the environment by human activity. Pollution by humans may harm the environment and the focus of pollution laws is to protect the environment by limiting or preventing human activity that may be deleterious to the environment. The Environmental Protection Act 1990 defines pollution as 'the release into any environmental medium from any process of substances which are capable of causing harm to man or any other living organisms supported by the environment'. In fact, defining the scope of environmental law is difficult and lacks precision. In part this is due to the difficulties faced by scientists in establishing environmental damage or harm.

Scientific definitions of pollution often contain phrases that relate to the ecological injury caused by pollutants. For example, Holdgate (1979) defines pollution as 'the introduction by man into the environment of substances or energy liable to cause hazards to human health, harm to living resources and ecological damage, or interferences with legitimate uses of the environment'. Traditionally, the harm attributed to a particular pollutant has been established in terms of its toxicity to humans and to selected species of animals, e.g. *Daphnia*, and plants, e.g. *Lemna*. This is far easier to assess and quantify than the less specific criterion of ecological damage. The interdisciplinary science of ecotoxicology has grown from the need to understand, quantify and predict the fate and potential adverse effects of pollutants in the environment. The procedures used to evaluate the environmental risk of a given pollutant are primarily based on the physicochemical properties of the pollutant and single-species or multi-species toxicity tests (see Chapters 8 and 10). There are clear advantages in an emphasis on the use of such procedures. They offer a relatively simple, rapid and reproducible assessment of safe environmental concentrations of any given pollutant. The results from such assessments can be incorporated into environmental regulation. The harm to one or even several species caused by a pollutant, however, may not give a true picture of the damage caused to other species or to any given ecosystem. This is more properly assessed in terms of the pollutants' impact on community dynamics and energy flow through an ecosystem, and pollutants' impact on species diversity. The interactions between organisms, community dynamics and energy flow through ecosystems are highly complex and difficult to determine (Figs 1.1 and 1.2). Even the diversity of species is difficult to establish. Even so it is for scientists to better define and assess ecological damage; to offer realistic schemes to predict the impact of pollutants on an ecosystem; and to indicate safe concentrations of a pollutant in the environment. This should be done on an ecosystem-by-ecosystem basis since some will be more vulnerable to perturbation than others. It may then be possible to extend the legal definition beyond 'harm to man and any other living organisms', to a broader ecological definition protecting the structure, function and biodiversity of ecosystems. Clearly, mistakes have been made in the past. For example, the damaging effect of organochlorine pesticides through their longevity, bioconcentration

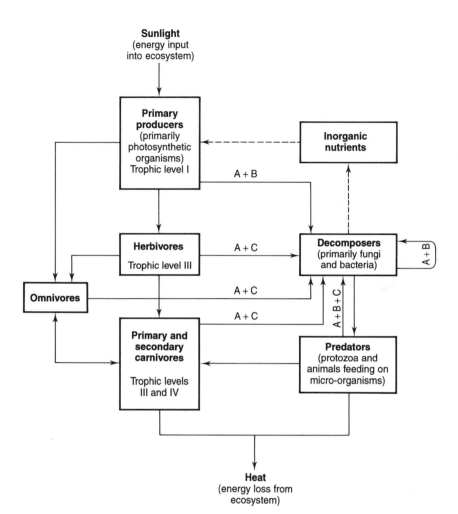

Fig. 1.1 Schematic diagram of energy flow through an idealised food web. A food web is a number of linked food chains. Arrows represent energy flow: A, dead cells and/or dead organisms; B, excretion; C, wastes.

and biomagnification (see Chapters 8 and 10) was not predicted. It is the scientific community that must devise appropriate procedures to predict accurately the environmental impact of pollutants and human activities, and to help devise an appropriate legal framework for environmental protection.

Environmental law receives more attention today than in the past. This is because during the past 20 years there has been a greater public awareness of environmental issues which have been brought to the

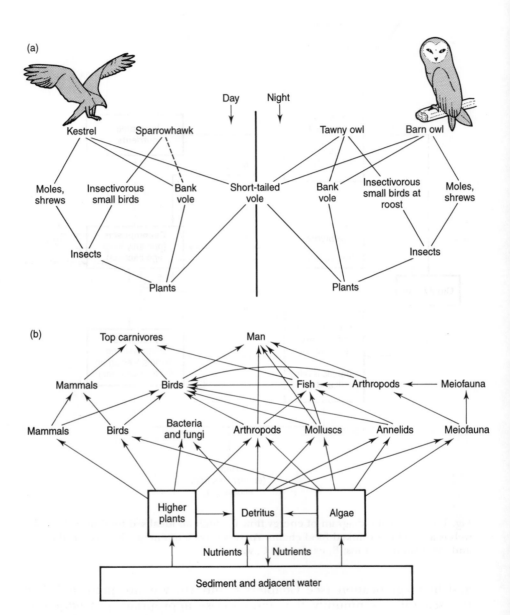

Fig. 1.2 (a) A highly simplified food web of an English oak wood. (b) Salt marsh. The complexity of community interactions is clear even in these simplified examples. (Reproduced from McEldowney *et al.*, 1993).

public's attention by major world events. The acute environmental, agricultural and health effects of the accidental release of large amounts of radioactive material into the atmosphere from the Chernobyl nuclear power plant and the subsequent contamination of large parts of Europe caused immense public concern. The chemical disaster at Bhopal, which caused the death or serious injury of thousands of people, starkly high-lighted the dangers associated with parts of the chemical industry. Pressure groups such as Friends of the Earth and Greenpeace bring media attention to specific environmental issues. Membership of the European Union provides a common forum for Member States to debate matters of common interest, including the environment.

The protection of the environment is an important issue in the politics of many European countries. This is reflected in election results favouring political parties that support measures to control and ameliorate environmental damage. Law depends on the social, political and economic context of society. In the United Kingdom, the political party in power has a strong influence over what laws are passed in Parliament. Public opinion influences what is socially acceptable. Laws are not always enforced or uniformly obeyed. Some laws are not respected and fall into disuse. There is always a difficult choice if the government of the day enacts unpopular laws that may not be obeyed. Currently, all the major political parties in the United Kingdom have linked environmental protection to their political agenda. This is a recognition that there is public concern about environmental issues. Even the international political agenda has been influenced by public consciousness. There are global environmental problems which are beyond solution at national level. The impact of large atmospheric con-centrations of carbon dioxide – primarily through fossil fuel burning and deforestation (see Chapter 12) – on global climate change is a topic for considerable public and scientific debate. The accumulation of chlorofluorocarbons (CFCs) in the stratosphere, associated with ozone depletion, an increase of UV irradiance at ground level and, therefore, greater risk of skin cancers, is another example of an environmental problem considered at an international level (see Chapter 12).

Law is rarely static. Environmental law is constantly changing to keep pace with developments and social change. In the eighteenth century, before major industrialisation in Britain, environmental problems were treated as part of the general law. Environmental law may be traced back to the need for public intervention as a response to public health problems in the nineteenth century. Pressure for the reform of public health from Edwin Chadwick (1801–90) resulted in major legislation such as the Public Health Act 1848. Proper sanitation, the prevention of diseases and the improvement of housing, through the adoption of minimum standards, were all concerns of subsequent legislation in the 1870s – notably the Local Government Board Act 1871 and the Public

Health Act 1875 and 1879. A balance had to be worked out between intrusive government intervention into the rights of private property and the need to require high standards of public health. The Alkali Acts 1863 and 1868 (see: the Alkali, etc., Works Regulation Act 1906) created a central inspectorate with wide discretionary powers including prosecution under the criminal law. Similar inspectorates were created for river pollution (Rivers Pollution Prevention Act 1876). Prosecutions were extremely rare and the inspectorate was responsive to the argument that unreasonable costs could not be borne by private manufacturers when jobs and profits might be put in jeopardy. A compromise was worked out between heavy-handed enforcement and incremental improvements. Gradually health standards improved. The 'best practicable means' ensured that the costs of new improved technologies were introduced as profits remained buoyant. The British approach to environmental regulation depended not on heavy judicial intervention or prosecution but on the spirit of a sensitive, albeit incremental, approach to change.

Today environmental law is found in various specialised laws dealing with specific areas of the environment such as water, air and land. Increasingly, environmental law is found in legislation, largely, though not exclusively, based on initiatives taken by the European Community.

Environmental law is also found in various subject areas of law such as criminal law, contract law, tort law, property law and administrative law. Today, many environmental lawyers believe, with justification, that environmental law as a distinct subject has developed in its own right. This means that environmental law possesses its own concepts which provide principles that are distinctive and unique to the subject. Science and scientific expertise are required for the study and development of environmental law to a greater extent than in many other legal disciplines. Kiss and Shelton in their *Manual of European Environmental law* (Cambridge, 1993, p.7) note that 'rules of nature, found in biology, chemistry and physics, are basic to environmental law'. Environmental law depends on science to assess and predict the environmental impact of many human activities. Scientific studies often seek explanations and analysis of environmental problems, and the data from such research may be used to suggest solutions to the problems. The scientific community has addressed the issue of environmental maintenance and amelioration in a variety of ways – from developing clean technologies, to remediation of contaminated land, to design of synthetic chemicals to ensure limited longevity in the environment. Equally essential, however, in the control and prevention of pollution is co-operation between scientists, lawyers and regulators. Environmental law must be flexible and adaptable to the changing needs of the environment. It must also respond to scientific advancement whether in environmental monitoring techniques or in the control and amelioration of pollution.

Interdisciplinary collaboration is essential if the environment is to be satisfactorily protected.

Despite the coming of age of environmental law, there is reliance on many of the principles developed from other branches of the law. Environmental lawyers must be skilled in understanding public and private law. A knowledge of European Community law (Chapter 3) is essential as the EC has developed environmental policies that have led to changes in environmental law. European environmental law is composed of national, regional and international laws. These reflect competing and sometimes contradictory national priorities. Since environmental problems do not recognise territorial boundaries, there is also a need to understand international law.

▶ Techniques of environmental law

Environmental law has as its main objective the protection of some aspect of the environment and its effects on people or wildlife. Achieving the goal of protecting the environment involves the activities of environmental protection agencies, such as the new Environment Agency under the Environment Act 1995, local and central government and various pressure groups. The policies pursued in protecting the environment are also important in understanding the basis of the legal rules. Policy considerations involve assessing public opinion, understanding commercial and economic constraints and often balancing the interests of the consumer, the citizen, and different lobbying groups on environmental issues. Environmental policies develop at different levels of government activity. Environmental law is found in the national law of the United Kingdom, European Community law and international law. Understanding environmental policy is essential as an aid to interpreting the application of legal powers and in providing the context for an understanding of environmental problems. Analysing environmental policy is an essential part of understanding the legal and scientific basis of environmental law.

Throughout this book the reader will discover the wide variety of means available for the enforcement of environmental law. Criminal sanctions may impose a fine or imprisonment. Civil remedies such as injunctions or damages prevent some harm from occurring or provide compensation for injury sustained. There are various controls over environmental pollution provided through legal means. Licences or contracts may regulate and set standards of behaviour. For example, the water companies are required to comply with standards set by contract *and* in legislation in the performance of their tasks of providing wholesome water. Enforcement agencies such as the National Rivers Authority (now the new Environment Agency under the Environment

Act 1995) are given wide statutory powers to inspect, report and take action in respect of river pollution.

In addition to the more traditional legal means to redress environmental problems there are new developments that set directions for the future of environmental law. The introduction of integrated pollution control (see Chapter 6) provides standards for products or processes rather than for discharges or emissions.

In recent years interest has grown in the use of economic means to regulate the environment. Experiments in this form of environmental control involve using taxation rather than legal sanctions. For example, the use of an energy tax to reduce consumption of energy may be more effective than either criminal or civil sanctions. There is some discussion of a proposed 'carbon tax' intended to reduce the burning of fossil fuels. Conservation is seen not only as environmentally friendly but cost efficient. The principle that 'the polluter pays' is seen as a preventive measure to encourage waste avoidance and prevent pollution. Encouraging the use of one energy resource in preference to another is contained in s. 32 of the Electricity Act 1989 in the form of a non-fossil fuel obligation. This provides a requirement on distributors of electricity produced from fossil fuels such as gas, coal or oil to contract for a specific minimum of electricity produced from nuclear and renewable sources of energy such as wind, solar, geothermal, tidal and biofuels including refuse and landfill gas (see Chapter 9). The likely cost of energy produced from non-fossil fuel sources is higher than electricity produced from fossil fuel. To bridge the cost gap, under s. 33 of the Electricity Act 1989 there is a fossil fuel levy. This acts as a compensation to the electricity distributor for the purchase of more expensive non-fossil fuel.

Lawyers require a knowledge of the economic, political and scientific nature of environmental problems. Scientists interested in understanding environmental law require an explanation of how laws are framed and the nature of legal analysis relevant to environmental problems. The starting point is to consider the sources of law.

Sources of law

The development of general rules or laws for society as a whole is a complex process. The United Kingdom is unique among other European countries in not having a written constitution. This has the result that the origin of legal rules that apply to the environment is the same as legal rules in general. There are two major sources of environmental law: legislation and judge-made or case law. Environmental law is also to be found in the wide policy discretion delegated to ministers and contained in a wide variety of circulars, guidance notes and rules of practice.

▶ Legislation and statutory interpretation

Legislation

Legislation, meaning Acts of Parliament, more commonly called statutes, is usually introduced on the initiative of government ministers. Parliament makes legislation in the form of public Acts that generally apply throughout the country or private Acts which apply restrictively to specific activities or individuals or groups. Before 1972 it was common for local authorities to make regular use of private Acts to enable them to perform many important tasks. Since 1974, many local authorities rely on widely drafted statutory powers contained in public Acts which consolidate the law.

Environmental law is to be found mainly in statutory form. This is a reflection of the recent enactment of many statutes in environmental law such as the Environmental Protection Act 1990, the Water Resources Act 1991, the Water Industry Act 1991 and the Environment Act 1995. Related areas of law which affect the environment, such as planning law, are also based on statute such as the Town and Country Planning Act 1990.

Major statutes that apply to the environment are usually found in consolidation Acts containing broadly drafted and generally expressed sections setting out principles of environmental law. A recent example of specific legislation is the recent Environment Act 1995 which contains 125 sections and repeals and amends much previous legislation. The 1995 Act clarifies certain areas of law such as the law relating to National Parks and introduces a statutory National Waste Strategy. There is an abundance of detail and technical law contained in such statutes. Often the framework of the statute includes long schedules containing complex legal information setting out processes and procedures. The complexity of the legislation is usually a feature of modern statutes. This is partly attributable to the difficulty of enacting laws to cover environmental problems. Legal definitions may be differently worded than if the same definition were expressed in scientific terms. It is often very difficult, in areas where there is scientific information and scientific criteria, to provide adequate legal expressions to take account of a scientific meaning. Environmental legislation in the United Kingdom must also comply with EC law. This adds to the complexity of the law. EC law is often drafted in a different style than UK law. Principles of EC law may contain conceptual differences from UK law. All these matters must be taken into account in the drafting of environmental legislation.

Environmental law statutes may contain unclear or wide definitions but they are supplemented by detailed rules contained in delegated legislation. Delegated legislation is a term which refers to rules, orders, circulars or schemes which supplement the primary or main legislation. Powers to make delegated legislation are contained in Acts of Parliament. In most statutes the power is given to the Secretary of State or some member of the government. Frequently the power to make delegated legislation involves the use of statutory instruments. For example, the Electricity Act 1989 provides for statutory instruments, the Fossil Fuel Levy Regulations 1990 (SI 1990 No. 266), to implement the details of the fossil fuel arrangements discussed above.

The widespread use of delegated legislation such as the General Development Order and the Use Classes Order in planning law is no different from other areas of law. Many lawyers express concern at the way statutory instruments are made and the lack of detailed Parliamentary debate on their contents.

A common difficulty encountered when using either statutes or statutory instruments is the question of when the law has come into force. Commencement dates may differ for sections of the statute and implementation of a particular section may require a statutory instrument. The publications *Is it in Force* (Butterworths) and *Current Law* (Sweet and Maxwell) provide useful information on the commencement dates of legislation.

Statutory interpretation

The interpretation of statutes is often of bewildering complexity. There is a constant search for the most suitable meaning of words. This can lead to disagreement and unpredictable results. Predicting how a court might interpret words in the general context of environmental problems involves considerable skill. Nowadays it is more common than in the past for the courts to look at reports of Parliamentary debates in Hansard as an aid to interpretation. The use of Hansard in certain circumstances as an aid to interpretation has recently been approved by the House of Lords in *Pepper* v. *Hart* [1993] 1 All ER 42. Lawyers find discussion and analysis contained in the reports of Parliamentary Select Committees very helpful. In addition, and as a unique institution, there is, since 1970, a standing Royal Commission on Environmental Pollution. To date it has produced 17 reports and its permanent secretariat has given it added authority. The Royal Commission has helped focus Parliamentary attention on the environment and promoted access to information on environmental problems.

Lawyers use various aids in the interpretation of statutes. These consist of rules or presumptions about how words in a statute may be interpreted. Taken together they form what are called principles of statutory interpretation that are generally applied in English law. Different rules apply in the interpretation of European Community law. The continental style of drafting only sets out general broad principles. This leaves the exact details to be filled in by the judges, who are expected to promote the general legislative purpose of the law.

In English law the principles of statutory interpretation consist of rules and presumptions as follows.

The literal rule

The literal rule is used to refer to the interpretation of words in a statute that seeks to give words their plain, ordinary or literal meaning. Courts set their objective as discovering the Parliamentary intention behind the statute. Reference to the dictionary meaning of words may be used as an aid to interpretation.

The golden rule

The golden rule may be used to modify the literal rule to avoid any absurdity. If the words used in legislation are ambiguous, the golden rule allows the court to avoid the absurdity and adopt a meaning that is suitable for the purpose intended rather than have an absurd outcome. The golden rule may also be used in preference to the literal rule. Where the courts decide that public policy requires an interpretation beyond the literal interpretation of the words, the golden rule may ensure effect is given to public policy.

The mischief rule

The mischief rule is also referred to as the rule in *Heydon's* case (1584) 3 Co. Rep. 7a. This rule allows the courts to examine the law before the statute was made in order to ascertain the nature of the *mischief* which the statute was intended to remedy. The mischief rule allows the courts some discretion in finding the construction of the statute that best applies to the facts of the case. For example in *Maidstone Borough Council* v. *Mortimer* [1980] 3 All ER 552 the defendant cut down an oak tree protected by a preservation order under s. 102(1) of the Town and Country Planning Act 1971. Maidstone Borough Council prosecuted the defendant in the magistrates' court. The defendant successfully defended cutting down the tree on the basis that knowledge of existence of the preservation order was a necessary ingredient of the offence under s. 102(1). The council appealed to the Divisional Court. Mr Justice Park held that knowledge of the existence of the preservation order was not an ingredient of the offence and convicted the defendant. Interpreting the 1971 Act, the mischief rule allowed the court to consider what s. 102(1) of the 1971 Act was intended to achieve. The court considered that it was of the 'utmost public importance that such trees should be preserved'. The mischief the statute intended to prevent, namely the felling of trees, should not be undertaken without the local authority's consent.

Ejusdem generis rule

In applying the rules of interpretation the court may read the statute as a whole to understand the overall context of the law. Normally the courts give attention to the *ejusdem generis* rule, meaning that general words which follow particular words are limited in meaning to those of the particular words. The courts may follow certain presumptions when interpreting a statute. Property rights or private rights are not impliedly interfered with unless there are very clear words. The individual's liberty is presumed not to be interfered with unless Parliament has provided clear words. Parliament is assumed not to have altered the common law unless the statute expressly makes this clear. There are also presumptions that for a criminal offence there must be proof of the requisite intention or guilty mind before the accused may be convicted. Statutes are generally presumed not to have retrospective effect. The courts presume that crimes are not to be created by Parliament retrospectively because it would be oppressive or abhorrent to do so.

There is no hard and fast rule as to the rule of interpretation or presumption the courts may wish to follow. Courts exercise a discretion according to the context of the law and the facts of the case. Deciding what factors may influence the courts' discretion in environmental law requires the possession of accurate information about the nature of environmental problems. Access to information is a recurrent theme in both UK and EC legislation (see: Environmental Information Regulations 1992 (SI 1992 No.32400) and EC Directive 90/313). Scientific expertise may assist the courts in understanding environmental problems.

▶ Reading a statute

Statutory interpretation is aided by the way the statute is drafted. The preamble to the Act sets forth the need for the legislation and sometimes the effect the legislation is intended to have. The long title of an Act may assist the court in cases of ambiguity. It explains the purpose behind the legislation. The short title to an Act provides a general description of the Act but rarely is a guide to interpretation. Modern Acts of Parliament may have headings delineating particular sections or parts of the Act. There are marginal notes and side notes. These are not part of the Act and are not discussed in Parliament. They may provide some help in finding the sense of a d'ff···lt ·ection but are not normally used by the courts. Finally, there are schedules to many modern Acts. There is an increasing tendency to use the schedules to contain more detail than is possible in the main part of the Act. This is to avoid the main part of the Act becoming unduly cluttered. This has the disadvantage that often reference must be made to the schedules of the Act to understand the main content of each of the sections.

▶ Judicial precedent

Case law or judge-made law is an important source of law. English law is based on a common law system. Judge-made law, with the exception of EC law, is inferior to and can be overruled by statute or delegated legislation. In the case of EC law the judgments of the Court of Justice of the EC are binding on member states. The significance of EC law is more fully explained in Chapter 3. It is important to recognise how EC law has shaped the policy, principles and future direction of environmental law in the United Kingdom.

The contribution of judge-made law to the legal system is significant. In subjects such as contract or tort law judicial precedents are developed in advance of statutory principles. When statutes were passed in the nineteenth century they often enacted principles that had been developed by judges over many centuries. In environmental law, cases decided by judges are likewise important in developing the law and establishing legal principles. It is, however, most unlikely that the vast amount of statutory powers applied in environmental law will ever be given exact judicial interpretation in a decided case. Environmental lawyers have to read much statutory material in the knowledge that it is unlikely that the courts will ever be called upon to interpret the meaning of the legislation. Reading statutory material without the benefit of any judicial guidance is the source of much environmental law.

The doctrine of judicial precedent is fundamental to English law. The doctrine involves application of the principle of *stare decisis*, meaning that like cases should be decided alike. This means that higher court decisions are usually binding on lower courts. For example the Court of Appeal is generally bound to follow its own previous decisions and each court is bound to follow the decisions of a court above it. In Chapter 2 there is an explanation of the court structure and the hierarchy of courts. It is sufficient to note how judicial precedent has developed.

▶ Reading and interpreting cases

There is considerable skill involved in reading and interpreting legal cases. As a preliminary matter a good case note is essential for the understanding of the case. The date of the case, the court where the case is considered, the name and status of the judge should first be noted. The head note in the law report of the case contains some key words and phrases which should also be noted. The head note is written by the law reporter and contains a brief summary of the case and the legal issues involved. This is a useful guide to understanding the case but it does not represent the law. The most reliable way to ascertain the current law and the legal significance of a case is to read the judgment in the case.

When reading the judgment in the case first it is useful to identify the sources of law interpreted in the case. Some legal decisions are based on statutory interpretation with few references to previous cases. The main sections of the statute should first be noted. Finding and understanding the relevant section of the statute may involve some detective work as judges sometimes do not include in their judgments the full details of the relevant section of the Act. It is also important to note the main cases cited in the judgment. These may have to be read in full at a later date to appreciate their legal significance. The case-law method in English law involves the reading of a large number of cases. When reading a judgment it is important to understand how a judgment is written.

The decision of a judge involves the *ratio decidendi* and *obiter dictum* of the case. The *ratio decidendi* of the case is the principle of law on which the decision is based. In delivering a judgment, the judge outlines the facts of the case proved from the evidence. The application of the law to the facts is accompanied by reasons for his or her decision. The judge may also speculate on other issues which may have made the case special or similar to other decided cases. If the facts of the case had been different the judge might have reached a different conclusion. This is an *obiter dictum*, or something that is said by the way. Only the *ratio decidendi* of a case is binding in later cases because it represents the relevant law applied to the particular facts. The *obiter dictum* is, however, persuasive in argument in future cases.

Deciding what part of the judgment is *obiter dictum* and not *ratio decidendi* may require several close readings of the judgment. Very often the *ratio decidendi* of a case is not discovered until subsequent decisions discussing the case set out what other judges think the *ratio decidendi* of the case is.

In cases where there is more than one judge, for example in the Court of Appeal, there may be three judgments, or in the House of Lords there may be five judgments. Each judgment requires very careful reading. There may not be common agreement between the judges. The views of the dissenting judge do not state what the law is at that time. Future courts may decide that the dissenting judgment expresses a principle of law better than the majority and make reference to the dissenting judgment.

In practice a higher court may overturn or reverse the decision of a lower court on appeal in the same case. Similarly a higher court may overrule a principle laid down by a lower court in a different case. It is possible for a court to distinguish a case on the facts or on the point of law involved. This is a useful device to avoid being bound by a decision which a court feels is inconsistent with the way the law should develop. Techniques in distinguishing cases provide the courts with the opportunity to re-think the law in the light of new facts or unforeseen consequences.

Experiencing difficulty in interpreting cases is not unusual. Judges may wish to draw a line between what the courts are entitled to consider when interpreting the law and what is best left to the Government of the day in terms of policy (see: *Tesco Stores Ltd* v. *Secretary of State for the Environment and others* [1995] 2 All ER 636). Textbooks and articles in law journals may provide some assistance in understanding how the law has developed and the significance of a particular case. Such works may be cited in court and while they may be influential they are not always persuasive.

References and further reading

Law

Understanding environmental law first requires consideration of the policy that underlines the law. See: *This Common Inheritance: Britain's Environmental Strategy* (Cm1200,1990). A provocative and informative analysis of environmental issues may be found in Ben Jackson, *Poverty and the Planet* (Penguin, 1990). A general introduction to law may be found in: Glanville Williams, *Learning the Law* (Stevens, 1987); Philip Kenny, *Studying Law* (Butterworths, 1991); Terence Ingman, *The English Legal Process* (third edition, Blackstone, 1993); P. Beaumont and Stephen Weatherill, *EC Law* (Penguin, 1993); L. Kramer, *EEC Treaty and Environmental Protection* (Sweet and Maxwell, 1990); L. Kramer, *Focus on European Environmental Law* (Sweet and Maxwell, 1992).

There are a number of useful environmental law texts and edited books: Murdie, *Environmental Law and Citizen Action* (Earthscan, 1993); Simon Ball and Stuart Bell, *Environmental Law* (second edition, Blackstone Press, 1993); David Hughes, *Environmental Law* (Butterworths, second edition, 1992); Owen Lomas (ed) and John McEldowney (Warwick law ed) *Frontiers of Environmental Law* (Chancery Law Publishing, 1991), Churchill, Gibson and Warren, *Law, Policy and the Environment (Journal of Law and Society*, 1991); Jane Holder, Pauline Lane, Sally Eden, *et al.*(eds), *Perspectives on the Environment* (Avebury, 1993); Rosalind Malcolm, *A Guidebook to Environmental Law* (Sweet and

Maxwell, 1994); Martin Polden and Simon Jackson, *The Environment and the Law* (Longman, 1994); William Birtles and Richard Stein, *Planning and Environmental Law* (Longman, 1994); Colin Reid, *Nature Conservation Law* (Sweet and Maxwell, 1994).

There are a number of useful specialised studies such as: G. Richardson, A. Ogus and P. Burrows, *Policing Pollution – A Study of Regulation and Enforcement* (Oxford University Press, 1983); S. Elworthy, *Farming for Drinking Water: Nitrate Pollution of Water – An Assessment of a Regulatory Regime* (Earthscan, 1994); D. Vaughan, *EC Environmental and Planning Law* (McGraw-Hill, 1986); A. Mumma, *Environmental Law* (1995).

Environmental law may also be found in a number of specialised loose-leaf encyclopaedias. See: *Garner's Environmental Law* (Butterworths); *The Encyclopaedia of Environmental Law* (Sweet and Maxwell). There are also a number of related encyclopaedias, for example, Bailey and Tudway, *Electricity Law and Practice* (1992).

International environmental law is examined in Birnie and Boyle, *International Law and the Environment* (Oxford, 1992). For European Community law see: A. Kiss and D. Shelton, *Manual of European Environmental Law* (Cambridge, Grotius Publishers, 1993).

Keeping up to date in matters environmental is particularly important and essential in environmental law. See ENDS Report that provides a monthly digest of current developments (published by Environmental Data Services Ltd).

There are a number of useful sources in specialised journals: *The Journal of Environmental Law* (Oxford University Press); *Environmental Law and Management; Water Law* and *Utilities Law Review* are all published by Chancery Law Publishing; *International Journal of Biosciences and Law* (published by ABA).

Legal practitioners often provide useful information. See: the *Environmental Law Series* (Cameron Markby); *European Legal Developments* (Baker and MacKenzie); and *Green and Clean in Europe* (Allen and Overy); *Environmental Law* (Journal of the UK Environmental Law Association, UKELA).

Science

There are a large number of texts which deal with ecology and ecological principles, for example J.L. Chapman, M.J. Reiss (1992) *Ecology: Principles and Applications,* Cambridge University Press, Cambridge; and M. Begon, J.L. Hanpen, and C.R. Townsend, (1990) *Ecology, Individuals, Populations and Communities,* Blackwell Scientific Publications, Oxford.

Specific consideration of the fate, impact, monitoring and control of environmental pollutants is contained in a diversity of literature. Some examples are set out below:

Freedman, B. (1995) *Environmental Ecology. The Impact of Pollution and Other Stresses on Ecosystem Structure and Function*, 2nd edn. Academic Press, San Diego.

Holdgate, M.W. (1979) and *A Perspective of Environmental Pollution.* Cambridge University Press, Cambridge.

Mason, C.F. (1995) *Biology of Freshwater Pollution*, 3rd edn. Longman, Harlow.

McEldowney, S., Hardman, D.J. and Waite, S. (1993) *Pollution: Ecology and Biotreatment.* Longman, Harlow.

Moriarty, F. (1990) *Ecotoxicology, the Study of Pollutants in Ecosystems*, 2nd edn. Academic Press, London.

Newman, E.I. (1993) *Applied Ecology.* Blackwell.

Peterken, G. (1993) *Woodland Conservation and Management* 2nd edn. Chapman & Hall, London.

Samiullah, Y. (1990) *Prediction of the Environmental Fate of Chemicals.* Elsevier Applied Science, London.

Speilerberg, I.F. (1991) *Monitoring Ecological Change.* Cambridge University Press, Cambridge.

The Scientific Committee on Problems of the Environment (SCOPE) under the auspices of The International Council of Scientific Unions (ICSU) has a mandate to assemble and review available information on man-made environmental changes, their impact on man, and to evaluate procedures for the measurement of environmental parameters. There have been a series of publications arising under this mandate under the general heading SCOPE. These give an excellent and up-to-date review of current knowledge of environmental perturbation often at the global level. For example, B. Warrick and D. Jager (eds) (1986) *SCOPE 29. The Greenhouse Effect, Climatic Change, and Ecosystems.* John Wiley, Chichester.

There are a range of scientific journals which publish articles relevant to the impact of human activity on the environment and techniques for the control of environmental damage, for example *Functional Ecology; Water Research; Water Science and Technology; Marine Biology; Science; Chemistry & Industry*, etc. Other journals deal specifically and solely with these topics, for example *Ecotoxicology and Environmental Safety; Environmental Research; The Science of the Total Environment; Ecotoxicology; Ambio; Environmental Pollution; Environmental Toxicology and Safety*, etc.

An introduction to the legal system

An overview of the legal system in England and Wales setting out the system of courts is necessary to an understanding of how environmental issues are the subject of litigation. In this chapter we examine the organisation of the courts, including how to take a case to court and the procedures necessary to make an application for judicial review. There is an explanation of how scientific evidence may be used in court cases.

At the outset it is important to remember the role of the courts in developing environmental law. The contribution of judge-made law to environmental law has already been noted in Chapter 1, especially in the development of property law, contract law, tort law and criminal law. Environmental problems may also be amenable to the remedies available in public law under judicial review.

Structure and organisation of the courts

There is an important distinction between civil and criminal disputes. Disputes between private citizens or between the citizen and the state are heard before civil courts. In environmental law this may involve tort, property rights or the wrongful exercise of public powers. A *tort* is a civil wrong that may give rise to an action for damages.

Criminal courts hear accusations involving a breach of the criminal law. In criminal law a distinction is made between summary offences and indictable offences. The former are generally less serious and are tried in the magistrates' court before magistrates without a jury. The latter are more serious and are tried in the Crown Court with a jury. Some less serious indictable offences, however, may be tried before a magistrates' court. The criminal jurisdiction and appeal structure for criminal cases is outlined in Fig. 2.1.

In civil cases the courts with a first instance jurisdiction are the High Court and county courts. The more important civil cases are heard in the High Court. Appeals from the High Court generally lie to the Court of Appeal (Civil Division) and thereafter to the House of Lords. Less

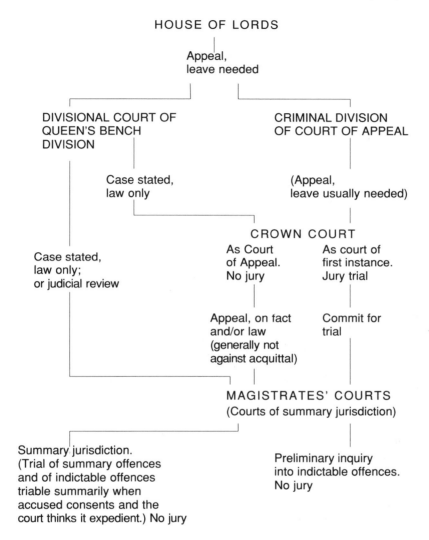

Fig. 2.1 The criminal jurisdiction and appeal structure. (Reproduced from p. 211 Spencer, J.R. (1989) *Jackson's Machinery of Justice* by kind permission of the author and Cambridge University Press. © Cambridge University Press 1989.)

important cases are heard in the county courts with appeals to the Court of Appeal and thereafter to the House of Lords (Fig. 2.2).

It is important to note that while there is a distinction between civil and criminal law, there is no rigid distinction between civil and criminal courts. Almost all the courts exercise jurisdiction over civil and criminal matters. The composition of the various courts mentioned above is different. Magistrates' courts are presided over by justices of the peace,

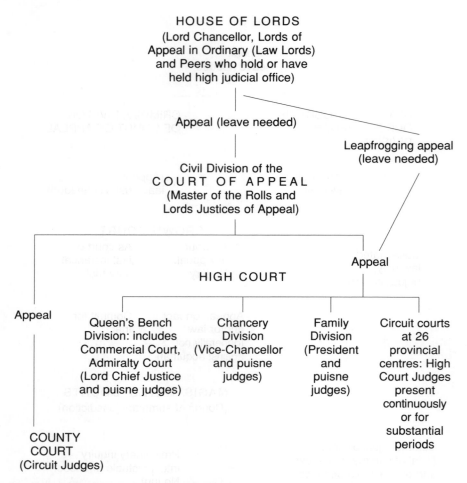

Fig. 2.2 The civil jurisdiction and appeal structure. (Reproduced from p. 39 of Spencer J.R. (1989), *Jackson's Machinery of Justice* by kind permission of the author and Cambridge University Press. © Cambridge University Press 1989.)

most of whom are lay but some are legally qualified and are called stipendiary magistrates. The magistrates' courts hear the majority of criminal cases. A person convicted of an offence may appeal to the Crown Court against conviction. Further appeal is possible to the House of Lords (Fig. 2.1). Magistrates' courts also exercise a civil jurisdiction in domestic proceedings. There is also jurisdiction over the recovery of charges for council tax and the community charge, and payments for water, gas and electricity.

The Crown Court is of recent origin. Set up in 1971, it replaced the old system of Assizes and Quarter sessions. The Crown Court is the major criminal court for serious cases. The judges of the Crown Court are High Court judges, circuit judges, recorders and justices of the peace. Normally High Court judges are from the Queen's Bench Division. Circuit judges are appointed by the Lord Chancellor from among barristers of ten years' standing or a recorder of at least three years' standing. Circuit judges may also sit in the county court to hear civil cases.

County courts have a jurisdiction based on a financial limit that is adjusted from time to time by Order in Council. Where cases exceed the financial limit they must be taken in the Queen's Bench Division of the High Court. In certain circumstances the parties may be able to waive this requirement by agreeing to have the case heard in the county court. Currently there are over 300 county courts in England and Wales. They are useful in hearing claims for damages arising out of contract or tort. All circuit judges are entitled to sit in the county court. More complicated civil actions are thought inappropriate for the county court and they must be set down for trial in the High Court. There is a useful scheme for the arbitration of small claims in the county court.

The High Court is a superior court of record and was created as part of the Supreme Court of Judicature by the Judicature Act 1873. There are three divisions: the Queen's Bench Division is the largest and comprises 63 judges; the Chancery Division; and the Family Division. Judges of the High Court normally sit in London but there are provisions for High Court judges to sit anywhere in England and Wales. The civil jurisdiction is the main work of the High Court. The Queen's Bench Division is a civil court where cases of contract and actions in tort may be heard, usually with a judge sitting alone. The Divisional Court of the Queen's Bench Division is composed of at least two High Court judges. The Divisional Court has jurisdiction to hear applications for judicial review used to supervise the activities of public bodies. The application for judicial review is important in environmental law because it provides important remedies to control any abuse by a public body. The importance of judicial review is explained in more detail below (page 30).

The Divisional Court may also hear appeals on points of law by way of case stated direct from the magistrates' courts or via the Crown Court. The Divisional Court may also punish contempts of court and hear applications for *Habeas Corpus*.

The Court of Appeal is composed of the Lord Chancellor and a number of designated judges such as the Lord Chief Justice, the Master of the Rolls, the President of the Family Division of the High Court, the Vice-Chancellor of the Chancery Division and 29 Lords Justices of Appeal. There are two divisions of the Court of Appeal: the Civil Division is headed by a President who is the Master of the Rolls; the Criminal Division is headed by a President who is the Lord Chief Justice.

The House of Lords is the highest court in the United Kingdom in cases not involving EC law. The full significance of EC law is explained in Chapter 3. The House of Lords as a court is headed by the Lord Chancellor and by between seven and eleven Lords of Appeal in Ordinary, often in popular usage called Law Lords. Every appeal heard by the House of Lords must be heard by at least three Law Lords but in practice it is usual for five to hear cases of importance.

▶ Taking cases to court

Criminal cases

Court cases involve different procedures for civil and criminal cases. In criminal cases there are detailed rules of evidence governing the conduct of a criminal case. The prosecution of the case is taken by the Crown Prosecution Service. In cases where a guilty plea is entered for the accused the prosecuting lawyers provide a brief description of the facts and the court may be told of the previous convictions, if any, of the defendant. The defendant may be granted legal aid and be represented by a lawyer. In cases of guilty pleas the defendant's lawyer may make a plea of mitigation. The circumstances of the case and the facts are explained before the court. Character witnesses are called on behalf of the accused.

In cases where the defendant pleads not guilty, the prosecution may call witnesses to give evidence on oath testifying to the guilt of the defendant. The defendant's lawyer has the opportunity to cross-examine witnesses and may call witnesses on behalf of the defence. The prosecution has the onus and burden of proof that the defendant committed the offence. The standard of proof in a criminal case is beyond a reasonable doubt. Recently, and controversially, the Criminal Justice and Public Order Act 1994, ss. 34–39, removes the accused's right to silence.

In environmental cases criminal proceedings are of minimal use and prosecutions are relatively uncommon. This is not to suggest that criminal law is unimportant. Pressure groups may view the criminal law as a useful means to force companies to take account of the environment. In some circumstances private prosecutions are possible but are rare.

Criminal prosecutions may arise from various statutory provisions imposing criminal liability. A common example is the offence of obstructing a regulatory agency from carrying out its powers of inspection. Sections 108–10 of the Environment Act 1995 provide the Environment Agency with a range of powers of entry and enforcement powers to carry out the duties under the 1995 Act. Section 110 makes it a criminal offence to intentionally obstruct an authorised person in the exercise of his or her powers or duties.

However, there is a growing recognition that it is only through adequate criminal sanctions that the environment will be protected. Such sanctions might include large fines or even imprisonment. This is an area of considerable controversy. The Law Reform Commission of Canada has argued that the criminal law is 'an instrument of last resort for reaffirming values'. Thus the criminal law must be used with some restraint in order not to undervalue its importance. Nevertheless the value of the criminal law helps 'to stigmatise behaviour causing disastrous damage with long term loss of natural resources'. This represents a fundamental value in society that can be protected through the criminal law imposing penalties.

The following example illustrates how the criminal law may be used. A prosecution may be taken for a public nuisance, which is a criminal offence as well as being a civil wrong. The question of what constitutes a public nuisance is widely defined. An act 'that is not warranted by law or an omission to discharge a legal duty' and where the 'act or omission obstructs or causes inconvenience or damage to the public in the exercise of rights common to all His Majesty's subjects'. One example is obstructing the highway, thereby interfering with the public. Another example is carrying on some offensive activity which results in the public being injured. Polluting a river with chemicals rendering the water unfit for human consumption or destroying the fish would come within the scope of the offence. Public nuisance is triable as a misdemeanour either in the magistrates' court or in the Crown Court. Environmental cases are not usually taken in the Crown Court where there are higher penalties including an unlimited fine or imprisonment.

Arising out of the criminal offence of public nuisance there may be civil proceedings. The Attorney-General may take out an injunction to stop the nuisance from continuing or to prevent the recurrence of the nuisance. Under s. 222 of the Local Government Act 1972, the relevant local authority may take action in the civil courts for damages arising out of the nuisance (see: *Gillingham Borough Council* v. *Medway (Chatham) Dock Ltd* [1992] 3 All ER 923 for a claim made in respect of nuisance caused by large movements of heavy lorries using the highway for access to a major sea port between 7 p.m. and 7 a.m.).

The enforcement of environmental law by means of the criminal law is commonly undertaken by regulatory agencies such as the newly established Environment Agency in England and Wales (hitherto, Her Majesty's Inspector of Pollution, HMIP, and the National Rivers Authority, NRA), and in Scotland the Environment Protection Agency, rather than the private citizen. In cases of water pollution, the scope of most criminal offences is found in statutory form. In February 1990 Shell (UK) was prosecuted for an oil spillage into the River Mersey which caused extensive pollution. The fine imposed by the court amounted to £1 million, one of the highest fines recorded in a case involving environmental pollution. This is regarded as an exceptional case. The need to increase the level of fines is recognised in the Environmental Protection Act 1990, which saw increases for fines in the magistrates' courts from £2000 to £20,000.

In recent years there is a trend in favour of bringing criminal prosecutions in cases involving environmental pollution. In 1992 Her Majesty's Inspectorate of Pollution took 19 prosecutions, representing double the number in the previous year (see Chapter 4). In March 1995 Welsh Water became the first water company prosecuted for breach of drinking water regulations (Regulation 28 of the Water Supply (Water Quality) Regulations 1989). The prosecution arose because of the use of epoxy resin in a relining operation of the water mains. It appears that six of the seven most frequently prosecuted water polluters are water companies (see: ENDS Report 242, March 1995 pp.44–5).

In English law many criminal offences that apply to the environment may be described as *strict liability* offences. This means that it is usually sufficient that the physical act or omission has taken place without having to prove that the defendant had full or even partial knowledge of the offence. The mental element of a crime of strict liability is not required to be proven. The definition of strict liability crimes is summarised by Smith and Hogan as follows:

> Crimes which do not require intention, recklessness or even
> negligence as to one or more elements in the *actus reus* are known as
> offences of strict liability or, sometimes, 'of absolute prohibition'.
> (Smith and Hogan, *Criminal Law.* Butterworths, 1994, p.99)

For example in *Ashcroft* v. *Cambro Waste Products* [1981] 3 All ER 699 concerning the disposal of controlled waste, it was not necessary for the prosecution to prove that the defendant knowingly permitted the deposit of controlled waste in breach of the law under s. 3(1) of the Control of Pollution Act 1974.

The scope of the criminal law is considerably broader than at first might appear. Criminal liability may extend from the person who actually committed the physical act involving the pollution to the directors of the company employing the individual. The legal principle that may extend liability from a single individual to a body corporate such as a company or partnership is known as *vicarious liability*. It is possible for statutes to contain their own specific formulation of this principle. For example the Environmental Protection Act (EPA) 1990 extends criminal liability to 'any director, manager, secretary or other similar officer of the body corporate or any person purporting to act in such capacity'. In the case of the EPA, it must be proved that the offence has been committed 'with the consent or connivance of, or to be attributable to any neglect' on the part of one of the persons mentioned above. Similar provisions may be found in ss. 217(1) and 210(1) of, respectively, the Water Resources Act 1991 and Water Industry Act 1991 and also s. 37 of the Health and Safety at Work, etc., Act 1974.

Criminal liability may include that of an accomplice where the offence has been aided and abetted. It is also a conspiracy where there is an agreement among two or more people to undertake an unlawful act. It is impossible to provide a definitive list of criminal offences in environmental law. Reference to the following statutes provides some of the main areas of criminal liability: the Environment Act 1995, the Water Resources Act 1991, the Water Industry Act 1991, the Environmental Protection Act 1990 (Parts I–VI), the Town and Country Planning Act 1990, the Planning and Hazardous Substances Act 1990 and the Control of Pesticide Regulations 1986, the Control of Pollution Act 1974 (Part III), the Health and Safety at Work, etc., Act 1974.

Civil cases

The procedures used in civil cases are to be found in the County Court Rules for County Court Actions and the Rules of the Supreme Court for High Court Actions. In the High Court an action is commenced by the person bringing the action, the plaintiff, issuing and serving a writ naming the defendant. The defendant is expected to acknowledge service of a writ. Exchanges between the parties on matters connected with the case are called pleadings. Discovery of documents that are necessary for the trial of the case in the possession of one party may be granted to the other party. The writ must be served within four months of its issue, though extensions of time may be granted by the court. Civil proceedings are subject to time limits as to when an action may be begun – usually within six years.

The trial of most civil actions is before a judge without a jury. The plaintiff opens the case and gives evidence calling witnesses in support of the case. Evidence is under oath and the witnesses may be cross-examined by the lawyer for the defence. The defence may also call witnesses and give evidence. In a civil case the standard of proof is not as high as in a criminal case. This is commonly expressed as meaning that in civil cases the standard of proof required from the plaintiff is on the balance of probabilities.

The use of a civil action may arise when an individual who has suffered harm or damage brings an action against the individual or institution that caused the damage or loss or harm. The complaint is based on tort or any other legal wrong. In environmental law the tort of nuisance is frequently the cause of action. This is where the plaintiff claims that there has been some unlawful interference with a person's rights involving the use or enjoyment of land. Nuisance is broadly defined to include actual physical interference with the land itself. This may arise where there is unnecessary noise or where the air is polluted. There are limitations on what is actionable. Mere interference with the use and enjoyment of land is only relevant in deciding *if* there may be actionable nuisance. It is not conclusive. Some level of noise discomfort may be considered an acceptable part of living in a busy street or some farmyard smells regarded as acceptable while living in the country. There is also the requirement that some real damage must be suffered by the plaintiff.

Liability may exist because of the rule developed in *Rylands* v. *Fletcher* (1868) LR 3 HL 330. This case established strict liability in certain defined circumstances. The rule applies when persons for their own purpose bring on to the land and maintain there anything which is likely to do mischief should it escape. Prima facie there is liability for all damage which is the natural consequence of the escape. There is a requirement that the use of the land must be 'non natural'. This means that the use of the land must be out of the ordinary and unusual. There is an implication that the bringing of something which has a special use on to the land increases the danger to the public. What constitutes the natural use of land is often highly complicated. Recently the House of Lords in *Cambridge Water Co Ltd.* v. *Eastern Counties Leather plc* [1994] 1 All ER 53, has considered the rule in an action by Cambridge Water claiming damages alleging negligence, nuisance and liability under the rule in *Rylands* v. *Fletcher* (see Chapter 10, p. 216).

On the question of defining non-natural use the House of Lords was reluctant to provide a binding definition. There was some discussion of examples which fell within the definition. The House of Lords considered that the storage of substantial quantities of chemicals on industrial premises is a classic example of non-natural use even in an industrial complex. For the future the question of extending the definition of non-natural use is unlikely to receive much attention after the House of Lords decision in *Cambridge Water*. The House of Lords held that strict liability for the escape of things likely to do mischief only arose if the defendant knew or ought reasonably to have foreseen that the escape would cause damage. This is an important qualification to the rule in cases where there is historic pollution, that is, where pollution has existed for some time and not been fully appreciated by anyone. The effect of the House of Lords decision is to treat the rule in *Rylands* v. *Fletcher* as part of the developing law of nuisance rather than a distinctive and separate development. This means that there is strict liability under the rule for damage caused by ultra-hazardous operations provided the harm was foreseeable. It remains to be seen what the future direction of the law will take after this important decision.

There are other grounds for civil action involving the tort of negligence or trespass and civil liability arising from the imposition of strict liability for ultra-hazardous activities. This list is not static as environmental protection is continuously creating situations where new liabilities may arise under EC law (Chapter 3). Currently the European Community, the Council of Europe and the United Nations Environment Programme (UNEP) are considering the future role of civil liability in environmental protection.

The common law developed the tort of negligence from the leading case of *Donoghue* v. *Stevenson* [1932] AC 562. Negligence requires proof of a number of distinct elements. There is first the requirement that there should be a duty of care towards the plaintiff. For there to be any legal liability there must be a breach of the standard of care, usually brought about by a failure to act reasonably. Damage which resulted must be due to a breach of the duty of care and not due to other causes. Negligence in environmental law is often difficult to prove. Environmental hazards may only indirectly have caused the harm complained of by the plaintiff. In making a claim for negligence, the plaintiff faces other problems. There may be contributory negligence on the part of the plaintiff which contributed to the harm. The effect of contributory negligence may result in a loss of damages awarded to the plaintiff should he succeed in proving negligence. This may make pursuing a claim in negligence financially not worth while or possibly too complicated to pursue.

In terms of remedies in environmental law, civil action may result in damages for the loss or an injunction. Damages are often claimed as the main remedy for any loss. Past losses may be compensated by damages as well as damages for any future losses. Injunctions are useful in the general area of environmental law. An injunction may be used requiring the abatement of a nuisance. Alternatively an injunction may be used in anticipation of any threatened illegality.

It is also possible to apply for a declaration. This is a remedy that merely sets out the legal position over the rights of the parties. Thus a declaration may help resolve ambiguities in the law. It is usual to combine a declaration with damages or an injunction depending on the nature of the facts raised in the case.

Individual iniatives on the part of a citizen to take action against some environmental harm are not uncommon. In the case of nuisance, occupiers may take reasonable and responsible action to abate the nuisance. Any action must not involve breaking the criminal law and notice is usually required before action is taken, for example to enter the land where the nuisance is caused.

As mentioned above, the European Community is actively considering the efficiency of civil liability laws. In March 1993 the Council of Europe agreed a Convention on Civil Liability. The Convention applies to dangerous activities that may affect the environment. Included in the

Convention are provisions relating to access to information, various compensation provisions and the grounds for civil liability. The Convention sets out some general directions for the future of civil liability in the protection of the environment.

▶ Access to Neighbouring Land Act 1992

There are many situations where it is desirable to gain access to land that would be otherwise a nuisance. Under the Access to Neighbouring Land Act 1992, which follows the recommendations of the Law Commission (see: *Law Commission Report* No.151), it is possible to apply to the court for an order to allow access for the carrying out of certain works. There is an important caveat that the works to be carried out must be reasonably necessary for the preservation of the land and it is subject to the strict enforcement of the court. There are technical and detailed specifications in the Act for the type of works that may be carried out and the rights that may be granted by the court. The range of rights is limited and may only be exercised with the authority of the court. Access orders must be registered under the Land Charges Act 1972 (see: Land Registration Act 1925). Such registered rights may be binding on various groups of people defined in the Act.

▶ Judicial review

Private and public law

In discussing liability for environmental harm we have focused on private law. It is also possible to obtain remedies in public law through the application for judicial review. This is a detailed and specialised area of law that has developed in importance over the last 30 years. Judicial review is available to challenge decisions or action taken by public bodies. It is important that public bodies are identified and distinguished from private bodies. Private law may be defined as regulating the relations of private persons, whether individuals, corporations or unincorporated associations, in their relationships with each other. Public law refers only to those individuals or bodies that exercise public law powers: the legislature, central and local government and the large number of fringe organisations that exercise governmental powers which are usually statutory powers.

The exclusive nature of the application for judicial review arises because judicial review is not available in private law matters. This point is exhaustively discussed in the House of Lords decision in *O'Reilly* v. *Mackman* [1982] 3 All ER 1124. This results in a separate procedure to be used for the review of public law matters than the use of the civil courts outlined above. The reason for a separate jurisdiction for public law is that the courts wish to distinguish the way activities of government or governmental agencies are reviewed from the review of private individuals. Traditionally the courts have viewed governmental powers differently than the citizen exercising private law rights. Government may exercise political authority and is accountable to Parliament in a way that is different from the citizen exercising private law rights. It is difficult to set out clearly defined rules for the distinction between public and private. To a large extent the courts will decide each case on its facts and on a case-by-case basis (see: *Mercury Communications Ltd.* v. *D.G. of Telecommunications* [1996] 1 All ER 575).

What is the role of judicial review for problems in environmental law? The enforcement of environmental law depends on various statutory bodies that are amenable to review by the courts. The private citizen may wish to seek a judicial review of a government decision. The vast number of planning laws that affect the environment often have a public law dimension and are susceptible to judicial review.

Making an application for judicial review

An application for judicial review is made to the Queen's Bench Division of the High Court, known as the Divisional Court. The application must be made promptly and within three months of the complaint. The procedures provided under the application for judicial review are found in Order 53 of the Rules of the Supreme Court and s. 31 of the Supreme Court Act 1981. There are two stages. The first stage requires the applicant to make out an arguable case and show that he or she has sufficient standing (*locus standi*) in the case. *Locus standi* requires that the aggrieved person has a sufficient interest in raising the case. At the first stage it is usual for there to be no hearing because the application is made on affidavit evidence and the defendant is not normally represented. If there is a hearing it is before a single judge. At the second stage there is a full hearing of the Divisional Court. Standing may be raised as part of the second hearing but there is also a full argument of the legal issues raised in the case. The remedies available to the litigant using the application for judicial review include all the private law remedies mentioned above on civil cases. These include damages and injunction or declaration. In addition, but exclusively available under the application for judicial review, are the various prerogative remedies. These are *certiorari* used to quash a decision, *prohibition* to prevent some illegality from taking place, and *mandamus* to command the performance of a public duty. There are technical rules as to which remedy is appropriate for the facts of a particular case.

Environmentalists may find that public law offers important remedies to protect the environment. Pressure groups may make use of public law remedies, though this is not always successful. In *R. v. Secretary of State for the Environment ex parte Rose Theatre Trust Co.* [1990] 1 All ER 754, developers granted planning permission to erect a block of flats uncovered what was thought to be an Elizabethan theatre, an archaeological site of great importance. The Secretary of State declined to schedule the site under the Ancient Monuments and Archaeological Areas Act 1979. The applicants consisted of well-known public figures in the world of the Arts who formed a company to campaign for the preservation of the site which they believed was the Rose Theatre where Marlowe's and Shakespeare's plays were performed. The Divisional Court held that the company did not have sufficient standing and declined to grant a *certiorari* against the Secretary of State.

In *R. v. Pollution Inspectorate ex parte Greenpeace Ltd (No.2)* [1994] 4 All ER 328 (also see: [1994] 4 All ER 321), the Divisional Court considered Greenpeace's objections to the safety of the Thorp nuclear reprocessing plant. The standing of Greenpeace was sufficient to satisfy the court that an application for judicial review should be considered. The issue of standing required the court:

> . . . to take into account the nature of Greenpeace and the extent of its interest in the issues raised, the remedy Greenpeace seeks to achieve and the nature of the relief sought.
>
> (See: Mr Justice Otton [1994] 4 All ER at p.349 h–j)

The grounds for judicial review

There are various grounds for judicial review. The main ground is that a public body has acted outside its powers or, as lawyers prefer, *ultra vires*. This may take the form of acting in the wrong manner, using the wrong procedures or behaving negligently. For example the use of guidance issued under an Act of Parliament must be consistent with the authority expressed in the Act of Parliament, otherwise it is *ultra vires*. The legal powers to make a decision must be correctly delegated to the requisite legal authority. If they are improperly delegated it may be regarded as *ultra vires*. The courts are vigilant as to the exact nature of the legal powers granted by Parliament including the purpose for which the powers are intended.

General principles of review may be found in *Associated Provincial Picture Houses Ltd v. Wednesbury Corporation* [1948] 1KB 223. The question of the improper exercise of discretion raises issues about whether the public body has acted reasonably. Relevant considerations must be taken into account and irrelevant considerations excluded from the decision. The decision maker must not act in breach of the rules of natural justice. This means the decision should be free from bias or prejudice (*nemo judex in sua causa*) and the citizen is entitled to a fair hearing and to be given an opportunity to be heard (*audi alteram partem*). The House of Lords discussed the principles of natural justice in *Ridge* v. *Baldwin* [1964] AC 40 and more recently in *CCSU* v. *Minister for the Civil Service* [1985] AC 374. In general terms there is a duty to act fairly that rests on public bodies exercising legal powers.

▶ Scientific evidence and environmental law

Scientists can have an important role in environmental cases. This role includes giving evidence in court and in the preparation of scientific materials and evidence to be used in court hearings. The proof of any alleged environmental harm often depends on scientific investigation and knowledge. Sections 111–13 of the Environment Act 1995 provide for information and evidence in connection with pollution offences.

Scientists may feel that there is a tension between what constitutes scientific proof and the requirements of proof in a court case. The law is often complex and sets precise demands which may not be readily met by scientific evidence. The standards set by legal tests do not always correspond with scientific knowledge or understanding. It is important to be aware of the potential for conflict. Scientists may find it bewildering that courts adopt a different evaluation of scientific evidence than do scientists. In recent years a great deal of controversy surrounding scientific evidence has arisen in cases involving DNA testing and in the work of the forensic science laboratories in carrying out tests on samples taken from terrorist suspects to discover if they have handled explosive substances. Both examples illustrate the difficulty the courts may have in relying on expert scientific evidence.

The courts have developed rules to deal with expert evidence. The general rule of evidence is that a witness must only give evidence on what is directly observed. There has developed a specific exception to this rule in respect of expert opinion. A witness is allowed to state his or her opinion on matters where he or she is an expert. Opinions on matters outside the particular expertise of the witness are not admissible. The word 'opinion' is legally defined to mean any inference from observed facts. In general the courts jealously guard the jurisdiction of the judge or jury to decide matters that come before the court. The explanation for this attitude, which can appear antagonistic to expert opinion, is that litigants are entitled to have their disputes settled by a judge or jury rather than by an expert witness. The courts are reluctant to allow expert witnesses to give evidence that may unduly influence the determination of the case. The rule appears to be that the admission of expert opinion is at the discretion of the court. Lord President Cooper, in *Davie* v. *Edinburgh Magistrates* [1953]SC 34 at p.40, noted that the function of expert witnesses:

... is to furnish the judge or jury with the necessary scientific criteria for testing the accuracy of their conclusions, so as to enable the judge or jury to form their own independent judgment by the application of these criteria to the facts proved in evidence.

In a well-known dictum Lord Justice Lawton explained in *R.* v. *Turner* [1975] QB 834 at p.841:

The fact that an expert witness has impressive scientific qualifications does not by that fact alone make his opinion on matters of human nature and behaviour within the limits of normality any more helpful than that of the jurors themselves; but there is a danger that they may think it does.

The question of whether an expert measures up to the necessary qualification of the particular expert required in a case is for the judge to determine. It may be necessary for the expert witness to demonstrate that he or she has undertaken specialist studies in connection with a particular issue raised in the case.

The courts are willing to take account of scientific publications and new developments in understanding environmental problems. In the recent House of Lords decision in *Cambridge Water* v. *Eastern Leather* [1994] 1 All ER 53 at p.65, Lord Goff explained how expert witness and scientific research provided the court in the conduct of the litigation with important scientific evidence on perchloroethene (PCE) present as a contaminant in the water supplies. In this case pollution could be traced back into the previous century. The development of better scientific knowledge over the past century was an important issue in determining legal liability. As Lord Goff acknowledged, 'the development of ... high resolution gas chromatography during the 1970s enabled scientists to detect and measure organochlorine compounds (such as PCE) in water to the value of micrograms per litre (or parts per billion) expressed as µg/litre.' (*Cambridge Water* v. *Eastern Counties Leather* [1994] 1 All ER 53 at p.65). This had not been possible in the past, which had a bearing on the outcome of the case (see Chapter 10).

Scientific understanding has a key role for the future development of environmental law. Scientists provide expert opinions to a number of important Select Committees and advisory bodies including the Royal Commission on Environmental Pollution. The various statutory regulators also receive evidence and information from scientists. The Countryside Commission and other government-funded bodies receive scientific information. Pressure groups such as Greenpeace employ scientists and conduct their own research programmes. The National Trust and other preservation societies also rely on scientific knowledge. Large construction companies employ and utilise scientific knowledge in putting forward planning applications and carrying out construction projects.

▶ Further reading

On the law of evidence see: *Cross On Evidence* (Butterworths, 1993); M. Grant, 'See you in environmental court?' (1991) 60 *Town and Country Planning* (6) 165; A. Mumma, *Environmental Law* (McGraw-Hill, 1995); P. McAuslan, 'The role of courts and other judicial type bodies in environ- mental management' (1991) 3 *Journal of Environmental Law* 195. *House of Lords Select Committee on the European Communities. Remedying Environmental Damage* 3rd Report (HMSO,1993)

On questions of constitutional and administrative law see J.F. McEldowney, *Public Law* (Sweet and Maxwell, 1994). Also see: Peter Cane, *An Introduction to Administrative Law* (Clarendon, Oxford Series, second edition, 1992); Clive Lewis, *Judicial Remedies in Public Law* (Sweet and Maxwell, 1992); Wade and Forsyth, *Administrative Law*, 7th edition (Oxford University Press, 1994); Michael Superstone and James Goudie (eds), *Judicial Review* (Butterworths, 1992); Holland and Webb, *Learning Legal Rules*, 2nd edition (Blackstone Press, 1993).

On nuisance liability see: F.H. Newark, 'The boundaries of nuisance' (1949) 65 LQR 480. Also see: Ogus and Richardson, 'Economics and the environment: a study of private nuisance' [1977] CLJ 284; J.P.S. MacLaren, 'Nuisance law and the Industrial Revolution – some lessons from history' (1983); *Oxford Journal of Legal Studies*, vol.3 No.2 pp.155–221. Kevin Gray, 'Equitable Property' (1994) *Current Legal Problems*, pp. 157–214.

On the use of the criminal law see: *The Law Reform Commission of Canada: Crimes Against the Environment Working Paper No.44; Pollution Control in Canada: the regulatory approach in the 1980s, A Study Paper; Sentencing in Environmental Cases Study Paper.*

Environmental problems do not recognise national territorial or geographical boundaries. Consequently environmental law involves consideration of treaty obligations in international law and the importance of various international organisations. Since 1972 the UK's membership of the European Community means that European Community (EC) law has an effect on almost every aspect of environmental law in the United Kingdom. This chapter is in two parts. First, there is an explanation of international law. Second, there is an explanation of EC law, the impact of EC law on the United Kingdom and the formulation of EC policy on environmental problems.

International law and the environment

Defining international environmental law

Birnie and Boyle (1992) in their *International Law and the Environment* noted how 'a distinct body of international law does now exist for the protection of the environment'. It is therefore necessary to give an outline of international environmental law. International law may best be defined in terms of its sources. The main sources of international law are custom, general principles of law recognised by prominent states, treaties and accepted principles of law from the International Court of Justice. Article 38(1) of the ICJ statute expresses the principles that the court should apply 'international custom, as evidence of a general practice accepted as law'. It is also the case that international environmental law crosses many distinct subject matter boundaries. This includes subject areas of law included in the law of the sea, international human rights law, or the law relating to international economic rights and duties of states. There are also resolutions of the General Assembly of the United Nations and other decisions by international organisations.

Customary international law

Customary international law recognises the territorial law of the state and the sovereignty of the state through its territorial jurisdiction. Environmental law based on international custom appears weak. This is because the sovereignty of each state and the incompatible nature of many vested interests may not facilitate the resolution of an environmental problem. Attempts to reconcile national sovereignty with international obligations are made. The 1972 Stockholm Declaration on the Human Environment contains Principle 21 of general application and represents custom. Principle 21 provides that states have '. . . the responsibility to ensure activities within their jurisdiction or control do not cause damage to the environment of other states or of areas beyond the limits of national jurisdiction'. Difficulties abound on precisely how such a declaration may be made enforceable, for example in the area of radioactive fall-out.

Treaty obligations

The limitations on the enforcement of customary international law have been acknowledged in recent years in the greater reliance on the use of treaty obligations. In the area of international environmental law, *treaties* are often concluded under the auspices of international organisations such as the United Nations. Treaties may be referred to in a number of ways. Some are called *conventions* and together with subsidiary agreements called *protocols* arguably provide the main source of international law.

International environmental law originally gave prominence to liability for damage as the main response to environmental harm. In recent years a transformation has gradually occurred and a greater emphasis is placed on environmental regulation to prevent environmental harm.

Increasingly, environmental policy is taking on an international perspective. Policy formulation and its implementation through international agreements may directly affect the United Kingdom. The Stockholm Conference on the Human Environment (1972) established the United Nations Environment Programme (UNEP) which has its headquarters in Nairobi and offices in Geneva. Under its jurisdiction fall a number of international conventions including the Vienna Convention for the Protection of the Ozone Layer agreed in March 1985. There is also the Basel Convention on the Control of Transboundary Movement of Hazardous Wastes and their Disposal of 1989 (22 March 1989).

Examples of important protocols include the Montreal Protocol in September 1987 on CFC production followed by more stringent controls agreed at the London Conference on the Montreal Protocol in July

1989. The United Nations Conference on Environment and Development held at Rio, Brazil, in 1992 (14 June 1992) resulted in conventions on Biodiversity and Climate Change. The implementation of these protocols and conventions is often problematic in practice. The 1992 Convention resulted in a Framework Convention on Climate Change intended to control global warming. Ratified by the United Kingdom in 1993, the Climate Change Programme set out how emissions of greenhouse gases might be controlled by the year 2000.

Under the UN Convention on Climate Change, the 'developed' countries had to submit a workable plan to reduce net emissions of greenhouse gases, e.g. carbon dioxide (CO_2), chlorofluorocarbons ($CFCl_3$ and CF_2Cl_2), methane (CH_4), nitrogen dioxide (NO_2), and ozone (O_3), by 21 September 1994 (see Chapter 12). The Administration in the United States has announced the US Climate Change Action Plan (CCAP). Forty-four specific actions are proposed to reduce net emissions of greenhouse gases to 1990 levels by the year 2000. In the plan it is anticipated that energy-related carbon dioxide emissions will only rise from the 1990 level of 1338 Mt of carbon to 1384 Mt in 1998 and decline to 1379 Mt by the year 2000. In addition it is considered that reduction in other greenhouse gases and sequestration of carbon will further reduce the total to 1335 Mt in 2000. The plan, however, may already require some revision. The US Newsletter *Energy, Economics and Climate Change* reported that by the end of 1993 emission levels had already reached those predicted for 1996, predominantly because of faster economic growth, lower energy prices and weather fluctuations. It is believed that 1994 levels may be even further from target. Eurosta, the European Commission's statistical office in Luxemburg, has indicated that Europe may find it hard to meet its obligation to limit CO_2 emissions to 1990 levels by 2000 even though estimates for emissions of CO_2 from fossil fuel burning in the European Union during 1993 were 3.2 per cent down on 1990. It is considered that the fall was primarily due to recession, which lowered industrial demand for energy and to restructuring in eastern Germany. As countries come out of recession the demand for energy is expected to rise substantially. In addition, as scientific understanding of the impact of greenhouse gas production and climate change on the biosphere increases, it may be necessary to reassess elements of the protocol (see Chapter 12). For example, it has been recognised for some time that methane (CH_4) emissions may be affected by changing climate; however, the potential interactions between CO_2 and CH_4 have only recently been assessed (Dacey *et al.*, 1994). It appears that our understanding of the global CH_4 budget may require modification since CO_2 can indirectly affect the carbon cycle. Methane is a potent greenhouse gas. It absorbs approximately 20 times more infrared than CO_2. Rice paddies and wetlands emit approximately 40 per cent of atmospheric CH_4. It has been found that increased CO_2 enhances the production of carbohydrates by photosynthesis in C_3 plants, that is, plants that fix CO_2 by the C_3 pathway during photosynthesis (see Chapter 12). *Scirpus olneyi*, a typical perennial sedge growing in marshes, has been used in a study of the impact of elevated CO_2 levels on CH_4 production from wetlands (Dacey *et al.*, 1994). It is a C_3 plant and, therefore, shows increased photosynthetic rate in response to elevated atmospheric CO_2 concentrations. The increased photosynthetic rate leads to increased growth much of which is associated with the root system where *S. olneyi* stores most of its organic matter, as do many other marsh plants. Microbial degradation of root material in the waterlogged sediment is through anaerobic processes and results in the formation of CH_4 through methanogenesis. The amount of CH_4 produced is dependent on the root material available for degradation: the larger the root the more CH_4 produced. In addition the higher plants, such as *S. olneyi*, inhabiting marshes often have well-developed internal gas spaces in their roots. These act to transport oxygen (O_2) from the air to the roots. They also have the effect of accelerating the transport of CH_4 from anaerobic sediment to the atmosphere. The larger the root, the larger the gas spaces and the greater the amount of CH_4 transported to the atmosphere. Thus increased CO_2 levels may have the effect of raising CH_4 production from wetlands. Rice is the staple diet of many nationalities, and the warm, well-fertilised conditions in rice paddies are likely to enhance CO_2-stimulated growth and therefore potentially the amount of CH_4 produced on degradation of the organic plant material (Dacey *et al.*, 1994).

The United Nations Conference on Environment and Development (UNCED) convened in 1992 identified environmental problems and the part international law may have in their resolution. Conservation strategies and attempts to regulate endangered species have come through the Convention for Conservation of Antarctic Marine Living Resources. Specific species may be protected, such as whales (see: 1966 International Convention for the Regulation of Whaling), but there appears to be no single convention that attempts to protect all wildlife globally (see Chapter 11).

There is a Convention on Biodiversity ratified by the United Kingdom in June 1994. In addition the United Kingdom has a Biodiversity Action Plan. There is also a Statement of Principle for the management, conservation and sustainable development of the world's forests. The United Kingdom Sustainable Forestry programme was introduced as a response. Finally there is Agenda 21, a programme of action to achieve sustainable development (see Chapter 9). The United Kingdom's Strategy on Sustainable Development covers this programme.

Enforcing international law

One important aspect of international treaties, conventions and protocols is that they are recognised and may be enforceable before the International Court of Justice. However, in domestic law in the United Kingdom such treaties are not directly enforceable unless there is national legislation passed to give the treaty domestic legal force. This does not always occur. A further complication is that, whereas the domestic law of the United Kingdom requires such primary legislation, international law does not. At first glance this position may appear an odd anomaly. The explanation lies in the historical development of English constitutional law. The sovereignty of the UK's Parliament means that international law requires an Act of Parliament for its introduction into domestic law.

In practical terms the result is that many internationally recognised and enforceable treaties binding on the United Kingdom in international law have no effect on the domestic law of the United Kingdom unless adopted by domestic law. Still further, it is possible for formally agreed policies within treaties not to be applied in practice because there are defects in domestic legislation or because there has not been any legislation.

A further complication arises from the contents of treaties, conventions and protocols. In many instances no legal or enforceable rules arise from such international obligations. Some lawyers categorise this as 'soft law' as opposed to formal rigid rules categorised as 'hard law'. This is a contentious description and to some lawyers it appears unhelpful as even 'soft law' may find acceptance in national legal systems and thus be implemented. A better way to understand the nature of some international law is to examine how the content of international treaties is created. Often statements of policy and intent are expressed in such consensual terms that for all practical purposes they are unenforceable. This is not to diminish their importance but to explain that different legal cultures are at work. Diversity and differences in national cultural and economic attitudes to law make this inevitable. The law-making process may involve different stages of negotiation. This involves various recommendations, guidelines and framework principles often expressed in discursive documents. In some European traditions establishing the correct policy is the precursor of legal rules. Obeying the high expectations set out in policy documents or in undertakings may result in more effective action than formal legal rules.

Apparently intractable environmental problems cover a wide spectrum of environmental issues. For example, as mentioned above, a United Nations Conference on Environment and Development (UNCED) convened in 1992 is a good example of the recognition of the width and diversity of environmental issues, from deforestation to biodiversity, when addressing questions of sustainable development in the world as a whole. International environmental law faces the twin problems of weakness in international law and complex and diverse issues arising from the environment.

An intrinsic difficulty of international environmental law is compliance. Disputes between states are often time consuming and beset by complex negotiation arrangements. The International Court of Justice has limited jurisdiction, and representation from non-governmental bodies is limited. Collecting evidence and presenting solutions through international law must confront the reality of weak enforcement procedures that are often bound up with international politics. Recognition of the extent and significance of such difficulties comes after the event. Solutions through the enactment of new laws appear as *ad hoc* law making after the event. The events following Chernobyl led to new laws on nuclear accidents, but this may be seen as too little too late.

International environmental law: future directions?

Reservations and criticisms about the weakness of international environmental law should not overlook its potential for future development. The Rio Declaration on Environment and Development adopted by the UNCED in June 1992 provides an example of international support for the development of general principles in environmental law. The Rio Declaration succeeded in adopting Conventions on Global Climate Change and Biological Diversity. Also included were principles agreed for future action. These include:

- The right of access to environmental information (Principle 10).
- That the precautionary principle should be widely applied and recognised (Principle 15).
- That national authorities should endeavour to adopt the principle of 'the polluter pays' in the cost of pollution (Principle 16).

There was also recognition of the need to carry out significant impact assessment when proposed activities may have an adverse impact on the environment.

The Rio Declaration attempts to reconcile future economic and social development with environmental protection. Attempting to integrate the two is likely to occupy the development of international environmental law for the foreseeable future. The capacity for international law to adapt to new challenges should not be doubted. As Birnie and Boyle (1992, p.546) note:

Having started as a system of rules limited largely to liability for transboundary damage, resource allocation, and the resolution of

conflicting issues of common spaces, international law now
accommodates a preventive, and in this sense precautionary,
approach to the protection of the environment on a global level.

Creating an international legal system to protect the environment is a
necessary prerequisite for future development. This requires both a
political will and various institutional responses. Existing international
institutions such as the United Nations appear weak and ill-suited to the
task ahead. Reliance on dispute resolution through the International
Court of Justice is limited. Both national and international courts
provide judicial review (see Chapters 1 and 2) over treaty operations
and international institutions. Occasionally disputes between states may
be settled, but courts have a minimal role to perform in the prevention
of environmental harm and changing the political process which
informs economic choices within national states. Using international
environmental law to impose restraints that inhibit growth and development is highly political. Ideas of common interest, global responsibility
and common heritage confront historical traditions of national interest,
economic and political sovereignty and state independence. Advancing
environmental issues through the development of the rights of the
individual to complain about the state's protection of the environment
is likely to further the controversy of the role of international
environmental law.

▶ European Community environmental law

Membership of the European Community since 1972 has brought into
existence in the UK's domestic law many Community treaties and
obligations. The EC is a party to many international environmental
obligations which are binding on Member States.

Currently the Community is referred to as the European Union and
is composed of 15 Member States, and this number is likely to expand
in the years ahead. The European Union incorporates three
Communities with common institutions. There is the Coal and Steel
Community set up under the Treaty of Paris 1951, the Economic
Community and an Atomic Energy Community under the Treaties of
Rome 1957. The Single European Act 1986 resulted in the
establishment of a single market and the Maastricht Treaty in 1992
established a European Union moving towards economic and monetary
union and greater inter- governmental co-operation.

It is first necessary to introduce some of the main institutions and
distinctive elements of the EC. Then it is possible to consider the
development of the EC's environmental policy.

An outline and introduction to EC law

As noted above the European Union is derived from a series of treaties:

- The 1951 Paris Treaty setting up the European Coal and Steel Community.
- The 1957 European Atomic Energy Community Agreement (EURATOM).
- The 1957 Treaty of Rome creating the European Economic Community (Common Market).

The Rome Treaty has been amended on a number of occasions, notably following an intergovernmental conference in 1986 resulting in the Single European Act and in 1992 the Treaty on European Union, the Maastricht Treaty.

The formulation of EC law, and the establishment of its aims and objectives, is undertaken by a number of institutions. There is a democratically elected Parliament, a Council representing the Member States and composed of government ministers, a European Council of the Heads of State or Government, a Commission which acts as custodian of the treaties, a Court of Justice to ensure that Community law is observed and a Court of Auditors to monitor financial arrangements and the management of the finances of the Community. It is expected that the role and function of these institutions will be reviewed as part of the consideration of the future strategy of the Community in 1996.

The European Commission

The European Commission consists of 20 members proposed by the Member States. It has a staff of about 15 000 divided into 30 Directorates. DGXI has specific responsibilities for environmental matters. The Commission has a President appointed by the governments of the Member States after consultation with the European Parliament. The Commission may set out proposals for Community policy and propose legislation. Legislative proposals are published in the *Official Journal of the European Communities* (OJ).

One function of the Commission is to ensure that Community law is obeyed. Thus the Commission can bring proceedings to challenge the legality of action taken by Member States or Community institutions. The Commission has a legislative function in that it may initiate legislation. It may submit proposals to the Council of Ministers. The Commission, under its President, may set out its agenda for the policy and objectives of the Community. In environmental matters the Commission may act against Member States when they are in default of environmental obligations. This may take the form of legal action before the European Court or suspension of regional development grants to a defaulting state, as in the case of Portugal in 1990.

The Council of Ministers

The Council of Ministers is composed of a representative of each Member State. The Council has wide decision-making powers. It lays down budgetary procedures, and concludes treaties on behalf of the Community. It helps formulate the policy of the Community. The Presidency of the Council is taken in turn for six months by each Member State. In the environmental area the Council usually operates in response to specific environmental problems. Overall, long-term environmental policies emerge through consensus and negotiation. There is a Committee of Permanent Representatives of Member States (COREPER) assisted by a General Secretariat. Agendas for Council meetings must conform to rules of procedure set down by COREPER. There is a European Council which meets at the end of each Presidency. The country holding the Presidency hosts a meeting of the political Heads of State representing the government of each Member State. Since the Single European Act 1986, there is wider use of qualified majority voting. Currently this is constituted by 62 votes out of 87 with the 62 votes being cast by at least 10 Member States. In major areas such as taxation unanimity is required and where the Council wishes to deviate from the Commission's proposals.

The European Parliament

Since 1979 the Parliament is directly elected by the electorate of Member States. It meets in plenary session about 14 times a year. Currently there are 626 members representing over 370 million people. Political groupings within the Parliament determine voting rather than national groups. Originally the Parliament's role was advisory. Gradually this is changing. The Single European Act 1986 and the Maastricht Treaty extended the powers of the European Parliament, allowing the majority of the Parliament the power to request the Commission to submit a proposal on matters for which the Parliament considers Community action is necessary. The Parliament may also veto certain environmental Acts. The Parliament may act through various committees, particularly through the Environment, Public Health and Consumer Protection Committee.

The Court of Justice of the European Community

The Court's primary function is to interpret and ensure the application of Community law is observed. There are 13 judges appointed by the governments of the Member States. Appointment is renewable for a term of six years. There are six advocate-generals who advise the Court independently of the judges on the basis of carefully argued submissions in open court. Such submissions are influential but are not binding on the judges. Procedures before the Court include both written and oral argument. The decision of the Court is binding on Member States. Interpretation of the judgments is left to the courts of the Member States. Hughes (*Environmental Law*, second edition, Butterworths, 1992, p.97) has noted that:

> The court had, by 1990, given 32 judgements in cases of infraction of environmental obligations with 35 cases pending, with an increasing number of 'second generation' cases, i.e. those involving allegations of specific infractions of directives, and sometimes involving evaluation of scientific and economic evidence.

The Court of Auditors

The Court of Auditors began life as two audit boards for the EC and Euratom. The Court of Auditors is now a Community institution (Article 4 EC) and has a staff of about 250 situated in Luxembourg. Its role is to ensure financial probity and rigour in accounts. The Court of Auditors is divided into four sections dealing with: the Agricultural Guidance Fund, the Regional Funds, Development Funds and Training and related matters. The Court of Auditors may help encourage the develop-ment of environmental policy indirectly through the publication of its reports.

The main sources of Community law

The Community treaties noted above are binding on all Member States. There is, in addition, Community legislation. The authority for legislation is derived from the various treaties of the Community. The Community institutions operating together and in accordance with the requirements of the treaties may make regulations, issue directives and take decisions.

- *Regulations* These are of general application. They are binding on Member States and apply automatically. This means that they require no national measure for implementation. They are directly applicable and ensure uniform application throughout the Community.
- *Directives* A Directive is binding on Member States when implemented by the Member State to whom it is addressed. In principle, in contrast to regulations, which are automatically appli-cable, Directives do not take effect until the Member State has taken action for their implementation. Most of the major laws relevant to the environment adopted since the 1960s have been through the use of Directives. Invariably Directives contain a timetable for the implementation of their various parts. Controversy surrounds Directives. In *Francovich and Bonifaci* v. *Italy* (Case C-6,C-9/90 19 November

1991) the European Court of Justice admitted the possibility that an individual may be able to sue if a Member State failed to implement a Community Directive. This provides considerable potential for the enforcement of Community rights.

● *Decisions* A decision may be applicable to Member States or individuals or institutions within the Community. It is binding but unlike regulations a decision is usually confined to the individual or institution that it specifically addresses.

The width and breadth of Community law calls into question issues of national sovereignty. In the United Kingdom attempts to reconcile' Parliamentary sovereignty and membership of the Community are difficult. All documents published by the Commission for submission to the Council are made available to both Houses of Parliament. There are two Parliamentary Committees established in 1974 for the purpose of examining Community legislation and proposals. These are the House of Lords Select Committee on the European Communities and the House of Commons Select Committee on European Secondary Legislation. Both committees provide a useful resource of information on Community proposals.

Member States must not only adhere to Community law in practice, they must also ensure that domestic law is not incompatible with Community law. This restriction applies to both local and central government in the United Kingdom. A particular problem arises with Directives that are of direct effect. Thus the approach to the inter-pretation of Community law by the EC Court of Justice must be adopted by the national court when considering whether a Directive has direct effect (see: *R.* v. *London Boroughs Transport Committee ex parte Freight Transport Association Ltd* [1991] 3 All ER 915).

European Community and the environment

In the early years of the Community the development of a Community policy on the environment was slow and *ad hoc.* Since the 1970s Community developments on the environment have been more con-siderable, more than probably any other aspect of Community policy. There are over 300 Directives, regulations and decisions currently in force covering such diverse areas of the environment as pollution control and wildlife.

In the early life of the Community environmental issues mainly arose through the interpretation of Article 100 of the Treaty of Rome relating to the harmonisation of national laws having a direct effect on the development of the Common Market. In addition Article 36 of the Treaty states that the protection of health and life of humans, animals or plants shall not be prohibited or restricted by any provisions of the

Treaty. However, this has been restrictively interpreted and generally most evironmental protection falls outside its ambit. In contrast, Article 235 is more widely interpreted. It permits institutions of the Community to take appropriate measures to achieve the objectives of the Community. It is frequently used to justify action on the environment. Articles 130R, 130S and 130T are used to develop environmental policy.

The Community has slowly developed environmental policies through the interpretation of the various articles noted above. In 1972 Community policy was formulated at the Paris Conference of the Heads of States and Governments. It was accepted that '. . . particular attention will be given to intangible values and to protecting the environment. . .'.

Specific Treaty obligations were added by the Single European Act 1986 and the Treaty of Maastricht 1991. Principles on the environment are found in the addition of Article 130R. These include:

- To preserve, protect and improve the quality of the environment.
- To contribute to the protection of the health of individuals.
- To ensure a prudent and rational utilisation of natural resources.
- To promote at international level, measures to deal with regional or worldwide environmental problems.

An additional element in the future development of environmental law is the principle of subsidiarity. Thus Community action on environment is to be taken only where the objectives can be attained through regional action rather than measures taken by each member state.

The Community has adopted various Action Programmes on the Environment. In all there have been five Action Programmes. The first three covered the period 1973–76, 1977–81 and 1982–86. The Fourth Programme covered the period 1987–92 and a Fifth Action Programme is now in place until the end of the century. The Fifth Action Programme makes the link between the protection of the environment and economic growth. The Community strategy is aimed at 'sustainable development'. This involves a wide range of institutions concerned with the environment. Public authorities, local and central government, various regulatory agencies and the general public are involved. It is expected that the Community will encourage sustainable development by taking account of the international dimension to environmental problems.

The concept of sustainable development originated in 1980 in the *World Conservation Strategy* formed by the International Union for the Conservation of Nature (IUCN) stressing sustainable development in ecological terms. The concept was redeveloped in 1987 to incorporate consideration of economic needs. The World Commission on Environment and Development (better known as the Brundtland Commission after its chair) produced a report entitled *Our Common*

Future (the Brundtland Report, 1987). In this report sustainable development was defined as:

Development that meets the needs of the present without compromising the ability of future generations to meet their needs.

A series of policy objectives were set for sustainable development:
● Reviving economic growth
● Changing the quality of growth
● Meeting essential needs for jobs, food, energy, water and sanitation
● Ensuring a sustainable level of population
● Conserving and enhancing the resource base
● Reorientating technology and managing risk
● Merging environment and economics in decision-making processes.

The Fifth Action Programme of the Community recognises that there are specific environmental problems that require specific action: climate change, air quality, nature protection, water protection, the urban environment and waste management. Also recognised in the Programme are sectors which are of particular concern to the environment. These are industry, energy, transport, agriculture and tourism. A distinguishing feature of the Fifth Action Programme is the development of a wide range of techniques to implement environmental policy. These include regulations, Directives, economic and fiscal indicators, including environmental audits and the recognition of environmental liabilities. Access to information and co-operation between different agencies within the Community is also to be encouraged. It is noteworthy that in the United Kingdom, the principal aims and objectives of the new Environment Agency established under the Environment Act 1995 include the objective of achieving sustainable development (see s. 4 of the Environment Act 1995).

Future directions

The Community appears to recognise the wide range of measures that are necessary to provide protection for the environment. Regulations and Directives are the main means of introducing legal change. Initiatives such as eco-labelling through Community regulation is an example of an attempt to provide consumers with more information on the environmental impact of products. In addition there is a proposed eco-audit system to encourage industrial companies to establish and implement environmental protection schemes.

The Community has also embarked on a number of new initiatives such as, in June 1991, a proposal for a Directive on Civil Liability for Damage caused by Waste. It is aimed at allowing compensation to be payable to victims of damage caused by waste. Compensation should be payable from funds set aside for that purpose. There are also expected to be detailed proposals from the Commission for civil liability for damage caused to the environment from certain types of pollution. Currently, however, the Commission appears to have moved its attention to liability for environmental damage. At the same time the United Kingdom has embarked on a substantial consideration of liability for contaminated land in ss. 57–60 of the Environment Act 1995.

An important aspect of the work of the Community is to provide access to environmental information. In May 1990 the Community (1210/90 EEC 7 May 1990) established the European Environmental Agency (EEA). The aims of the EEA are to ensure there is 'objective, reliable and comparable information' to the Member States and the EC. This is to facilitate the implementation and appraisal of Community measures and the taking of appropriate measures to protect the environment. There are delays in finding a location for the EEA. In the United Kingdom legislation implementing the EEA has been delayed and is expected in the next session of Parliament. It is unlikely that the agency will be operational before mid-1996. At the same time a new Directive (90/313 EEC) gives the public greater freedom of access to information on the environment (see: the Environmental Information Regulations 1992).

The Community continues to develop environmental policies. Starting from the premiss that national laws must be harmonised within the Community, there is now a recognition that different regulatory approaches should be *used* within the Community. Tensions remain between reconciling differing Community objectives and resolving the future of the Community with the principle of subsidiarity after Maastricht. There is also an attempt to provide some codification and adopt a more comprehensive approach to environmental planning. Since the 1980s the Community has adopted a more strict approach to environmental protection. The 'precautionary principle' allows more stringent measures to be taken even where there is scientific uncertainty about the likelihood of harm or the risk to the environment is not quantifiable. Preventing pollution, e.g. through clean technologies, waste minimisation processes, waste recycling etc., is seen as preferable to having to take measures once the pollution has occurred. Assessing the risk to the environment is therefore based not on the available scientific evidence but on an estimation of what the scientific evidence might be in the future. The precautionary principle is in Article 130R of the Maastricht Treaty and in Principle 15 of the Rio Declaration.

The combination of law, policy and general guidelines outlined above may give rise to further developments in advancing principles to protect the environment. Various attempts to prevent environmental harm arise through the implementation of the best available technology (BAT) or the best environmental practices (BEP) or the best practicable environmental option (BPEO). An added dimension to these is the adoption of a cost–benefit analysis through the best available technology not entailing excessive costs (BATNEEC).

In general, environmental laws remain fragmented. Aspects of Community law will be dealt with in the relevant chapters of this book covering land, water and air.

The European Environment Agency

The European Environment Agency was established as a legal entity on 30 October 1993. It was established under Council Regulation No. 1210/90 (OJ No. L 120/1). The Agency has a role in collecting, processing and analysing environmental information which may be disseminated throughout the Community. Technically the Agency is not one of the Community's institutions under the Treaties.

The Agency's first Executive Director Señor Domingo Jimenez-Beltran was appointed in 1994. The Agency aims to provide EC institutions and Member States with information to enable them to take measures to protect the environment. This will permit an assessment of information and the dissemination of information to the public. There is a Management Board with a Scientific Committee. The Agency's tasks include establishing and co-ordinating an Environmental Information and Observation Network, the collection of data on a comparable basis throughout Member States, to promote the broad dissemination of information about Europe's environment and to provide the application of environmental forecasting.

The Agency is also intended to act as an exchange for the best available technologies (see: ENDS Report 240, January 1995, p.22). The Agency intends to develop guidelines for assessing and drawing up indicators for the environment in a number of priority economic sectors. There will also be an important policy role for the Agency. This is likely to be contentious as in the past there has been resistance to a European Environmental Inspectorate. The Agency is expected to be confined to the question of implementation to discover if Member States have implemented environmental laws. Areas that are likely to be included in the Agency's remit are criteria for awarding eco-labels, the use and transfer of environmentally friendly technologies within the Community and in developing countries, and establishing environmental impact assessment of projects.

The state of the environment in 46 European countries is reviewed in one of the first reports from the new Agency published in 1995 (see: *Europe's Environment 1993: The Dobris Assessment.* HMSO, 1995). It is expected that there will be a series of reports published every three years monitoring the environment within Europe.

The Agency has divided its work on certain projects among consortia or research groups throughout the Community. Awarding such research contracts is often a point of contention among Member States, who wish to favour their own national research organisations. The likely success of the Agency will depend on its willingness and success at setting and initiating its own agenda and not becoming a delegated body for the various EC institutions or the Member States. One danger is that the sheer magnitude of the task may disable the Agency from effective action. Another difficulty is that dissemination of environmental information has the potential to bring the Agency into conflict with interested groups throughout the Community. Competing tasks within the Agency will require careful consideration of the priority to be given to its various roles.

▶ References and further reading

Birnie, P. and Boyle, A.(1992) *International Law and the Environment.* Oxford University Press, Oxford.

Bolin, B., Döös, B.R., Jäger, J. and Warrick, R.A. (eds) (1991) *Scope 29. The Greenhouse Effect, Climate Change and Ecosystems.* John Wiley, Chichester.

Caldwell, L.K. (1982), *Science and the National Environmental Policy Act: Redirecting Policy through Procedural Reform.* Cambridge University Press, Cambridge.

Carnwath, 'Environmental enforcement – the need for a specialist court' [1992]JPL 799.

Church, C.H. and Phinnemore, D. (1994) *European Union and European Community.* Harvester, London.

Craig, P. and de Burca, G. (1995) *EC Law Text, Cases and Materials.* Clarendon Press, Oxford.

Dacey, J.W.H., Drake, B.G. and Klug, M.J. (1994) Stimulation of methane emission by carbon dioxide enrichment of marsh vegetation. *Nature,* 370: 47–9.

Haigh, N. (1992) *EEC Environmental Policy and Britain,* 2nd edn. Longman.

HMSO (1995) *Europe's Environment 1993: The Dobris Assessment.* HMSO.

Hughes, D. (1992) *Environmental Law,* 2nd edn. Butterworths, London, p.97.

Johnson, S.P. and Coercelle, G. (1989) *The Environmental Policy of the European Communities.* Graham and Trotman, London.

Kiss, A. and Shelton, D. (1991) *International Environmental Law.* Dordrecht. Graham and Trotman, London.

Kiss, A. and Shelton, D. (1993) *Manual of European Environmental Law.* Grotius Press, Cambridge.

Kramer, L. (1992) *Focus on Environmental Law.* Sweet and Maxwell, London.

Kramer, L. (1993), *European Environmental Law*. Sweet and Maxwell, London.

McEldowney, J.F. (1994) *Public Law*. Sweet and Maxwell, London.

Mumma, A. (1995) *Environmental Law*. McGraw-Hill, London.

Nugent, N. (1994) *The Government and Politics of the European Union*, 3rd edn. Macmillan, London.

Office for Official Publications of the EC (1995) *The Institutions of the European Union*. Luxembourg.

O'Keefe, D. and Twomey, P. (1994) *Legal Issues of the Maastricht Treaty*. Sweet and Maxwell, London.

Preston, B.J. (1989) *Environmental Litigation*. Law Book Company.

Sands, P. (1995) *Principles of International Enironmental Law*. Manchester University Press, Manchester.

Snyder, F. (1990) *New Directions in Community Law*. Sweet and Maxwell, London.

Soussan, J.G. (1992) 'Sustainable development'. In A.M. Mannion and S.R. Bowlby (eds), *Environmental Isuues in the 1990s*. John Wiley, Chichester, pp.21–36.

Weatherill, S. and Beaumont, P. (1993) *EC Law*. Penguin, Harmondsworth.

World Commission on Environment and Development (1987) *Our Common Future*. Oxford University Press, Oxford.

Wurzel, R. (1993) 'Environmental policy'. In J. Lodge (ed.), *The European Community and the Challenge of the Future*, 2nd edn. Pinter, London, pp.178–99.

4 Regulatory bodies and the environment

The development of environmental law depends not only on the courts but also on a variety of agencies and institutions. Each may make its own individual and distinctive contribution. Many agencies operate nationally but they may also function both regionally and internationally. The main institutions of the European Community have already been noted in previous chapters. This chapter provides a brief introduction to some of the agencies in the United Kingdom that have a specific specialism and expertise in relation to the environment. The plan of the chapter is as follows: there is some discussion of the establishment of a unified Environment Agency under the Environment Act 1995; this is followed by an outline of the main central government departments and their responsibilities for the environment.

▶ A unified Environment Agency

Responsibility for the protection of the environment in the United Kingdom is not to be found in any single institution or body. Various responsibilities for the environment are held by a plethora of governmental and non-governmental bodies. Some bodies are advisory. For example the Royal Commission on Environmental Pollution advises the government on pollution problems and makes suggestions in the area of policy for the protection of the environment.

Some bodies with environmental responsibilities are elected and some are non-elected. Central and local government are elected. In the example of local government under s. 222 of the Local Government Act 1972 a local authority may bring an action in respect of a public nuisance if it considers that it is expedient for the promotion or the protection of the interests of the inhabitants of its area.

Appointed bodies with environmental responsibilities are not elected. The National Rivers Authority (NRA) and Her Majesty's Inspectorate of Pollution (HMIP) were established in an attempt to give some coherence to *ad hoc* developments in the protection of the environment. Both bodies had considerable statutory enforcement powers. The NRA under the Water Resources Act 1991 exercised nearly all water regulatory powers with regard to pollution and water resource management covering flood defence and land drainage, fishery and river navigation. HMIP was formed in 1987 from an amalgamation of the Industrial Air Pollution Inspectorate from the Health and Safety Executive and the Radiochemical and Hazardous Waste Inspectorate. It had important powers under various legislation (Alkali, etc., Works Regulation Act 1906, the Health and Safety at Work, etc., Act 1974) and also the Environmental Protection Act 1990 for the control of radioactive substances, atmospheric emissions and the monitoring of waste disposal.

Both NRA and HMIP are currently being transferred to a new Environment Agency established under the Environment Act 1995. The 1995 Act attempts to make a radical break with the past with the establishment of an Environment Agency for England and Wales and for Scotland a separate Scottish Environment Protection Agency (SEPA). The 1995 Act makes detailed provision for the transfer of functions and property rights to the new Agencies from the National Rivers Authority and Her Majesty's Inspectorate of Pollution (Fig. 4.1).

The new Agencies have been in existence since August 1995 but are not expected to be up and running with their statutory framework until April 1996. In November 1994 the Environment Agency Advisory

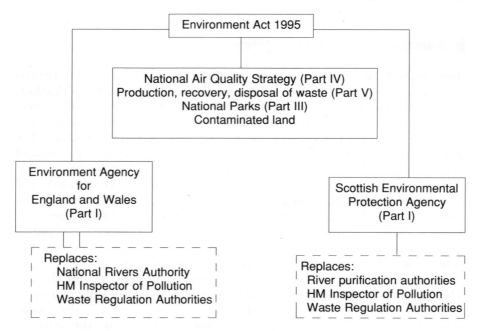

Fig. 4.1 Schematic diagram to show regulation under the Environment Act 1995.

Committee was appointed. Comprising 15 members it is chaired by Lord De Ramsay.

The Environment Act 1995 comprises 125 sections and 24 schedules. It amends and consolidates many recent Acts that apply to the environment. During the passage through Parliament of the Environment Act 1995, there was considerable controversy over the exact functions that should be given to the new Agencies. As a result of extensive debates a large number of amendments to the Act were made in the Lords and in the Committee stage in the House of Commons.

Part V of the Environment Act 1995 provides for a national waste strategy for England and Wales and for Scotland (see Chapter 9). The Environment Agency has been given a principal aim 'to protect and enhance the environment' taken as a whole so as to contribute to sustainable development, subject to other legislation and 'taking into account any likely costs'. There is no equivalent aim set out for the Scottish Environment Protection Agency (see: *Guidance to the Environment Agency on its Objectives, Including the Contribution it is to Make Towards the Achievement of Sustainable Development* (DoE, 1995)).

▶ Central government and the environment

Government departments

There are a number of government departments and agencies with responsibilities that include the environment. Central government departments that are relevant include the following.

The Department of the Environment (DoE)

The Department of the Environment has responsibilities for the development of policy for the environment as well as maintaining important links with other government departments where environmental issues are raised. Included within its remit are responsibilities for planning matters, including inner cities, environmental protection, conservation and water. There is a specialised division dealing with Environmental Impact Assessment and divisions dealing with conservation and the countryside. There is an Environment Protection Group containing Her Majesty's Inspectorate of Pollution (HMIP). As noted above HMIP was formed in 1987 as a result of the merger between the Industrial Air Pollution Inspectorate part of the Health and Safety Executive and the Radiochemical Inspectorate and Hazardous Waste Inspectorates of the Department of the Environment. HMIP was part of the DoE and there were various proposals (see: Cm 1200) that HMIP should be a separate agency. The future of HMIP has now been settled. Under the Environment Act 1995 HMIP is to be transferred to the new

Environment Agency. There are some 8000 premises controlled by HMIP under the Radioactive Substances Act 1960 (now contained in the Radioactive Substances Act 1993). These include research, defence, manufacturing and industrial sites. Its proactive functions are to ensure that in developing policy the 'best practicable environmental option' (see Chapter 5 for a discussion) is included in certain areas such as pollution control, and in radioactive waste management strategies.

There is also within the DoE a Directorate of Air, Climate and Toxic Substances. As noted above, pollution and its control are also within the department's remit. Under s. 80 of the Environment Act 1995 there is a national air quality strategy which will require an assessment of the quality of air and consultation with the new Environment Agency outlined above. There is also within the DoE a division for the central development of environmental protection and sustainable development.

The Ministry of Agriculture, Fisheries and Food (MAFF)

This department has many responsibilities over the environment. Primarily responsible for government policies on agriculture, horti-culture and fisheries in England, it is also involved in safety measures for food including labelling and supervision of additives. MAFF also exercises responsibilities for the protection and enhancement of the countryside and marine environment. It undertakes responsibilities for policy on the control of animal, plant and fish diseases. There is a Countryside, Marine Environment and Fisheries Directorate that oversees the national and international protection of the marine environment. An Environment Task Force oversees environmentally sensitive areas, including environmental aspects of the Common Agricultural Policy of the European Union.

The Department of Trade and Industry (DTI)

This department has wide-ranging responsibilities for government policy on energy, including electricity, coal, gas and oil, the environment and industry. It is primarily responsible for trade policy, but the department has an Environment Division which co-ordinates the DTI's strategic policy on environmental issues. Environmental management, eco-audit regulation and BS 7750 standard setting are all included within the remit of this division. There are also a number of related energy divisions: the Atomic Energy Division, the Coal Division, the Oil and Gas Division and an Electricity Division. There is an International Energy Unit that co-ordinates European Community energy matters and matters within the European Energy Charter.

The Department of Transport

The Secretary of State for Transport is the highway authority under the Highways Act 1980 (SI 1981 No. 238). This means that there are responsibilities for the main 'trunk roads'. Often this work is undertaken by local authorities on the basis of contractual or agency arrangements. The Department of Transport also has responsibilities that include coastguard and marine pollution, vehicle testing, oversight of road transport and of local authorities' planning. There is within the department a Marine Pollution Control Unit that provides contingency planning and the co-ordination of counter-pollution measures. There is a Road Programme Directorate that provides oversight of the road construction programme.

The Department of Health

This department has responsibilities for the administration of the National Health Service. One of its divisions is the Health Aspects of the Environment and Food, which deals with many aspects of general environmental issues such as radiation and chemical pollution of the environment. It also has responsibilities over toxicology and the chemical safety of food and consumer products.

The Overseas Development Administration (ODA)

The ODA provides assistance to overseas countries. One of its executive agencies is the Natural Resources Institute, which contributes assistance through sustainable management of natural resources through the application of science and technology. It has a number of divisions relevant to environmental issues, such as the Applied Ecology Division and the Resource Management Division.

Government departments in Wales

The Welsh Office (WO) exercises responsibilities for the environment for Wales. Water, sewerage, environmental protection, agriculture and fisheries and roads all come within its remit. There is a Transport, Planning and Environment Group with an Environment Division. One of its newly formed Executive Agencies is the Planning Inspectorate responsible for planning, public inquiries, and environmental protection for Wales. There is a Countryside Council for Wales, which is the Government's statutory adviser on wildlife, countryside and maritime conservation matters in Wales. It is answerable to the Secretary of State for Wales and receives an annual grant in aid. There is a Science and Policy Development Directorate responsible for managing all aspects of policy formulation, research and advice on the natural resources of Wales.

Government departments in Northern Ireland

In Northern Ireland environmental issues are primarily the responsibility of the Department of Environment for Northern Ireland. Environmental protection, nature reserves, areas of outstanding natural beauty, the preservation and conservation of historic sites and buildings are all responsibilities of this department. Water, planning and roads also fall within the department's remit. In addition the Department of Economic Development for Northern Ireland has a function in the development of energy policy, the regulation of the future gas industry, energy efficiency, promotion of renewables and responsibilities over minerals and hydrocarbon exploration and licensing. The Department of Agriculture for Northern Ireland is responsible for the development of the agriculture, forestry, and fisheries industries in Northern Ireland including the application of EC policy to Northern Ireland.

Among the regulatory agencies in Northern Ireland there is the Office of Electricity Regulation Northern Ireland (OFFER NI), which is responsible for the promotion of competition in the generation and supply of electricity, including the promotion of energy efficiency in Northern Ireland.

The Scottish Environment Protection Agency (SEPA)

Chapter II of the Environment Act 1995 provides for the establishment of a Scottish Environment Protection Agency on a similar basis to the Environment Agency for England and Wales (see: pp.53–55). Section 21 provides that the functions of river purification authorities and waste disposal authorities, as well as pollution control, shall be exercised by the new agency. The new agency shall also exercise the functions of local authorities in relation to the release of substances into the air and a variety of powers to ensure clean air. The 1995 Act makes detailed provision for the transfer of property, rights and liabilities to SEPA to enable it to carry out its functions.

Government departments in Scotland

The Secretary of State for Scotland is responsible in Scotland for a wide range of regulatory matters which in England are the responsibility of various central government departments.

In Scotland, on matters concerning the environment, there is the Scottish Office Agriculture and Fisheries Department with responsibility for agricultural policy at both UK and EC level. There are within this department a number of Executive Agencies including the Scottish Fisheries Protection Agency for enforcement of fisheries regulations and the Scottish Agricultural Science Agency responsible for the regulation and protection of the environment over plant health, crops and food. The Scottish Office Environment Department has a remit that includes policy and function affecting the environment and the physical development of Scotland. This covers town and country planning, water supplies and sewerage, air and river pollution, nature conservation of the countryside and historic monuments. Within this department there are various divisions such as HM Industrial Pollution Inspectorate for Scotland, with responsibilities over the control of hazardous waste, radioactive waste management and air pollution control. There is also the Rural Affairs and National Heritage Atmospheric and General Environmental Protection HMIPI with regulatory responsibility for air pollution. All these powers have been transferred to the newly established Scottish Environment Protection Agency under Chapter II of the Environment Act 1995.

There is a Scottish Natural Heritage established by the Natural Heritage (Scotland) Act 1991 and responsible to the Secretary of State for Scotland. Its role is to take over the responsibilities of the Nature Conservancy Council for Scotland and the Countryside Commission for Scotland. Its aims are to secure the conservation and enhancement of Scotland's natural heritage and promote the enjoyment of the country-side. It has a statutory duty to care for sites and areas for the protection of natural habitats and wildlife such as National Nature Reserves, Sites of Special Scientific Interest and National Scenic Areas. It advises the Secretary of State for Scotland on the designation of Natural Heritage Areas in Scotland. Section 35 of the Environment Act 1995 provides amendments to the powers given to Scottish National Heritage to take account of the creation of the new Scottish Environment Protection Agency established under Chapter II of the Environment Act 1995.

Miscellaneous bodies

There are a number of bodies, which are not part of government departments, but which have an important role in the protection of the environment. Many of these are research councils that provide financial support for environmentally related research. These include the Economic and Social Research Council (ESRC), and the Natural Environment Research Council (NERC). In the past the Science and Engineering Research Council (SERC) and the Agriculture and Food Research Council (AFRC) sponsored projects related to the environ-ment. The SERC and AFRC were reorganised into three new research councils on 1 April 1994. The new councils are the Biotechnology and Biological Sciences Research Council (BBSRC), the Engineering and Physical Science Research Council (EPSRC) and the Particle Physics and Astronomy Research Council (PPARC). In the case of EPSRC, the Rutherford Appleton and Daresbury Laboratories have been brought under a unified management structure. In general, the BBSRC is key among the new research councils in supporting some environmentally associated research.

There are a number of bodies that undertake research in particular areas of specialism such as Horticultural Research International (HRI) which is a charity operating under Next Steps Agency status and sponsored by the Ministry of Agriculture (see: J.F. McEldowney, *Public Law*, Sweet and Maxwell, 1994 for a discussion of the role of the Next Steps Agencies; also see: *The Financing and Accountability of Next Step Agencies*, Cm 914, HMSO, 1989; and *The Strategic Management of Agencies Models for Management Next Steps Team*, HMSO, 1995). Its work on plants and biology is important to the environment. There is a Pesticides Safety Directorate which became an Executive Agency of the Ministry of Agriculture, Fisheries and Food (MAFF) from 1 April 1993. Its main aims are to protect the health of human beings, creatures and plants, and safeguard the environment. Its role is to ensure the safe, efficient and humane control of pests and to advise MAFF on pesticides.

The Countryside Commission is responsible for the conservation and enhancement of the beauty of the English countryside (see: the Wildlife and Countryside Act 1981 s. 47 and Sch. 13). The Commission is independent of the DoE and its members are appointed by the Secretary of State for the Environment. One part of its function is to keep under review the management of National Parks (see: the National Parks and Access to the Countryside Act 1949). English Heritage, formerly the Historic Buildings and Monuments Commission for England under the National Heritage Act 1983, advises the Government on the preservation of England's historic monuments and buildings. English Nature (Nature Conservancy Council for England), advises the government on nature conservation in England. It promotes the conservation of England's wildlife and nature. Extensive statutory powers under the Health and Safety at Work, etc., Act 1974 are provided to the Health and Safety Commission which is responsible for the implementation of the legislation. The National Radiological Protection Board carries out research and provides information to those responsible for radiological protection. The Royal Commission on Environmental Pollution advises the government on matters concerning pollution and the environment. The Forestry Commission is the government department responsible for forestry policy in Britain. It is responsible to MAFF and the Secretary of State for Wales and the Secretary of State for Scotland. It is distinct from other government departments as there is a statutorily appointed Chairman and Board of Commissioners (see: the Forestry Act 1991) and it is charged with the duty to implement the Forestry Act 1967. It sets the standards for the forestry industry and regulates plant health, conservation, and the management of forests under its control. There is a statutory duty to achieve a reasonable balance between the development of the forestry industry and the environment.

There is a UK Eco-Labelling Board which was set up on 2 November 1992. It is the body which is responsible for the administration of the European Communities eco-labelling scheme within the United Kingdom. This scheme is intended to promote the use of goods that have a reduced impact on the environment and to provide better information to the consumer on products from an environmental perspective. The remit of the Board is to encourage industry, retailers and the consumer to be conscious of the environmental impact of products.

The Public Health Laboratory Service comprises a network of 52 microbiology laboratories and 22 specialist epidemiological and reference units throughout England and Wales. Its function is to detect patterns, trends and outbreaks of infectious disease. An important function is to provide methods of disease control and strategies of prevention. It may help detect and provide solutions to environmental dangers that could affect public health.

The Joint Nature Conservation Committee was established by the Environmental Protection Act 1990 for the purpose of understanding conservation in Great Britain as a whole. It is a committee of the Countryside Council for Wales, English Nature and Scottish Natural Heritage. There are independent members drawn from Northern Ireland and the Countryside Commission. Its aims are to provide common scientific standards and to undertake the commissioning of research related to conservation in the United Kingdom.

There is the UK Atomic Energy Authority established by statute in 1954 as a statutory corporation (see: the Atomic Energy Authority Act 1954 as amended by the Atomic Energy Authority Act 1971). Its aims and functions include the production, use, disposal and storage of atomic energy. It undertakes research associated with the nuclear industry and also ensures the manufacture and transport of atomic material under strict conditions. One part of the Authority's trading activities is undertaken by British Nuclear Fuels Ltd (BNFL). The design, operation and supply of plant and equipment are undertaken by this company. There has been a controversial development of extensive reprocessing facilities at BNFL's plant at Sellafield. The reprocessing facilities separate reusable materials from irradiated fuel produced during nuclear fission. The facilities operate on a commercial basis and there is the planned import of nuclear waste from other countries.

Another aspect of the Authority's work is undertaken by Radiochemical Centre Ltd, set up under the Atomic Energy Act 1971 and renamed in 1981 as Amersham International. It is operated as a commercial enterprise, which supplies radiolabelled materials to research hospitals and industry. There are plans to privatise parts of the Atomic Energy Authority (see: Atomic Energy Authority Act 1995).

Finally, under the Deregulation and Contracting Out Act 1994 there is a Deregulation Task Force. Its remit is to identify regulatory burdens on industry and make recommendations for their removal. In its first report, the Task Force identifies some of the areas where business is carrying a heavy regulatory burden. Controversially it asserts that legislation in the environment area may place major burdens on industry and business. The new Environment Agency is likely to have to grapple with the problems of deregulation at a time when there is increasing pressure for improvements in environmental standards (see: Deregulation Task Force, report 1994/95).

There are a number of voluntary organisations active in the environmental area, such as Greenpeace and Friends of the Earth mentioned in previous chapters. Specific organisations that protect rights, such as the Ramblers' Association, also deserve mention. This was founded in 1935, following the setting up of a National Council of Ramblers' Federation in 1931, and the creation of a number of distinct federations in London. Its role is to preserve the national footpath network and support the creation of national parks. Such organisations perform an educative function as well as providing for the interests of members. The National Trust, through ownership of a number of historic buildings and parkland, also makes an important contribution to the protection of the environment. Founded on 16 July 1894, it was six months later registered under the Companies Act 1862 as 'The National Trust for Places of Historic Interest or Natural Beauty'. The Trust has become one of the largest private landowners in Britain and currently owns about 1 per cent of the land. It cares for over 200 historic houses. Independent of government the Trust, through endowments and gifts, seeks to conserve and preserve the historic aspects of its many buildings and the land that it owns. In 1993/94 its income was £139 million, nearly 30 per cent coming from membership fees. In recent years it has had to respond to the increase in public awareness about the environment (see: Robin Fedden and Rosemary Joekes, *The National Trust Guide*, The National Trust, 1973).

▶ Local government and the environment

Local authorities have wide-ranging duties and responsibilities that have an impact on the environment. They are 'competent authorities' for many EC Directives and regulations. This means that local authorities have a wide range of legal obligatons placed upon them by virtue of membership of the European Union. In addition local authorities have important enforcement powers over many environmental matters. For example, as mentioned in the early part of the chapter, local authorities possess wide powers under s. 222 of the Local Government Act 1972 to bring an action for public nuisance. Under s. 80 of the Environmental Protection Act 1990, where the local authority concludes that noise amounting to a nuisance exists or is likely to recur in its area, it must serve a notice on the person responsible for the noise.

Local authority powers range from public health, food hygiene, building control and planning policy to trading standards and statutory nuisances. At local authority level the planning department makes important planning decisions within the framework of the Town and Country Planning Acts. Local authorities have also a role in transport, waste collection and management, and construction projects, including mineral extraction and change of use. There is usually a planning committee with powers delegated from the full council. Account is taken of the various environmental assessment statements under the Town and Country (Assessment of Environmental Effects) Regulations 1988.

There is also an environmental health department under the jurisdiction of environmental health officers; it has various statutory powers relevant to food and health. The control of smoke, noise and air pollution is also monitored by the local authority in partnership with Her Majesty's Inspectorate of Pollution (now the Environment Agency). Finally there are various statutory duties exercised by trading standards officers relevant to con- sumer protection. Local government also has an important policy role on environmental issues. There are various local government associations throughout Scotland, England, Wales and Northern Ireland.

▶ Pressure groups

The significance of pressure groups in the development of environmental policy should not be overlooked. At the national and international level, Friends of the Earth, Greenpeace and the World Development Movement have been active campaigners and have been engaged in the lobbying process for better protection of the environment. They are often successful in challenging government action (see: *R. v. Secretary of State for Foreign and Commonweath Affairs ex parte World Development Movement* [1995]1 All ER 611). Greenpeace has been particularly active in monitoring radioactive waste. Mr Justice Otton, in *R. v. Pollution Inspectorate ex parte Greenpeace* [1994] 4 All ER 321 at p.349, described how the organisation had nearly 5 million supporters worldwide with 400 000 supporters in the United Kingdom; about 2500 of these lived in the Cumbria region where the British Nuclear Fuels plant was situated.

Local groups campaigning about a particular issue may campaign alongside national pressure groups. There are many national groups such as the Campaign for Rural England, the Ramblers' Association and the Royal Society for the Protection of Birds. The National Trust, a charity which owns many buildings and areas of natural beauty, may also lobby for the protection of the environment.

The role of pressure groups or lobby groups is often controversial. In recent years their importance has become more significant in the area of legal challenge. The Law Commission, in its recent report on administrative law (Law Com. No. 226) acknowledges that interest groups may have good grounds for having standing, in the public interest, to make an application for judicial review. This might apply in cases where the pressure group feels that the public are adversely affected by an administrative decision of a government agency or government itself (see Chapter 2).

Privatisation and the environment

The government's privatisation policy and its impact on the major utilities such as water, gas and electricity has importance to the environment. The significance of the regulation of the newly privatised industries is discussed in Chapter 5.

Information on the environment

There are a number of diverse bodies that provide information about the environment. In addition currrent legislation on the environment requires a number of environmental registers to be kept by various pollution control agencies and local authorities. Reference to the appropriate part of the book may be made to discover further details. Access to information not covered by a specific register may be found through one of the central government departments mentioned above. Generally see the Environmental Information Regulations 1992 (EC Directive 90/313, OJ No L 158/56) and in the United Kingdom, the Environmental Regulations 1992 SI No. 3240 (see: *R* v. *British Coal Corporation ex parte Ibstock Building Products* unreported 21 October 1994, ENDS report 247, August 1995, p. 41.

The following are some of the more important registers for information under various environmental legislation.

● *The Environmental Protection Act 1990* Registers under Part I on pollution control. Information relating to integrated pollution control is maintained by Her Majesty's Inspectorate of Pollution (now the Environment Agency) and various Local Authority Air Pollution Agencies (see: Environmental Protection (Prescribed Processes and

Substances) Regulations 1991). Under the supervision of the various Waste Regulatory Authorities there are registers under Part II that relate to waste on land, Part IV relates to litter and Part VI to genetically modified organisms. Finally under s. 143 there are registers relating to contaminated land.

- *Town and Country Planning Act 1990* Registers are maintained of planning applications under s. 69 and of enforcement and stop notices under s. 188.
- *Water Resources Act 1991* Registers are provided by the National Rivers Authority (now the Environment Agency) that relate to pollution. These are pollution control registers under s. 190 and registers of abstraction and impounding licences under s. 189.
- *Water Industry Act 1991* The water regulator, the Director General of Water Services, maintains a register on information relating to the appointment and regulation of water and sewerage operators (s. 195), water quality registers under ss. 67–69 and 213 (also see the Water Supply (Water Quality) Regulations 1989). Registers for the purpose of works discharges are maintained under s. 197. Registers relating to deposits at sea and incineration at sea are maintained under the Food and Environment Protection Act 1985.
- *The Clean Air Act 1993* Local authorities in England and Wales have registers containing information on the emission of pollutants and other substances into the air.
- *The Environment Act 1995* Changes introduced by the new Act include under s. 113 provision for the disclosure of information to the newly created Environment Agency and the Scottish Environment Protection Agency. Section 51 provides that the new Agencies must make available to the relevant minister information on matters within the responsibility of the Agencies. This section is widely drafted to include information that is not within the possession of the Agency but which it is reasonable to expect it to acquire.
- *Miscellaneous legislation* Finally, there are a number of registers to be found under a miscellaneous collection of legislation. For example, under the Control of Pollution (Amendment) Act 1989 and under the Controlled Waste (Registration of Carriers and Seizure of Vehicles) Regulations 1991, the Waste Regulation Authority has a register of waste carriers. The Control of Industrial Air Pollution (Registration of Works) Regulations 1989 (see the Alkali Act 1906 and Health and Safety at Work, etc., Act 1974) provide for industrial air pollution registers to be maintained. There are registers under s. 39 of the Radioactive Substances Act 1993 and under the Environment and Safety Information Act 1988. Registers of noise levels are maintained by a local authority under s. 64 of the Control of Pollution Act 1974 (also see: the Control of Noise (measurement, etc.) Regulations 1976).

Public access to information on the environment and openness about environmental information enable the public to participate in the government process and allow government to be better informed about the environment. In 1984 the Royal Commission on Environmental Pollution favoured a presumption of unrestricted access for the public to information on pollution control. This idea has not been acted upon.

▶ Useful addresses

Advisory Committee on Business and the Environment, Room C11/18, 2 Marsham Street, London SW1P 3EB.

Biodiversity Action Plan Steering Group, Room 105, Tollgate House, Houlton Street, Bristol BS2 9DJ.

Department of the Environment (DoE), 2 Marsham Street, London SW1P 3EB.

Deregulation Unit, Room 715, Ashdown House, 123 Victoria Street, London SW1E 6RB

Ministry of Agriculture, Fisheries and Food (MAFF), Whitehall Place, London SW1A 2HH.

Department of Trade and Industry (DTI), 123 Ashdown House, Victoria Street, London, SW1E 6RB.

Department of Transport (DoT), 2 Marsham Street, London SW1P 3EB.

Department of Health, Richmond House, 79 Whitehall, London SW1A 2NS.

Energy Efficiency Office, 1 Palace Street, London, SW1E 5HE.

Forestry Commission, 231 Corstorphine Road, Edinburgh EU12 7AZ.

Her Majesty's Inspectorate of Pollution (HMIP), Romney House, 43 Marsham Street, London, SW1P 3PY.

National Rivers Authority, Rivers House, Waterside Drive, Aztec West, Almondsbury, Bristol BS12 4UD.

OFFER, Head Office, Hagley House, Hagley Road, Birmingham B16 8QG.

Royal Commission on Environmental Pollution, Church House, Great Smith Street, London, SW1P 3BZ.

The Government's Panel on Sustainable Development, Room A124, Romney House, 43 Marsham Street, London SW1P 3PY.

▶ Pressure groups and organisations

Anglers Conservation Association, 23 Castlegate, Grantham, Lincs NG31 6SW.

The Council for the Protection of Rural England, Warwick House, 25 Buckingham Palace Road, London SW1 0PP.

The Environmental Law Foundation, Lincoln's Inn House, 42 Kingsway, London WC2B 6EX.
Friends of the Earth, 26–28 Underwood Street, London N1 7JQ.
Greenpeace, Canonbury Villas, London N1 2PN.
National Society for Clean Air, 136 North Street, Brighton, BN1 1RG.
Royal Society for Nature Conservation, The Green, Witham Park, Waterside South, Lincoln LN5 7JR.

▶ Useful sources of information

Civil Service Year Book – available as an annual publication from HMSO (1995–).
ENDS Reports – Monthly publication from Environmental Data Services Ltd, Finsbury Business Centre, 40 Bowling Green Lane, London, EC1R 0NE.
The British Ecological Society, 26 Bloades Court, Deodar Road, London, SW15 2NU.
The Geological Society, Burlington House, Piccadilly, London W1V 0JU.
Guidance to the Environment Agency on its Objectives, including the contribution it is to make towards the achievement of sustainable development (DoE, 1995).
The Consumer Association, 2 Marylebone Road, London, NW1 4DF.
Business and the Environment Programme: The Environment Council, 21 Elizabeth Street, London, SW1W 9RP and Business in the Environment, 8 Stratton Street, London W1X 5FD.

▶ Reports from the Royal Commission on Environmental Pollution

1st Report: Cmnd 4585 (1971).
2nd Report: Three Issues in Industrial Pollution, Cmnd 4894 (1972).
3rd Report: Pollution in some British Estuaries and Coastal Waters, Cmnd 5054 (1972).
4th Report: Pollution Control: Progress and Problems, Cmnd 5780 (1974).
5th Report: Air Pollution Control: An Integrated Approach, Cmnd 6371 (1976).
6th Report: Nuclear Power and the Environment, Cmnd 6618 (1976).
7th Report: Agriculture and Pollution, Cmnd 7644 (1979).
8th Report: Oil Pollution and the Sea, Cmnd 8358 (1981).
9th Report: Lead in the Environment, Cmnd 8852 (1983).
10th Report: Tackling Pollution – Experience and Prospects, Cmnd 9149 (1984).

11th Report: Managing Waste: The Duty of Care, Cmnd, 9675 (1985).

12th Report: Best Practicable Environmental Option, Cmnd 310 (1988).

13th Report: The Release of Genetically Engineered Organisms to the Environment, July 1989.

14th Report: Genhaz – a System for the Critical Appraisal of Proposals to Release GMOs into the Environment, June 1991.

15th Report: Emissions from Heavy Duty Diesel Vehicles, September 1991.

16th Report: Freshwater Quality, June 1992.

17th Report: Incineration and Waste, May 1993.

18th Report: Transport and the Environment, October 1994

19th Report: Sustainable Use of Soil, February 1996.

5 Privatisation and the environment

Since the 1980s large-scale privatisation of many of the major utilities has been undertaken by the government. In this chapter the environmental implications of privatisation are outlined when considering the structure, organisation and role of the newly privatised industries. One of the crucial questions for the future development of environmental protection is the extent to which regulatory bodies will develop sufficient long-term strategies for the protection of the environment.

▶ Introduction

The government's privatisation policy has implications for the environment. The process of privatisation is where the ownership of utilities such as gas, water and electricity has been transferred from the public sector to the private sector through the creation of newly formed Company Act companies. A good example, where the environmental implications have become obvious, is the privatisation of the water industry. Privatisation has had the effect of bringing to the public's attention certain environmental problems. For example, water privatisation has involved high capital costs to update the existing water and sewerage facilities inherited by the newly privatised water companies. A large part of such costs has been passed to the consumer and this has resulted in consumers experiencing higher water charges than under the nationalised industry. It is estimated that water bill increases will amount to 5 per cent a year from 1995 to 2000, mainly due to waste treatment costs. Proposals for metering water have been made in an effort to find an equitable distribution of water charges.

Privatisation has also highlighted greater regional variations in water charges than hitherto. Consumers in different parts of the country have higher bills, reflecting the differences in the existing infrastructure and in some cases higher clean-up costs. In particular, sewerage clean-up costs for coastal regions are higher because of European Community standards for cleaner beaches (see Chapter 11).

In general, privatisation policy has resulted in greater transparency in real costs and in the calculation of prices paid by the consumer to the privatised industry. Very often environmental-based costs were not fully calculated pre-privatisation. At the early planning stage of many privatisations, however, environmental matters were not fully considered. This was partly because environmental matters were given a lower priority than commercial requirements such as a wider share ownership or competition. The environmental consequences of privatisation arise in many issues that may be found in the sections of the book on land, water and air. In this chapter it is useful to note some of the regulatory bodies and their role as regards the environment.

Privatisation: regulatory bodies

The established pattern of privatisation legislation has involved formulating statutory powers and combining these with regulatory responsibilities. There is an implicit trade-off between legal powers and operating responsibilities. The newly privatised operators are given sufficient legal powers to carry out their commercial activities. This includes contractual and licensing powers. In return regulatory standards are expected to be met and obligations to carry out an efficient and competitive industry are agreed.

The enabling privatisation legislation provides legal powers to the regulators and licensing arrangements for the newly formed utility companies. The regulators include OFFER for electricity, OFWAT for water, and OFGAS for gas. Each regulator has specific regulatory powers under the relevant privatisation legislation. The various powers of the main regulators have been brought into common form by the Competition and Service (Utilities) Act 1992. Powers include: the issuing of licences or exemptions; setting performance standards; regulating disputes between customers and companies; the investigation and publication of information; the monitoring of standards and their appraisal; and to change conditions of licences and review those conditions. In addition various duties are commonly enjoyed by regulators such as: to ensure that all reasonable demands for utility services are satisfied; to ensure licence holders have financial probity; to promote competition; to safeguard the interests of consumers; and to regulate prices.

Central government policies: privatisation and the environment

The absence of any coherent or well thought-out general plan regarding the implications of privatisation for the environment is most obvious in the case of some of the public utilities. Some of the main public utilities privatised in the 1980s fall within the energy sector. As the examples of coal, electricity and gas illustrate, the environment was a secondary consideration in the privatisation process.

In the 1980s the main central government department responsible for the development of national policies on coal, electricity and atomic power was the Department of Energy. In the period of privatisation of gas and electricity its main concern was the creation of markets in energy. Energy conservation and energy efficiency received secondary attention compared to the need to provide competition within the energy industries. Since April 1992 the Department of Energy has been wound up and the functions of the Secretary of State for Energy merged with those of the Department of Trade and Industry.

Following the privatisation of the main utilities such as gas and electricity, policy on the environment has altered. The environment has attracted more political attention. In the 1990s there is greater awareness of the need for energy efficiency, stricter regulation and more effective pricing arrangements intended to achieve environmental objectives. Recent examples include differential taxes in favour of 'green' petrol, consumption taxes through the addition of value added tax (VAT) on gas and electricity. Water charges since privatisation in 1990 have included clean-up costs to bring the UK standards more closely in line with standards set in the European Community. There is also the cost of rebuilding and updating the water distribution systems to modern standards.

Environmental issues are likely to be important in the remaining major privatisation of railways and in the recently privatised coal industry. In the case of both railways and coal the privatisation legislation includes consideration of the environment. In the case of railways the Railways Act 1993 and the British Railways Act 1994 contain specific provisions for the upkeep of roads, footpaths and other maintenance works.

The proposed privatisation of the railway industry has come at a time when the government's policy on building motorways has been heavily criticised, largely on environmental grounds. Environmental issues have promoted government grants for rail to be connected to industrial facilities and to encourage rail as a means of delivering industrial goods. (Policy Statement from the Department of Transport, 28 May 1991). This policy was introduced to encourage rail usage and enhance Rail Freight as a company prior to privatisation.

The privatisation of British Coal, completed in January 1995, has resulted in the industry undergoing restructuring. As part of this restructuring, environmental issues have been addressed to make the coal industry suitable for the market (*Report of the Royal Commission on Energy and the Environment: Coal and the Environment*, 1981). This has resulted in some attention being given to environmental concerns.

Specific industries and privatisation

As a general principle privatisation statutes have not always included specific requirements that take into account environmental issues. The following are examples of where the protection of the environment is considered as part of the privatisation legislation.

▶ Coal

Prior to January 1995, the newly privatised coal industry was operated by British Coal. Particularly sensitive issues such as opencast mining have raised environmental issues. Previously 90 per cent of all opencast mining was under the control of British Coal, and in 1989 opencast mining contributed to 19 per cent of production of British Coal. Opencast mining falls under the Housing and Planning Act 1986 (see: the Opencast Coal Act 1958 amended by the Housing and Planning Act 1986) and requires planning permission. Specific sites such as National Parks and Areas of Outstanding Natural Beauty fall within specific protection under the planning laws (see Chapters 7 and 8). Privatisation of the coal industry has been accomplished by management buyout and sale. It is likely to bring demands for commercial exploitation of more opencast mining on economic grounds. This is likely to test the existing laws on environmental protection to the limits.

The Coal Industry Act 1994 has two sections devoted to the protection of the environment. Section 53 sets out duties in connection with planning matters and responsibilities for the protection of the environment. Section 54 sets obligations to restore land affected by coal-mining operations. Section 58 of the Environment Act 1995 inserts a new section 91a, into Chapter II of Part III of the Water Resources Act 1991 and provides for the regulation of abandoned mines by the newly established Environment Agency.

▶ Gas

The newly privatised gas industry has certain environmental responsibilities under the Gas Act 1986. Contained in s. 9 of the Gas Act 1986 there is a duty to develop an efficient, co-ordinated and economic system of gas supply and to supply gas to premises. Section 18 of the 1986 Act imposes high standards of safety and under the Health and Safety at Work Act 1974 there are requirements for the protection of the public against fire, explosions or other injurious dangers. The 1986 Act does not make any specific environmental demands on the British gas industry other than general environmental protection concerned with pollution control and planning. Natural gas is in fact less polluting than coal or oil, emitting lower levels of pollutants including carbon dioxide (an important greenhouse gas) on combustion. Since the privatisation of the electricity industry there has been a large expansion in the use of natural gas to generate electricity, primarily because of its relatively low cost. There are plans to continue expanding this use of gas through the construction of small gas-fired electricity stations. This is justified by both cost and environmental considerations.

The Office of Gas Supply (OFGAS), established under the Gas Act 1986, is responsible for monitoring the activities of British Gas plc and its powers include the enforcement of the price formula. The Director has a duty to promote efficiency and economy on the part of gas suppliers. The Gas Act 1995 provides for the reorganisation of the gas industry.

▶ Water and sewerage

The newly privatised water companies under the Water Act 1989 and under Parts III and IV of the Water Industry Act 1991 are given some general duties. There is a general duty to maintain and develop an efficient and economical system of water supply under ss. 37 and 94 of the 1991 Act. Section 52 imposes a specific duty on water undertakers to provide a 'wholesome supply' of water for domestic purposes (see: SI 1989 No. 1147 and SI 1989 No. 1384). There is a Directive 80/778/EEC on standards of water for human cconsumption. It is an offence to supply water unfit for human consumption and there are delegated powers given to the Secretary of State under s. 67 of the 1991 Act to lay down standards for wholesome water. In addition the Director General of the industry, as the regulator of the industry, has functions which include environmental as well as commercial matters. In practical terms the commercial running of the industry appears to have been given more emphasis than environmental concerns.

As noted in Chapter 4 the National Rivers Authority (NRA) was established by the Water Act 1989. It was an independent body with wide statutory powers covering water resources, pollution control (such as microbiological and chemical), flood defences, fisheries, recreation, conservation and navigation in England and Wales. It also has responsibilities for the marine environment around the coast of England and Wales. Flood defence includes sea defences but not coastal protection, which falls under local authority jurisdiction. The NRA has links with the main government departments such as Environment, and Agriculture, Fisheries and Food. It is now subsumed into the new Environment Agency under the Environment Act 1995 (see Chapter 4).

▶ The onshore oil and gas industries

Environmental issues have been of central importance in the development of oil and gas exploration in the North Sea since 1986. In this example licences are provided to allow commercial undertakers to exploit the natural resources of the country. There is clearly potential conflict between the protection of the environment and the exploitation of resources for the benefit of the community as a whole. Local community interests may also be in conflict with national interest. Various circulars have attempted to provide a framework for the resolution of these matters (see: DoE Circular 2/85 Planning Control over Oil and Gas Operations).

▶ Electricity

Privatisation of the electricity industry under the Electricity Act 1989 raised a number of environmental issues. Various duties have been placed on the generation, supply and efficient use of electricity. Licences for the generation, supply and transmission of electricity may contain conditions under s. 7 of the 1989 Act and there is a general duty to develop and maintain an efficient, co-ordinated, economical and competitive electricity supply and generation system. Schedule 22 of the Environment Act 1995 amends s. 38 of the Electricity Act 1989 to encourage the development of combined heat and power systems to be introduced by a public electricity supplier.

The main environmental duties therefore fall on the main electricity generators – PowerGen and National Power. Originally under the nationalised industry arrangements, 90 per cent of electricity production came from coal-fired generation stations, raising major environmental concerns. Environmental controls were necessary since coal-fired generation stations emit sulphur dioxide, nitrous oxide and carbon dioxide. Such harmful emissions are subject to stringent European environmental controls. These gases have a considerable environmental impact (see Chapter 12). Sulphur dioxide and other gases have a direct effect on plants. They tend to reduce the efficiency of carbon fixation during photosynthesis and reduce the growth of plants even when direct damage is not evident. In addition, sulphur dioxide together with the nitrogen oxides contribute to the formation of 'acid rain' (pH 4.0–5.0) and the acidification of terrestrial and aquatic habitats. Acidification not only damages the environment through hydrogen ion (H^+) accumulation, but also has a severe impact on the biogeochemical cycles. Some essential nutrients become limiting for plant growth as a result, while others accumulate to potentially toxic levels. The end result is a decline in species diversity and abundance at all the trophic levels within an ecosystem (see Chapter 12). In addition, the nitrogen oxides are greenhouse gases and contribute to the ozone depletion in the stratosphere. Carbon dioxide is of course a key greenhouse gas. The imposition of strict controls on the emission of these gases has had the effect of encouraging electricity generation from other sources, notably gas turbine and combined cycle. Currently, there are also developments which are less polluting. These are advances in wind technology, combined heat and power systems and in alternative energy sources such as waste incineration and solar power.

The Electricity Act 1989 contains a detailed regulatory framework for the industry. Some of these legal powers have the effect of providing a framework for the protection of the environment. Controls on generating stations that exceed 50 megawatts (MW) are contained in s. 36(1) of the 1989 Act requiring the consent of the Secretary of State. In the case of large power generating stations, where the capacity is 300 MW or more, there is the requirement of an Environmental Assessment (see Chapter 6). Consent is also required for the installation of power lines. Schedule 9 of the 1989 Act applies to proposals for the building of new generating stations and electricity works. There is the requirement that the natural beauty of a site should be preserved. This includes conserving flora, and the geological and physiographical features of special interest, including sites and buildings, have to be protected (see: the Electricity (Applications for Consent) Regulations 1990 No. 455 and SI 1990 No. 443. Also the Electricity Generating Station (Inquiries Procedures) Rules SI 1990 No. 528, DoE Circular 14/90).

There are detailed requirements for the building of electricity generating stations that set important environmental controls, including licences issued by the Health and Safety Executive under the Nuclear Installations Inspectorate. The forum of a public inquiry is used to discuss many of the environmental issues related to nuclear power (see: the Sizewell B inquiry and the report by Sir Frank Layfield, 27 January 1987). The form of the inquiry is carried out according to the terms of Cmnd 7133 (1978) containing guidance to inspectors on the conduct of inquiries (see: Cm 43 (1987) for a recent discussion of the reform of the procedures).

Section 32 of the 1989 Act provides that there is a non-fossil fuel obligation. This requires electricity suppliers to acquire a specified percentage of electricity from non-fossil fuel generating stations. Fossil fuel is defined as coal and its products, natural gas, crude liquid petroleum or its products. A non-fossil fuel generator is therefore one which is driven by power other than fossil fuel. Examples include hydro-electric, wind power, solar power, nuclear power or gas from a landfill or waste deposit site. The inclusion of nuclear power is to ensure that electricity distribution companies purchase the output of nuclear power stations. This means the nuclear industry is effectively subsidised by the fossil fuel levy. Since 1990 there is a 10 per cent surcharge on fossil fuel-generated power, which is a subsidy to nuclear power.

Environmental issues regarding the use of energy for both industrial and domestic purposes have attracted a great deal of attention after the decision of the Chancellor of the Exchequer in 1993 to raise value added tax on utilities such as gas, electricity and water. This tax has in part been described as an environmental tax, encouraging energy conservation and thereby reducing pollutant emissions.

▶ Privatised utilities and European Community law

One important aspect of European Community law is the question of how Community Directives impose obligations on Member States. The primary responsibility for ensuring that Member States introduce national laws to implement Directives is entrusted to the Commission. However, there are circumstances where it is possible to invoke provisions of a Directive directly before a national court where the Directive is precise and unconditional. The precise obligations are usually directed against the Member State because it is the Member State that may be in default (see Chapters 1–3).

The crucial concept adopted by the Court of Justice is 'emanations of the state'. What precisely is covered by the term 'emanations of the state'? The concept includes government departments, local authorities and public sector corporations. The High Court in *Griffin and others* v. *South West Water Services Ltd* (25 August 1994) held that a privatised utility came within the definition. A statutory water company with public functions laid down under the Water Industry Act 1991 was held to perform a public service as a water and sewerage undertaker under the control of the state. If this approach is followed in other cases it places obligations directly on privatised utilities. This may have significant consequences when there are delays or incomplete provisions in national laws when incorporating important Community Directives, in particular the obligations under the 1990 Directive on Environmental Information (90/313/EEC OJ 158 23 June 1990 and the Environmental Information Regulations 1992, SI 1992 No. 3240). Member States have obligations to ensure that information relating to the environment is made available to the public. This may now require a direct obligation on the privatised utility to ensure the Directive is complied with correctly to the full.

▶ Conclusions

Privatisation and regulation have provided an alternative to state ownership of the major utilities. One of the most contentious issues that face the future of the privatised industries is whether sufficient competition will be provided under the new arrangements. Competition is thought to provide benefits to the consumer as well as profitability to the industry. Keener pricing, better quality of service and greater efficiency are expected under privatisation than under the nationalised industries. The success of privatisation is likely to depend on assessing competiton within each industry. The emphasis given to competition has consequences for the environment. The evaluation of environmental concerns appears to have a lower priority than competition. Despite the fact that the creation of new regulatory structures and new industries provides greater opportunities than before to prioritise environmental issues, it is possible these opportunities will not be exploited to the full.

▶ Further reading

General background

Baldwin, R. (ed.) (1995) *Regulation in Question: The Growing Agenda.* London School of Economics, London.

Beesley, M. (ed.) (1994) *Regulating Utilities: The Way Forward.* London Institute of Economic Affairs, London.

Bishop, M., Kay, J., and Mayer, C. (1995) *The Regulatory Challenge.* Oxford University Press, Oxford.

CRI Regulatory Review (1994) (available from 3, Robert Street, London WC2N 6BH).

Ernst, J. (1994) *Whose Utility? The Social Impact of Public Utility Privatisation and Regulation in Britain.* Open University Press, Milton Keynes.

Garbutt, J. (1995) *Environmental Law,* 2nd edn John Wiley, Chichester.

McEldowney, J.F. (1994) *Public Law.* Sweet and Maxwell, London.

Ogus, A.I. (1992) 'Regulatory laws: some lessons from the past'. 12 *Legal Studies* 1.

Ogus, A.I. (1994) *Regulation: Legal Form and Economic Theory.* Clarendon Press, Oxford.

Woolf and McCue, 'Who regulates the regulator?' the great debate [1993] 4 *Utilities Law Review* 199.

Energy policy

Coal and the Environment, Cmnd 8877 (HMSO, 1983)

House of Lords Select Committee on the European Communities 13th Report Session 1990/91, *Energy and the Environment.*

Royal Commission on Environmental Pollution *Nuclear Power and the Environment*, Cmnd 6618 (HMSO, 1976).

6 Environmental assessment and integrated pollution control

In previous chapters the main elements of environmental law have been outlined. In this chapter the assessment of the environmental impact of a proposed project or development is considered. In the United Kingdom environmental impact assessment is part of planning law. Environmental harm is a material consideration in the granting or refusal of planning permission. Assessing the environmental impact of a development is therefore a first step in the calculation of whether there will be a detrimental effect from the proposed development.

This chapter is focused on the mechanisms that may be used to assess the impact of a development on the environment. There are three aspects of this subject relevant to modern environ- mental law. First, there is the definition of environmental impact assessment. How is environmental assessment undertaken and when is it carried out?

Second, there have been advances in the development of integrated pollution control (IPC). This approach reflects a change from previous practice in the direction of pollution controls over the environment. In earlier chapters the development of environmental controls appears pragmatic. There are a diverse number of administrative and enforce- ment agencies involved in pollution control. The fact that many agencies act only in a reactive mode inhibits longer-term action to prevent environmental harm. The historical development of environ- mental law has resulted in separate controls existing for emissions into the atmosphere, environmental problems on land and pollution of water. The creation of specialised statutory arrangements for specific problems, such as the Clean Air Acts or the Alkali Acts, has resulted in a fragmented approach to environmental problems. An attempt to provide a more proactive and preventive approach is found in the development of integrated pollution control.

Third, there are techniques available to make developers take account of environmental concerns. Environmental audit is increasingly popular. The use of insurance to cover high compensation payments in the event of accidents provides incentives to encourage companies or developers to take account of good environmental practices. Account must be taken of the multidisciplinary skills evident in the techniques of environmental assessment.

▶ Environmental assessment

An outline

Environmental impact assessment was introduced in the United States in 1969 (see: the US National Environmental Policy Act (NEPA) 1969; Kiss and Shelton, *Manual of European Environmental Law*, Cambridge, 1993, p. 58). In the United States the 1969 Act incorporated a requirement for assessing the environmental impact of major federal actions significantly affecting the quality of the human environment. The aims of environmental assessment are to ensure that information on the environment is assessed as part of development projects. Alternatives that mitigate harm to the environment are included in the assessment of the potential effects on the environment of a proposed development. In the European Union, EC Directive 85/337 on the Assessment of the Effects of Certain Private and Public Projects on the Environment established the requirement of a preparatory statement outlining the effects on the environment of a particular development. The implementation of the Directive in July 1988 was achieved in the United Kingdom through the Town and Country Planning (Assessment of Environmental Effects) Regulations 1988 (SI 1988 No. 1199). Member States were given some time to prepare implementation arrangements. The first European Court ruling on environmental assessment (Case C-396/92, 9 August 1994; see: ENDS Report 237, October 1994; p. 43) adopted a strict approach to ensuring that Member States did not delay the implementation of the Directive which they were all expected to achieve by July 1988.

Powers to extend the remit of environmental assessment have been granted to the Secretary of State who may make regulations setting out the categories of projects that fall under the requirements of environmental assessment. There are a number of statutory instruments that apply environmental assessment to a wide variety of activities.

Major projects such as those listed in Annex I of the Directive, including developments such as power stations, oil refineries, motorways and major roads, thermal power stations, radioactive waste disposal sites and toxic waste disposal sites *must* always be subject to prior environmental assessment. In Annex II, developments that *may* fall within the scope of environmental assessment are listed. Examples include pig or poultry farming units, mineral extraction, metal processing, glass-making, food manufacture, holiday villages, tanneries and paper manufacturing. A project does not automatically have to have an environ-

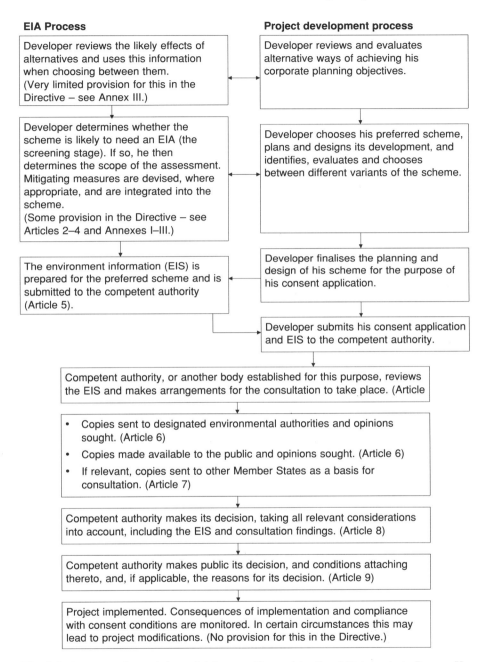

EIA Process

Developer reviews the likely effects of alternatives and uses this information when choosing between them. (Very limited provision for this in the Directive – see Annex III.)

Developer determines whether the scheme is likely to need an EIA (the screening stage). If so, he then determines the scope of the assessment. Mitigating measures are devised, where appropriate, and are integrated into the scheme. (Some provision in the Directive – see Articles 2–4 and Annexes I–III.)

The environment information (EIS) is prepared for the preferred scheme and is submitted to the competent authority (Article 5).

Project development process

Developer reviews and evaluates alternative ways of achieving his corporate planning objectives.

Developer chooses his preferred scheme, plans and designs its development, and identifies, evaluates and chooses between different variants of the scheme.

Developer finalises the planning and design of his scheme for the purpose of his consent application.

Developer submits his consent application and EIS to the competent authority.

Competent authority, or another body established for this purpose, reviews the EIS and makes arrangements for the consultation to take place. (Article

- Copies sent to designated environmental authorities and opinions sought. (Article 6)
- Copies made available to the public and opinions sought. (Article 6)
- If relevant, copies sent to other Member States as a basis for consultation. (Article 7)

Competent authority makes its decision, taking all relevant considerations into account, including the EIS and consultation findings. (Article 8)

Competent authority makes public its decision, and conditions attaching thereto, and, if applicable, the reasons for its decision. (Article 9)

Project implemented. Consequences of implementation and compliance with consent conditions are monitored. In certain circumstances this may lead to project modifications. (No provision for this in the Directive.)

Fig. 6.1 Annex to the opinion of Advocate General in *Bund Naturscutz in Bayern eV, Richard Stahnsdorf and Others* v. *Freistaat Bayern* (Case C396/92). A simplified flow chart of the EIA process and its relationship to project appraisal, authorisation and implementation.

mental assessment. The question of whether to have an assessment or not depends on whether a project is judged to have significant environmental effects by virtue of its size, location and characteristics (DoE Circular 15/88). The test of whether environmental assessment will take place is whether the project will leave 'significant' effects on the environment. There is guidance as to what is meant by 'significant'. Each case is to be decided on it merits and eventually there is likely to be clarification as to the type of project where an assessment will be carried out. The local planning authority decides whether an environmental assessment will be required but must give a reasoned statement for its decision. Activities that are likely to require an environmental assessment are trout farms, water treatment plants, wind energy projects, motorway services, golf courses, coastal protection works and toll roads subject to private financing. Developers are free to volunteer an assessment.

Environmental assessment is an important part of the planning process (see Chapter 7 for an overview of planning and the environment). In projects where environmental assessment is required to be carried out, planning permission may not be granted unless the assessment has been taken into consideration. In terms of priority, this does not mean that the assessment is the most influential factor in the final decision to grant planning permission. It does mean, however, that it must be taken into account.

The significance of environmental assessment is that it provides a more proactive and preventive approach to limiting environmental harm. Unlike the law on the control of pollution, which is subject specific, environmental assessment takes account of a wide range of issues associated with the environment. Throughout the Community, Member States have varied in the number and extent of environmental assessments carried out. 'These ranged from a dozen or fewer in Denmark and Portugal, a couple of hundred in the UK, 1000 in Germany, to 5500 in France' (ENDS Report 232, May 1994, p. 38). Different interpretations have been given to the Directive and there are national differences in initiating an assessment (see: ENDS Report 199, pp. 12–15 on the survey carried out by Manchester University's EIA Centre on the planning register and the failure to have environmental assessment in cases where it appears it ought to be justified).

In the United Kingdom the aims of environmental assessment are incorporated into the existing planning procedures. This enables relevant information on the environment to be considered as part of the planning process. In cases where there is a dispute as to whether an assessment should be carried out there is an appeal procedure for the developer to the Secretary of State for the Environment. The courts appear reluctant to intervene in the actual merits of the decision reached by the planning authority (see: *R.* v. *Swale Borough Council and*

Medway Ports Authority ex parte The Royal Society for the Protection of Birds [1991] JPL 39; *R.* v. *Poole Borough Council ex parte Beebe and others* [1991] JPL 643). The Secretary of State may request an environmental assessment after he has called in an application or even where the application has gone on appeal.

The environmental statement

Local authorities have been given detailed advice as to how to draw up an environmental assessment (see Fig. 6. 1). The main component is the environmental statement. There is at present no statutory basis as to the form of the statement. However, in Annex III of the Directive there are detailed requirements that include a description of the proposed development, such as the site, the design, the size, scale and outline of the development. There should be included various data on the main effects the proposed development will have on the environment. Specific details should be given on the effects of the proposed development on human beings, fauna and flora, soil, water, air, climate and landscape and on the cultural heritage of the country. It is expected that the statement should have a non-technical summary of relevant information. This provides an important obligation on developers to explain the significance of their project. There is a DoE checklist of the items to be included (see: Department of Environment, *Guide to Environmental Assessment,* HMSO, 1989). This comprises information describing the process; information describing the site and its environment; assessment of the effects; mitigating measures and their likely effectiveness; and risk of accidents from the development.

In practice consultants have been critical of the way environmental statements have been drawn up (see: ENDS Report 235, August 1994, p. 33) and that many statements lacked balance and were unclear in predicting the outcome of the development. There are proposals for improvements from the Commission, discussed below, which include better consultation and advance definition of the potential environmental problems. In response to the Commission's proposals, the DoE has published a *Draft Guide on Preparing Environmental Statements for Planning Projects* (DoE, 1994). This is intended to encourage a more detailed and carefully constructed statement than are currently prepared. The Draft Guide envisages a five-stage process beginning with a baseline survey and culminating in an outline of proposals to modify the project so as to reduce its environmental impact. Calculation and prediction of the effects of a proposal are to be undertaken, adopting the 'best practical techniques' available to developers. The Draft Guide seeks to distinguish predicted impacts from an evaluation of their significance. Alternatives to the project or the need for the project are expected to be carefully set out and any variations noted.

The Draft Guide is detailed and contains ten appendices setting out issues which developers need to consider in the environmental statement. There is also a separate guide published by English Nature on environmental assessment of nature conservation (see: *Nature Conservation in Environmental Assessment*, English Nature, 1994).

The developer and environmental assessment

Developers embarking on a planning application must be aware that, where an environmental assessment is required, failure to submit a statement renders the process *ultra vires* this means that it is unlawful. Where an environmental statement is required as part of the planning application, the planning authority is not permitted to consider the application without the environmental statement.

As noted above a developer may volunteer to undertake an assessment. This has led to a proliferation of voluntary environmental assessments. Environmental consultants, who specialise in the preparation of an environmental statement, are regularly employed in the preparation of planning applications involving environmental assessments. As a result developers are increasingly aware of the need to address the likely impact of their proposed development. It is by no means clear that this will result in more sensitive environmental planning. Where an environmental statement is required the developer is responsible for its contents. If necessary the planning authority can request further information if the statement is inadequate. The environmental statement is prepared and submitted together with the planning application. The Secretary of State has powers to exempt particular developments from the need for an environmental assessment. One drawback is that it is not possible for a third party to initiate the environmental assessment process.

Recent developments

Some recent changes have been introduced in England and Wales. From 3 June 1995 projects that benefit from permitted development rights became subject to the normal planning process if they require environmental assessment. This change may affect small numbers of industrial, agricultural and land reclamation projects (see: SI 1995 No. 418, Town and Country Planning (General Permitted Development Order) 1995; SI 1995 No. 417, Town and Country Planning (Environmental Assessment and Permitted Development) Regulations 1995; DoE Circular 3/95; and ENDS Report 242, March 1995, p. 36). In such circumstances developers will have to apply to the planning authorities for a decision as to whether the proposed project requires environmental assessment under the new arrangements.

▶ **Proposals for amendment to the 1985 EC Directive on Environmental Assessment**

The European Commission has recently issued proposals for amendment to the 1985 Directive (see: OJC 130, Vol. 37, 12 May 1994). This comes as a result of the Commission's finding that there was insufficient co-ordination of approach to assessment throughout the Community. The Commission proposes that for Annex II projects, that is, those that *may* require an environmental assessment, there should be some form of screening process to ensure consistency in approach. In particular, attention would have to be given to projects that would have a significant effect on special protection areas designated by the Member States (for example, the 1979 Directive on the Conservation of Wild Birds and the 1991 Directive on Habitats).

The Commission also proposes that for Annex II projects the relevant planning authority would have to determine whether an environmental statement is required, on the basis of thresholds set and the selection criteria laid down by Member States. In effect, this would mean a new Annex II with more details on the characteristics of the project, and the sensitivity of the environment liable to be affected. Ecosystems vary in their vulnerability to disruption. It is, therefore, essential in an EIA to consider the ability of ecosystems affected by a given project to maintain their structure and function during the disturbance. The capacity of an ecosystem to be re-established when the project is completed should also be considered.

The main rationale of the Commission's proposals is to bring greater awareness to the relevant planning authority of the need for an environmental assessment. A duty on all planning authorities to consider assessment through a screening process and to publish their decisions is intended to provide a more systematic approach to environmental assessment throughout the Community.

The Commission has also identified failures in many environmental assessment statements to contain sufficient information. The intention of the Directive is to provide a scoping exercise to permit interested parties, the planning authority and other statutory parties to ascertain the scope of environmental assessment and the degree of investigation required. Deficiencies in information and the degree of adequate consultation have led the Commission to propose a duty on the planning authority to define in advance the information required from the developer. This might be achieved through agreement with other interested bodies, such as planning consultants, industry and developers. The Commission has proposed a number of other changes to the Directive in addition to the scoping and screening arrangements noted above. A new duty of consultation is proposed to ensure that both the public and any relevant statutory bodies are consulted about the project.

The Commission has made two new proposals that are currently not required in the United Kingdom. On decision making the Commission proposes that there should be an implicit duty on planning authorities to 'take into consideration' the information obtained from the developer, the opinion of statutory bodies and the public when making their decision on a project. Finally, it is proposed that reasons and considerations on which a decision to refuse or grant consent, despite receiving unfavourable opinions, is based, must be published.

There are proposals for better consultation between Member States over projects that give rise to 'significant adverse effects' on the environment in another Member State. This is part of the treaty signed at Espoo, Finland, on 25 February 1966, where all European states except Malta and Turkey signed the agreement. Generally, the treaty provides for environmental assessment found in the domestic arrangements of most European states. The aim of the treaty is to provide notification for the party affected by any transboundary activity to be informed as early as possible. The state affected may then participate in the environmental assessment. Information must be provided on the proposed activity and alternatives considered. Included in the treaty are arrangements for monitoring the management of the planned development and any conditions that must be met for the proposal to go ahead.

▶ The significance of environmental assessment

Environmental assessment permits public opinion and expert advice to be combined in the evaluation and calculation of the impact of a proposed development on the environment. This provides the potential for transparency and openness in the planning process. The criteria for deciding whether or not to carry out an environmental assessment in projects that are under Annex II are open to widely different interpretations. This results in uncertainty and differences in practice between Member States (see: *Bund Naturscutz in Bayern V, Richard Stahnsdorf and Others* v. *Freistaat Bayern* – Case 396/92).

There are drawbacks in the present arrangements. Developers are given a wide latitude in drawing up the environmental statement. Choice of consultant or adviser is left to the developer. Though planning departments may use their own consultants and external advisers, public sector resources may not match private sector finance. Environmental assessments may favour the wealthy investor who is able to choose the most skilled advisers and present the most favourably written assessment.

There is considerable vagueness in the terms and objectives of the assessment. This results in variable practices throughout the country.

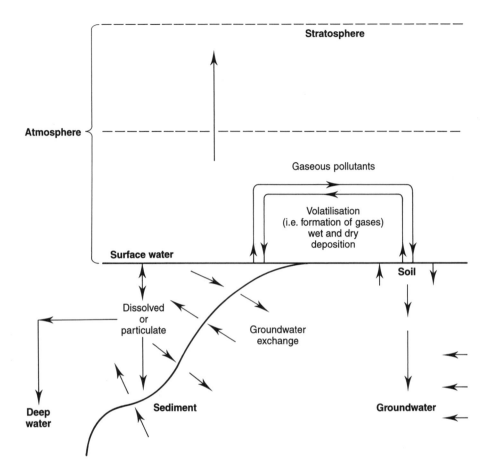

Fig. 6.2 Potential pathways for pollutant transfer between the atmosphere, terrestrial and aquatic environments. Arrows indicate possible routes followed by pollutants.

There are wide variations in the quality and standards of environmental assessment. This may be a reflection of the nature of the activities under review and of the different expertise employed in each assessment. There is a large element of self-assessment involved in the process. This permits developers to set their own requirements and criteria, which may form the basis of the environmental assessment. It is also the case that any assertions and objectives set out in environmental assessments may be impossible to justify or verify. Greater weight may be given to the environmental assessment than to other parts of the planning application. Does this not imply a presumption in favour of the development if the environmental assessment is written in a favourable form?

▶ Integrated Pollution Control (IPC)

Definition and origins

Integrated pollution control (IPC), owes its origins to the Royal Commission on Environmental Pollution in 1976. The introduction of a system of IPC marked a break with the past tradition of legislating on specifically targeted problems. In the nineteenth century the protection of public health was the focus of much legislation. The Alkali Inspectorate was created in 1863 to provide expertise and resources targeted on highly noxious chemical processes and industries. The approach of identifying specific problems and legislating on the basis of identifiable shortcomings continued into the twentieth century. As late as 1974 the Health and Safety Executive was formed to safeguard the health of workers.

Following the 1976 Royal Commission on Pollution report, and despite government hesitations, the Environmental Protection Act 1990 contains the legal framework of integrated pollution control (IPC). Adopting the view that no one part of the environment is separate from another, IPC attempts to take an integrated approach to the environment. IPC takes account of the fact that the pollution from one activity in one medium may have implications in another. There has been a proliferation of regulatory agencies which may lead to ineffectiveness in controls over pollution. There is also the concern that overlapping jurisdictions of different agencies may lead to lack of transparency in finding out about environmental harm.

There is a variety of routes by which pollutants may transfer between the atmosphere, terrestrial and aquatic environments (Fig. 6.2). The routes are complex and the rate and extent of transfer depend on a variety of abiotic and biotic factors. The following two examples serve to illustrate in brief the complex interrelationships between the atmosphere, aquatic and terrestrial environments in the disposal of waste and the release of pollutants which make IPC an appropriate policy.

1. In the United Kingdom a substantial amount of household waste (up to 90 per cent), much of which is biodegradable, is disposed of to controlled and uncontrolled landfill sites (see Chapter 10 for a more detailed consideration of landfill disposal). Controlled sites are in fact in the minority and comply with a strict Department of Environment Code of Practice as to depth and required sealing, etc. Several pollutant problems have arisen as a result of the use of landfills. It became evident that uncontained landfills produced leachate containing a cocktail of toxic compounds, e. g. toxic metals. This leachate travelled considerable distances from the site, contaminating surrounding soil, infiltrating surface waters and

perhaps most significantly causing considerable groundwater pollution in chalk and fissured rock. In 1986, partly as a response to pressure from EC legislation, the DoE issued a guidance document on landfill practice (Waste Management Paper [WMP] No. 26). This paper indicated a change from the 'dilute and disperse' philosophy of UK landfill to a philosophy based on waste minimisation and containment in order to protect groundwater. Another problem associated with the use of landfill has become evident recently and arises from the pollution of yet another medium as a result of landfill disposal – the atmosphere. Biodegradation of the organic waste in landfill results in the production of carbon dioxide, CO_2, and methane, CH_4 (up to 40 per cent of UK CH_4 emissions arise from landfill), both of which are greenhouse gases. The use of landfill, therefore, must now be assessed in the light of the UN Framework Convention on Climate Change. The United Kingdom is required to cut CH_4 and CO_2 emissions to 1990 levels by the year 2000. As a result, in the United Kingdom, incineration is now considered a more suitable method of waste disposal than landfilling (Royal Commission on Environmental Pollution, 1993). This example serves to illustrate pollution of the atmosphere and water from the disposal of solid waste to terrestrial environments and, therefore, the inherent advantages of an IPC system.

2. In the 1960s Scandinavian ecologists first recognised the problem and impact of acidification in ecosystems. This is primarily related to the atmospheric emission of sulphur dioxide and nitrogen oxides from anthropogenic (and to a lesser extent natural) sources. Currently in the United Kingdom 60 per cent of sulphur emissions arise from power stations and 30 per cent from industrial processes, while approximately 45 per cent of nitrogen oxide emissions arise from power stations. Vehicles are of growing importance in the release of nitrogen oxides to the atmosphere, currently accounting for up to 30 per cent of releases. The remainder of nitrogen oxide gases arise from other industries including agriculture. These gaseous emissions are currently controlled under various legislation (see Chapter 12). Sulphur dioxide and nitrogen oxide gases dissolve in rain, producing sulphurous and sulphuric acids together with nitric and nitrous acids. Rain acidified in this way has a variety of environmental repercussions, including an impact on cloud formation which influences local and regional climate; and acid precipitation causing soil and surface water acidification. There is a clear decline in species diversity and abundance, at all trophic levels, in acidified waters. For example, acidified lakes support few if any fish. Acidification has also been linked to forest decline, although this has yet to be clearly demonstrated. (For a more detailed analysis see Chapter 12.) Clearly, the release of gaseous pollutants to one

medium, the atmosphere, has considerable consequences for the other environmental media, i.e. the aquatic and terrestrial ecosystems. This example again illustrates the interrelationships between different parts of the biosphere and the significance of IPC.

Since 1991, the system of IPC applies to a wide range of processes and substances. There is currently a five year rolling programme to bring existing processes within IPC. It is expected that 5000 processes will fall under IPC (see: *Integrated Pollution Control – The First Three Years* (ENDS, 1994, p. 1)). IPC is also supported through Community law. The Fifth Action Programme of the Community, *Towards Sustainability*, has designated IPC as a priority field of action. IPC adopts a scientific approach to environmental problems which do not recognise geographical boundaries and may require a pooling of scientific knowledge. An integrated approach to the environment has been favoured in many Member States throughout the European Union. Integrated approaches to environmental issues may be found in eco-labelling of products, the environmental auditing of installations and common pollution controls over processes (see: Directive 85/337/EEC Environmental Assessment of Certain Projects; Directive 82/501/EEC Impact of Major Accident Hazards of Industrial Activities). Generally the Community has moved in the direction of a proactive and preventive approach to environmental harm, adopting the precautionary principle. In contrast, the United Kingdom has generally adopted a more reactive style. Invariably policy differences emerge as a more integrationist approach to the Community is adopted in the approach to 1996. Despite any difference in approach between the United Kingdom and the Community, IPC has been adopted in the United Kingdom.

There is a proposed Directive on Integrated Pollution Prevention and Control or IPPC (see: Commission of the EC COM(93)423 final 14 September 1993). IPPC is intended to be introduced and implemented in all Member States within a framework Directive leaving the details to be implemented in each Member State. The proposal follows the pattern set in the United Kingdom for IPC. However, the proposed Directive is likely to be more widely drawn and affect more processes and substances than the UK arrangements at present. This may require additional legislation in the United Kingdom to supplement the 1990 Act. The proposed Directive contains a list of industrial activities which would be the subject of detailed legislation in each Member State on the basis of a 10 year implementation period. Once an authorisation is granted it is proposed that there should be a condition requiring the restoration of the environment when a process has permanently ceased operation.

The aims and objectives of IPC

The aims and objectives of IPC fall into two categories as follows. First, it is intended 'to prevent, minimise or render harmless releases of prescribed substances – using the best available techniques not entailing excessive cost'. Secondly, an objective of IPC is 'to develop an approach to pollution control that considers releases from industrial processes to all media in the context of the effect on the environment as a whole – the "best practicable environmental option" '.

In the first category, the 'best available techniques not entailing excessive costs' is commonly known as BATNEEC. BATNEEC is not defined in the 1990 Act. In fact the principles that define its objectives and explain its usage have been subject to change. In the early stages the 'best available technologies' was replaced with 'best available techniques'. There is no clear definition of what is 'best'. In practice the word is interpreted to mean what is practical and available. However, there are economic factors in the evaluation of what is available. Costs of applying one particular technique have to be considered over any alternative that is available. The Department of the Environment issued guidance in 1991 which it has revised in 1993. In particular the revised guidance considers that for new processes the economic condition of an industrial sector may be considered relevant when evaluating what is required. This view is broadly supported by HMIP, now the new Environment Agency, under the Environment Act 1995, which may look at the most up-to-date standards applied to new processes but recognise older standards applied to older processes. At one point it was considered that a revision of an old plant would result in new standards being applied to the plant as a whole. The current view is that excessive cost should not be entailed and each case will be looked at on its own merits. Specific requirements are contained in Codes of Practice issued by HMIP for various processes.

The second category of objective for IPC, mentioned above, is the 'best practicable environmental option' commonly referred to as BPEO. Its origins are with the Fifth Report of the Royal Commission on Environmental Pollution in 1976. BPEO has been described as 'the option that provides the most benefit or least damage to the environment as a whole, at acceptable cost, in the long term as well as the short term'. There is no statutory definition of BPEO but the 1990 Act does encapsulate the principle but only 'where the process is likely to involve the release of substances into more than one environmental medium'. Limits on the principle appear from the fact that the 1990 Act does not appear to permit fundamental questions to be raised about the policy merits of a process or the need for a process. Revised Department of the Environment guidance was issued in 1993. In the 1991 version consideration of the effects of a local environmental issue and the effects the proposed process would have on the local environment require to be considered.

The implementation of IPC

In England and Wales, Her Majesty's Inspector of Pollution (HMIP), now the new Environment Agency, is responsible for implementation of IPC. This includes authorisation and regulation of the processes. It is significant that this responsibility covers all of the environment, that is water, air and land. Some aspects of area air pollution control (APC), however, are given to local authorities. There are two lists, 'A' and 'B'. List 'A' is subject to IPC and falls under the jurisdiction of HMIP. List 'B' is subject to local authority regulation with respect to atmospheric pollution (see: Schedule 1 of the Environmental Protection (Prescribed Processes and Substances) Regulations 1991, SI 1991 No. 472; also note amendments such as SI 1994 No. 1271 and SI 1994 No. 1329).

In Scotland responsibility for implementation of IPC is undertaken by HM Industrial Pollution Inspectorate (now the Scottish Environment Agency under the Environment Act 1995). Implementation of IPC in Scotland is expected to take place at a slower pace than that planned for England and Wales.

The radical nature of IPC involved the early expansion of HMIP, which had to grow in terms of staff recruitment and expertise. Now that HMIP has been subsumed into the new Environment Agency, the process of change is likely to continue. IPC has also required a change in the culture of many industrial companies and in the processes and systems in operation.

The legal structure of IPC is complex. The main outline of IPC is to be found in Part I of the Environmental Protection Act 1990. However, the application of IPC to specific processes and systems is found in a number of regulations (see: the Environmental Protection (Prescribed Processes and Substances) Regulations 1991, SI 1991 No. 472; the Environmental Protection (Applications, Appeals and Registers) Regulations 1991, SI 1991 No. 507; the Environmental Protection (Authorisation of Processes) (Determination Periods) Order 1991, SI 1991 No. 513; and also recent changes contained in SI 1994 No. 1271 and SI 1994 No. 1329). There are a large number of guidance notes issued by HMIP for the setting of standards for particular processes to be brought within IPC. Similarly guidance and regulations may be issued by the Department of the Environment defining the requirements of IPC to local authorities in the control of air pollution.

The procedures for implementing IPC were over a five year period from 1991 to 1995. The time-table for implementing IPC was as follows (note that many processes have already been implemented): the fuel and power industry (1992); the waste disposal industry (1992); the mineral industry

(1992); the chemical industry (1993/94); the metal industry (1995); and other industries such as paper manufacturing (1995).

Applications, authorisations, enforcement and appeals

The five year timetable for implementing IPC establishes specific guidance for a large number of processes. This includes detailed guidance notes as to what may be taken into account in determining an application for an authorisation. Generally the notes point to the environmental quality standards that are relevant to the particular process, the standards that are achievable and that will satisfy HMIP; how such standards can be reached; the rationale of designation of the process under IPC; guidance on the authorisation and what may amount to a substantial change requiring a variation procedure. The latter applies to a substantial change in a process.

It should be remembered that IPC is personal to the applicant or operator. There are procedures for transfer of an authorisation and/or which provide variations to the existing arrangements. HMIP (now the Environment Agency) has powers to revoke an authorisation provided this is done in writing (s. 12 of the Environmental Protection Act 1990). Also to be found in the Environmental Protection Act are variation powers (s. 12 and Environmental Protection (Applications, Appeals and Registers) Regulations 1991, SI 1991 No. 507); Prohibition and Enforcement notices (see ss. 13 and 14) and powers of inspectors (see s. 17). There are detailed provisions on appeals (see ss. 15 and 22 of the 1990 Act).

▶ An assessment of Integrated Pollution Control (IPC)

The first three years

IPC is now in its fifth year of operation. During its first three years the experience of operating IPC has been the subject of research and scrutiny. Research undertaken by Environmental Data Services (ENDS, see: *Integrated Pollution Control – The First Three Years* (ENDS, 1994, p. 1)) has investigated, using surveys and interviews, the operation of IPC over the first three years. Case studies and in-depth analysis were used to provide an assessment of IPC in operation. The ENDS study has revealed a 'varied picture'. In some industries there is a willingness to adopt the IPC approach; in others there is considerable reluctance. HMIP has had to take account of variable practices and expectations have been accordingly adjusted. While there is little doubt that 'IPC is setting the pace of environmental improvements', doubts remain as to its effectiveness. In that respect there is one significant finding in the

ENDS research conclusions (see: *Integrated Pollution Control – The First Three Years* (ENDS, 1994, p. 194)):

> It is still too soon for any clear improvement in the quality of the receiving environment to be apparent. The overall success or failure of IPC will depend on the speed at which the existing processes are upgraded to new plant standards – and on this issue the jury is still out.

The effectiveness of IPC in large measure depends on the enforcement of standards set by HMIP (now the Environment Agency). Currently, government concern is that, in general, there is too heavy a regulatory burden on industry and business. This concern has resulted in the passage of the Deregulation and Contracting Out Act 1994 which permits Orders in Council to amend primary legislation as a means of reducing unnecessary regulation. Is there a potential conflict between the further development of IPC and government policy in favour of deregulation? IPC expressly involves a government commitment to strengthening the regulatory structure and improving the efficiency and effectiveness of pollution controls on industry. It would appear that IPC faces a considerable challenge from government policies that favour deregulation. Recently the Department of the Environment has made proposals to relax emission monitoring requirements for processes subject to local authority air pollution control (see: ENDS Report 235, August 1994, pp. 30–1).

Environmental information

Environmental Information Regulations 1992

Access to information about the environment is fundamental to its proper management. In general the Community favours greater openness. EC Directive 90/313 (adopted 7 June 1990, OJ 1990, No. L 158/56) is implemented in the United Kingdom by the Environmental Information Regulations 1992 (SI 1992 No. 3240) (see: William Birtles (1993), JPEL 615–626 and Birtles and Stein (1994, pp. 122–9)). The Directive provides that 'practical arrangements' should be put into place aimed at making available information on the environment by all public authorities with responsibility for the environment. Public authorities include the Department of the Environment, local authorities, water service companies and local authority waste disposal companies. In the 1992 Regulations (SI 1992 No. 3240) environmental information is very widely defined to include information on the quality and state of air, water, soil, flora, fauna and natural sites and other land.

If the request for information is refused, that refusal must be in writing and be accompanied by reasons. There are exceptions which include commercial and industrial confidentiality, personal information or data and information which would increase the likelihood of damage to the environment if it was disclosed. There are also certain categories of information such as national security where it would not be in the public interest to disclose the information. The procedure in requesting information provides that once a request for information is made it must be responded to promptly and no later then two months from the request. Reasons for refusal must be given and this must be done in writing. Although there appears to be no right of appeal against the refusal to disclose information, the procedure for request is subject to judicial review. It is also possible to make a complaint by way of letter to an MP or to the local or central government ombudsman.

Public registers and access to information

IPC has promoted greater openness in the management and operation of industrial processes. HMIP operates public register offices in Bristol, Leeds and Bedford. Recent increases in public complaints to HMIP about industrial processes regulated by HMIP (see: ENDS Report 236, September 1994, p. 8) indicate a greater public awareness about the environment and the role of HMIP. It is assumed that current arrangements will operate under the new Environment Agency.

However, there are shortcomings in the present arrangements. Parts of the application that the operator of the process does not want to reveal may be withheld on the grounds of commercial confidentiality. When HMIP issues a Schedule 1 notice before determining an application for IPC the effect is to deny the public access to information provided as a condition of the notice. Requirements for publicity are not always met. Companies applying for an IPC authorisation are required to advertise in 'one or more' local newspapers. A common complaint is that the advertisement is not placed for a long enough period and rarely is more than one newspaper used by companies.

An important aspect of protecting the environment is the provision of reliable statistics and information on the environment throughout the Community. The European Environment Agency provides this useful resource approved by the Council (OJ 1994, C213).

Techniques in environmental standard setting

Setting standards in the implementation of environmental management systems provides an opportunity for improvements in the environment. There are a number of techniques available. United Kingdom companies which set out to introduce environmental management systems may implement standards contained in BS 7750 (roughly similar in shared principles of European and international management found in EN 29000 and ISO 9000). They may also qualify for registration of sites under the EC regulation on eco-management and audit (EMA). Ultimately EC regulations that set out standards to meet EMA may lead to the withdrawal of BS 7750. At the present time the EC regulations may be met by UK companies applying an extended form of BS 7750. It was expected that differences between BS 7750 and the Community standards would be worked out, and in February 1996 agreement was reached (ENDS Report 253, p.43).

In order to meet BS 7750 certification must take place ensuring objectives and targets are set for any documented environmental policy. The management system must provide a management structure with key personnel acting under specific responsibility and authority. There must be a programme for achieving objectives and targets and assessing the direct and indirect environmental effects caused by the organisation. The certification process is very detailed, with a system of records, management and periodic reviews of the environmental management system.

Standard setting may also be achieved through the development of insurance for environmental risk. Financial institutions regularly take into account environmental risks of companies when considering loans and insurance. Ensuring that there is sufficient insurance coverage contained in comprehensive general liability policies is a complicated task given recent court cases on the extent of pollution costs (see: *Cambridge Water Company* v. *Eastern Counties Leather* [1994] 1 All ER 53 and for a discussion see Chapter 10). High-risk industries may have to seek specialist insurance advice with Lloyds or, outside the UK, with leading Swiss insurance companies. The implication is that insurance principles may encourage companies and others to act in an environmentally responsible way.

One limitation on insurance is that it does not normally cover deliberate acts or omissions of the insured. Liability is therefore normally confined to accidental damage (see: Kiss and Shelton, 1993, pp. 78–80; John H. Wasink, 'Environmental insurance in Europe and the United States, an Introduction' *Environmental Liability Law Quarterly*, 3/89, p. 71 quoted in Kiss and Shelton). The scope for expansion in the market of environmental insurance is considerable. Recently environmental impairment liability policies have been issued with larger premiums than normal insurance. Such policies have a specific coverage, usually excluding clean-up costs of hazardous waste sites and limited liability for particular harm only. The policies are usually drawn up after a site survey and are specific to that site. The dates of cover are usually carefully stipulated and exclude claims made before a certain date. Usually such insurance policies are on a 'claims made' basis covering only claims brought by a third party within the policy period.

This form of insurance may set the pattern for future developments in the insurance industry. Specialised insurance policies drawn up with the needs of a particular industry, specified exemptions and carefully calculated liabilities may become common practice. Setting higher premiums and risk assessments involves a multidisciplinary approach with lawyers, actuaries, environmental specialists and environmental scientists working in close collaboration.

Insurance liabilities are normally left to market forces. Governments, however, may assist with letters of credit, indemnity arrangements, licences and loans. In the event of no insurance being available at a reasonable cost there is the possibility of companies creating a large fund to pay damages in the event of liability, with annual sums payable to sustain the fund in the event of damages being payable.

Since June 1993 there is a draft Convention on Civil Liability for Damages Resulting from the Exercise of Activities Dangerous for the Environment. General standards are contained in the draft Convention based on principles such as the 'polluter pays'. This principle has been agreed among OECD countries since 1972. It was agreed that subsidies should not be provided to cover pollution control costs. Instead, such costs should be paid by the polluter who in general may pass costs on to the consumer. In common with this principle both the Single European Act and the Maastricht Treaty have upheld the view that the cost of preventing and eliminating nuisances should be borne by the polluter.

The draft Convention applies to persons, companies and agencies within contracting parties. If the damage occurs outside the contracting state there are provisions for the filing of reciprocal remedies. Nuclear damage is provided for by the Paris Convention on Civil Liability 1960 and the Vienna Convention 1963.

Voluntary environmental auditing is encouraged in the Member States of the Community. An environmental audit is a means of assessing the cost–benefit of a proposed development or scheme. One sign that this is recognised as an important development is in the area of eco-audit strategies. There is a proposed Council Regulation allowing voluntary participation by industrial companies in a Community eco scheme. This arrangement encourages industrial companies to undertake an officially accredited audit. In each audit there should be an environmental statement that is applicable to a particular site. The policy of the company on environmental issues as applied to that particular site is examined as part of the audit system.

▶ Conclusions

Environmental assessment provides an evaluation of the likely effects of a major project on the environment. It also allows projects to be analysed from an environmental perspective rather than solely on commercial criteria. At present EIA operates largely under the influence of the operator though there are signs that EIA may become a substantial hurdle to be overcome before planning permission is considered likely. The development of EIA should not be restricted by having to pass the obstacle of planning permission. EIA should therefore be seen as a positive development that may help encourage a responsible approach to the protection of the environment (see Fig. 6.2).

In a recent Institute of Directors survey (IOD, 1994, pp. 10–11) '14 per cent of companies were carrying out environmental audits, 9 per cent were considering them'. It is clear from the survey that environmental audit is principally an issue for larger companies, with smaller companies being less active in this regard.

Integrated pollution control offers an opportunity for a radical change in culture and attitude to the environment. Although it is still in its early years, many processes are being brought within its remit. IPC is likely to set the pace for the future development of environmental law. In common with EIA, IPC must transform the culture of industry and business in the pursuit of environmental awareness. Curiously, the climate of deregulation (see: the Deregulation and Contracting Out Act 1994) is set to challenge any gains achieved in the early life of IPC in the United Kingdom.

▶ References and further reading

Alder, J., Environmental impact assessment: the inadequacies of English law. *Journal of Environmental Law*, **5** (2), 203–21.

Birtles, W. and Stein, R. (1994) *Planning and Environmental Law.* Longman, Essex.

Biswas, A.K. and Agarwala, S.B.C. (1994) *EIA for Developing Countries.* Butterworths, London.

Bradley, K. *et al.* (1991) *Environmental Impact Assessment – A Technical Approach.* DTPS Ltd, Dublin.

Clark, M. and Herington, J. (eds) (1988) *The Role of Environmental Impact Assessment in the Planning Process.* Mansell, London.

Department of the Environment (1994) *Environmental Assessment – A Guide to the Procedures.* HMSO, London.

DoE (1994) *Guide on Preparing Environmental Statements for Planning Projects Consultation Paper.* Department of the Environment.

English Nature (1994) *Nature Conservation in Environmental Assessment.*

Goldin, I. and Winters, A. L. (ed.) (1995) *The Economics of Sustainable Development.* Cambridge University Press, Cambridge.

Goudie, A. (1993) *The Human Impact on the Natural Environment*, 4th edn. Blackwell, Oxford.

Holder, J. (1995) European Law and Environmental Impact Assessment. Unpublished PhD thesis, University of Warwick.

Holdgate, M.W. (1979) *A Perspective of Environmental Pollution*, Cambridge University Press, Cambridge.

Institute of Directors (1994) *Business Opinion Survey of the Environment.* IOD, London.

Jones, C.E., Lee, N. and Wood, C. *UK Environmental Statements 1988–1990 An Analysis.* EIA Centre, University of Manchester, 1991, Occasional Paper 29.

Kiss, A. and Shelton, D., (1993) *Manual of European Environmental Law.* Grotius Press, Cambridge.

Kramer, L. (1994) *European Environmental Law Casebook*, Sweet and Maxwell, London.

Pearce, D., Barbier, E. and Maikandya, A. (1994) *Sustainable Development: Economics and Environment in the Third World.* Earthscan Publications, London.

Royal Commission on Environmental Pollution (1993) *Incineration of Waste: Seventeenth Report.* HMSO, London.

▶ Miscellaneous regulations applicable to environmental assessment

SI 1988 No. 1241 Trunk Roads and Motorways.
SI 1989 No. 167 Electricity Power Stations.
SI 1990 No. 367 Overhead Electricity Power Lines, Oil and Gas Pipelines.
SI 1988 No. 119 Mandatory Annex 1 Assessments.
SI 1989 No. 1207 Afforestation Projects.
SI 1988 No. 1336 Port and Harbour Projects.
SI 1988 No. 1218 Marine Salmon Farming Projects.
SI 1988 No. 1221 Scotland.
SI 1994 No. 2010 Provides an extension of the Environmental Assessment rules to Scotland.

▶ International agreements

OECD, Guidelines in Respect of Procedures and Requirements for Anticipating the Effects of Chemicals on Man and in the Environment 7 July 1977 C(77)97 (Final).
1991 Espoo Convention on environmental impact assessment in a transboundary context. ENDS Report 207, pp. 34–5.

UNEP, Environmental Auditing (report of the United Nations Environment Programme) (1989).

▶ Useful sources of information

Environmental Data Services Ltd, London.
Environmental Impact Assessment Centre, Department of Planning and Landscape, University of Manchester, Manchester M13 9PL.
Natural History Museum, London.
Directorate of Environmental Policy and Analysis, Department of the Environment, London.
Environment Protection Group, Department of the Environment, London.
Institute of Directors, Business Opinion Survey, *The Environment* (IOD, 1994).

PART II
Land

In the United Kingdom, town and country planning is a means of land use control. Planning law is of central importance to the development of the built environment. Since the planning legislation of 1947, the development of planning law has been an important achievement in the social, economic and political life of the nation. For example, the creation of 'green belt' areas around our towns and cities represents a major contribution to the controls over land use, and the recognition that land is a scarce resource. About one-third of land in England is within areas designated as green belts, National Parks and Areas of Outstanding Beauty (see: *This Common Inheritance*, HMSO, 1990, para. 6.2). Planning law forms a specialised law subject in its own right and there are many specialised books dealing with planning law. This chapter provides, in brief outline only, the main elements of the planning system as a means of understanding how the planning process may protect the environment. In July 1994 the government issued a wide-ranging discussion document: *Quality in Town and Country*. There is also a recent White Paper, *Rural England* (Cm 3016, HMSO, 1995). Further details on planning law may be found in the various specialist reference books listed at the end of this chapter.

An outline of the planning system

The challenges of planning in the 1990s

The aftermath of the Second World War encouraged a positive examination of the redevelopment of bombed and wrecked towns and cities. In 1947, general responsibility for re-planning the affected cities and towns fell to local authorities at the level of county and borough local government (see: the Town and Country Planning Act 1947). The cornerstone of the post-war approach to planning was the requirement to adopt a Development Plan for the area. Designated within the plan was the allocation of specific activities to the land available. Uses for which land could be allocated included agriculture, open spaces, industry, housing and educational purposes. Local authority permission was required for most land to be developed within the local authority area. In addition statutory controls existed for the retention of woodlands, the maintenance of waste disposal sites, slum clearance and the preservation of historic buildings and areas of archaeological interest or importance. There was also concern about ribbon development which was curtailed in areas designated as 'green belt'.

Planning has proved controversial because it attempts to reconcile many contradictory aims and objectives. Setting priorities is difficult when conservation and development appear in conflict. The desire for economic growth and development is countered by the need to conserve and preserve – especially good agricultural land. The seemingly endless pursuit of suburban housing developments and the growth of commercialisation of town centres is resisted by those who point to the need to regenerate town centres as living spaces and resist urban sprawl. Post-war planning ills are listed as the growth in urban motorways, the development of city tower blocks and the destruction of historic buildings. Out-of-town shopping complexes may add further decline to impoverished urban centres. Inner-city deprivation is seen as partly a planning failure and vandalism and crime as endemic to urban degeneration.

The expectation that any single planning system can hope to reconcile or provide solutions to all these problems appears unrealistic. In fact English planning law is remarkably reactive rather than pro-active. In the current fashion for centralisation planning is surprisingly locally based, with local authorities having substantial planning responsibilities. There is, however, a gradual shift in powers from local to central government. Central government sets the boundaries of development control. Primarily, central government operates through the Department of the Environment (DoE) which continuously monitors planning policy and decisions. The DoE also has to oversee new activities and, where relevant, take account of new technologies. One example of new developments that need to be considered in the planning system is the use of television satellite dishes and digital telephone antennae.

Grant has noted that the aims of planning laws are to provide 'a system of guidance and regulation of a predominantly private development market' (Grant, 1986, p. 1). He also notes:

Planning law establishes the framework for power through which planning control over land use is exercised, but the policies which are pursued in the name of planning and the choices which are made between competing alternatives for development are the product of a variety of largely unregulated influences, some of them powerful others weak. Planning law prescribes the procedures – it sets the battle lines for the resolution of conflict over land use between the interests of private property and the prevailing 'public' or 'community' interest.

The government sees the present arrangements as a balance between councils that can use planning controls to protect '. . . local character and amenities, while individuals have a reasonable degree of freedom to do what they wish with their property' (see: *This Common Inheritance*, HMSO, 1990, para. 6.13). This approach emphasises the traditions of the planning system. How environmental considerations may be prioritised within that tradition remains to be seen.

The United Kingdom has a high population density of 236 inhabitants per km^2. Current population is about 57.6 million in a land area of 244 111 km^2. This compares to other European countries with inhabitants per km^2 as follows: Italy, 192; Germany, 225; France, 105.2; Spain, 77; Belgium, 328. The White Paper on *Rural England* (Cm 3016, HMSO, 1995, p. 8) acknowledges the United Kingdom 'as one of the most urbanised countries in Europe'.

Since the 1980s the United Kingdom has undergone considerable change in its commercial, industrial and working practices. The United Kingdom was the first major industrialised country. Older industries such as coal, iron, steel, textiles and shipbuilding have been reorganised to take account of the global economy. The United Kingdom is self-sufficient in oil and North Sea oil production also provides a major contribution to the balance of payments. Today 68.6 per cent of the working population are employed in the service sector, with only 27.9 per cent in industry and 2.2 per cent in agriculture. Leisure amenities such as new golf courses are important in future planning decisions.

Demands on the planning system range from urban city renewal, industrialisation and waste management, to large centres or con-urbations with increased intercity road networks which, in particular, proliferated in the 1980s. Currently, transportation problems have created fundamental questions about the government's road transport policies (see: Royal Commission on Environmental Pollution 18th Report. *Transport and the Environment* (HMSO, 1994)).

▶ Planning law and practice

Planning legislation

The modern planning system originated in the Town and Country Planning Act 1947. This legislation has remained as a blueprint for planning law today. The legislation which permits the making of plans is found in the Local Government Act 1972, ss. 182–4 and Sch. 16 (as amended by the Local Government, Planning and Land Act 1980). In addition there have been important and substantial amendments contained in the consolidation of the law in the Town and Country Planning Act 1990 and the Planning and Compensation Act 1991, the Planning (Listed Buildings and Conservation Areas) Act 1990 and the Planning (Hazardous Substances) Act 1990. The latter represents some comprehensive changes following an inquiry into planning enforcement (see: Robert Carnwarth QC, *Enforcing Planning Control*, HMSO, February 1989). Significantly, there are differing views as to the objectives that ought to be set in any planning system that may require consideration of environmental matters.

Planning functions are shared between the two different tiers of local authorities, that is, counties and districts. Counties are involved in the preparation of structure plans, the control of developments concerning mineral and aggregate workings and processing, waste disposal sites and developments that involve National Park boundaries.

District councils prepare local plans for their areas. There is no national system of regional plan making and local plans have to work consistently alongside any statutory-based plan. There are specific arrangements for urban development corporations and these are provided under the Local Government, Planning and Land Act 1980.

Development plans and the environment

The key instrument for the future guidance of planning is the use of development plans. Introduced in 1947, development plans were radically revised under the Town and Country Planning Act 1968. Development plans have two elements: the structure plans containing strategic issues and policies which require the approval of the Secretary of State; and the local plan formulated within the general framework of the structure plan. Development plans are not mandatory, but often are a crucial factor in determining an individual's planning application. Arguably there is a presumption in favour of the development plan when planning decisions, including change of use, are reached. The local planning authority is required under s. 70(2) of the Town and Country Planning Act 1990 'to have regard to the provisions of the development plan so far as material to the application and to any other material consideration'. It is well to remember that there may be material considerations apart from the development plan and some attention is required to be given to these in a planning decision. The intention under a new s. 54A of the Town and Country Planning Act 1990 (see: s. 26 of the Planning and Compensation Act 1991), is to increase the status of the development plan. The development plan becomes *the* key matter unless material considerations indicate otherwise. It remains to be seen the extent to which a plan-led rather than a market-led planning system will emerge from present arrangements (see: Gatenby and Williams, 'Section 54A: The legal and practical implications' [1992] JPL 110).

The planning system is not intended to be an arbitrary one. The adoption of statutory development plans by the local authority allows the local authority to develop criteria to judge individual proposals to build on land or make a change of use. The public is thereby given some guidance as to what plans are likely to meet with local authority approval and this may act as an incentive for well considered developments.

Account is taken of development plans by the courts (see: s. 287(2) of the Town and Country Planning Act 1990). There are a variety of different kinds of plans recognised in the planning legislation that have statutory recognition. Structure plans are undertaken by the 'shire' counties and districts, local plans by the shire counties and districts, and unitary development plans by the metropolitan areas. Such statutory plans are in addition to the discretion of local authorities to initiate their own voluntary plans for their area.

Structure plans

A structure plan falls under s. 30 of the Town and Country Planning Act 1990 (hereinafter TCPA 1990). The local planning authority for the locality must undertake a review of certain matters specified in s. 30(2). These include 'the principal physical and economic characteristics of the area'. Review invariably should be continuous, involve surveys of the needs of the community and under s. 31 of the TCPA 1990 structure plans must contain a written statement of the authority's policy and proposals for the area. Structure plans should include a key diagram for the area together with insets on the map of the area setting out the plan. The Secretary of State may offer guidance (see: *Memorandum on Structure and Local Plans*, DoE Circular 22/84) on the contents of structure plans which should include: housing; green belts; the rural economy; major industrial, business, retail and other employment-generating developments; strategic transport and highway facilities; mineral working; waste disposal; land reclamation and reuses; tourism; and leisure and recreation. There are detailed procedures for the alteration of structure plans once they have been finalised (s. 32 of the TCPA 1990). There is a publicity requirement for the plans (s. 33 of the TCPA 1990) and also for the withdrawal, alteration or repeal and replacement of structure plans (s. 34 of the TCPA 1990).

There are also detailed procedures for the approval or rejection of structure plans. There is a period of up to six weeks after the publication of the structure plans for the Secretary of State to receive objections. An examination in public may be undertaken to hear objectors (see: s. 35 of the TCPA 1990 and detailed rules for the examination in public contained in *Structure Plans. The Examination in Public*, HMSO, 1978 as amended). In the case of structure plans the Secretary of State must give approval for the plan (see: *Severn Trent Water Authority* v. *Secretary of State for the Environment* [1989] JPL 21). The Secretary of State has wide discretion as to how to deal with proposals, but he is under a clear duty (see s. 35(10) of the TCPA 1990) to give proper, adequate reasons for the decision which are clearly intelligible and deal with the principal points of the plan.

Local plans

Section 36 of the Town and Country Planning Act 1990 requires local planning authorities, within directed time-limits set by the Secretary of State, to prepare a local plan for their area. The plan must contain a written statement of detailed policies for land use including conservation policies. These are defined to include conservation of the natural beauty and amenity of the land, the improvement of the physical environment and management of traffic in the area of the plan. Specific plans about minerals and waste are to be treated separately as detailed below.

Local plans must include maps, diagrams, illustrations and the various material considerations relevant to the planning authorities. Local plans are invariably the responsibility of the district council. The local plan must conform in general to structure plans. It is possible for plans to designate specific areas for action to be taken on comprehensive development or improvement.

The public may participate in the planning process by contributing to the consultation in the drawing up of plans. Representations may be made and must be considered by the planning authority. The Secretary of State may act as an objector to the plan or to an alteration to a plan. A plan may not be accepted unless objections have been carefully considered. In certain cases where objections are made there may be a public local inquiry held by a person appointed by the Secretary of State. Indeed the role of the Secretary of State is of some importance. In formulating the plan regard must be given to any information provided by the Secretary of State. Powers exist for the Secretary of State to intervene (ss. 43–44 of the TCPA 1990) and call in a local plan for his consideration. Ultimately this may mean that the local authority is unable to take any action on the plan until the Secretary of State has made a decision. Once approval is granted the local authority is not required to adopt the plan. In cases where further proposals are made by the local authority, the Secretary of State has the ultimate discretion whether to accept or reject proposals provided such proposals or amendments are properly considered (s. 45 of the TCPA 1990).

If there is any conflict between a local plan and a structure plan then under s. 46 of the TCPA 1990, the local plan must prevail (subject to one exception under s. 35C of the TCPA 1990 for notification of changes to structure plans).

In addition to local plans there are two types of specialist plans provided for under the TCPA 1990. County planning authorities are required to produce mineral local plans (see: s. 37 of the TCPA 1990 as amended). The one exception is National Parks, where the mineral plan is prepared specially or mineral policies may be included in specific cases within a local plan.

Minerals plans drawn up by the local authority must have regard to the directions of the Secretary of State. The plans must have detailed maps and policies for the extraction and working of minerals. Included within the mineral plan must be policies that take account of the environment.

The second type of specialist plans are local waste plans. Local plans must contain policies relating to the disposal of waste or refuse. Normally such plans must fall within a five year cycle. In formulating such plans account must be taken of the plans drawn up by waste regulation authorities under s. 50 of the Environmental Protection Act 1990. The local waste plan is also expected to take account of land use and the Department of the Environment issues guidance on how to draw up such plans (see: ENDS Report 234, 1990, pp. 21–5). S.92 of the Environment Act 1995 provides that the Secretary of State will introduce a waste strategy which will replace waste disposal plans.

Unitary development plans

Unitary development plans came about after certain changes to local government under the Local Government Act 1985. This resulted in the setting up of unitary local authorities in London and in the metropolitan counties, including West Midlands, Greater Manchester, Merseyside, South Yorkshire, Tyne and Wear and West Yorkshire.

The unitary development plan is the sole plan for the area and supersedes any other plan. Its remit includes all the planning matters for the area, such as a framework for development, conservation, development control and general land use policy. The form of the plan follows in part the example of the local plan outlined above. The plan is in two parts. Part I is a framework document and provides a written statement of the local authority's land use policies and general development strategy. Included are matters relevant to the environment such as conservation of natural beauty and the environment, amenities and improvement in the physical environment, including an assessment of traffic flows. There is an assumption that planning will take place on a 10 year cycle and authorities must consult with the Department of the Environment, the Countryside Commission and the Nature Conservancy Council in their area (see DoE Circular 3/88).

Part II of the plan must take account of the contents of Part I and give detailed guidance on the matters that are likely to inform planning decisions for individual applications. It is possible to designate certain areas within the plan as action areas in need of redevelopment. There are similar procedures for drawing up the plan as outlined above for local plans. Consultation procedures and procedures for making objections are intended to ensure that account is taken of public representations before the plan is adopted. The Secretary of State may make objections and there are requirements that draft copies of the plan be sent to the Secretary of State for consideration. The Secretary of State has wide powers to consider objections and may modify or call in the plan where appropriate. If a whole or part of a plan is called in then there must be a local public inquiry to hear objections (see: ss. 13, 17–20 and 24–6 of the TCPA 1990).

Material considerations

Section 70(2) of the TCPA 1990 requires the local planning authority to have regard to the provisions of the development plan that are material to the planning application (see below for a detailed explanation of the procedures for making a planning application). While there is wide discretion given to the planning authority, there is a requirement that the circumstances of each case must be carefully considered and representations taken into account in the final decision. The question arises as to the priority to be given to the development plan and what, if any, are the material considerations that must be taken into account. Generally account must be taken of the development plan when considering an application for planning permission. Also included in planning discretion are circulars and planning policy guidance. For example, a recent DoE guidance note (see: PPG13, DoE) encourages transport-efficient land use by curtailing carbon dioxide emissions. This is intended to make transport considerations a part of land use planning, for example in planning a shopping centre the transport implications of the chosen site must be calculated. As the development plan takes shape the principles that are used in its inception may receive greater attention as the plan emerges in reality.

The breadth of 'material considerations' implies that the planning authority has a wide discretion. Almost any consideration which relates to the use and development of land is capable of forming a material consideration for the purposes of planning law (see: *Stringer* v. *Minister of Housing and Local Government* [1971] 1 All ER 65). In an important decision the House of Lords has clarified the role of the courts, and that of the planning decision maker. In *Tesco Stores Ltd* v. *Secretary of State for the Environment* [1995] 2 All ER 636 three companies applied to the local planning authority for planning permission to build a retail food superstore, each on a different site. Settling the competing demands of each developer was difficult. Some of the concerns of the planning authorities and at the subsequent planning inquiry were the costs of a substantial road scheme, the West End Link (WEL), needed to accommodate the proposed developments. The town was the subject of severe traffic congestion and the inspector at a previous inquiry, concerned with revisions of the local development plan, recommended that a major link road should be added to the plan to relieve traffic congestion. The local highway authority had indicated that it could not fund the new link road. One of the competing developers, Tesco Stores, offered to fund the WEL even though its proposed store was not expected to add to traffic congestion. The inspector expressed an informal view that Tesco's application should be favoured. One of the other developers, Tarmac, appealed to the Environment Secretary and Tesco's application was called in. The Secretary of State granted planning permission to Tarmac despite the informal views of the inspector in favour of Tesco. Tesco appealed to the courts. The main issue before the House of Lords was the extent to which the Secretary of State was legally obliged to consider Tesco's offer to pay for the link road and what weight ought to be attached to such an offer. This depended on whether a consideration was relevant. The House of Lords held that Tesco's offer to finance the link road was not a material consideration. The key factor is that there has to be some connection between the proposed development and the offer made by the developer. The House of Lords upheld the Secretary of State's decision to approve Tarmac even though the result would be the building of a superstore without any link road.

The *Tesco Stores* decision must be put into the context of planning law. In the 1970s local planning authorities had increasingly used the power to enter into agreements (called s. 52 agreements) to exact payments or benefits which could not be imposed as part of the planning conditions. Such agreements were entered into by local planning authorities, despite guidance contained in Circular 5/68 that such agreements between planning authority and developer could not be made a condition of the planning permission. In practice planning permission was refused until the developer entered into the agreement. Then planning permission was granted unconditionally. These arrange-ments became known as planning gain and the Department of the Environment has issued guidance in Circular 22/83 and now Circular 16/91. The aim of the circular is to impose a 'necessary relationship between the development and the benefit' before any obligation may be entered into.

The *Tesco Stores* case is significant because, in general, it will make it more difficult for planning authorities to seek various benefits from developers as part of the proposed development. In a wide-ranging review of planning law in this area, Lord Hoffman stressed the reluctance of the courts to enter into questions of buying and selling planning permission. These matters are generally for the planning authorities and not the courts. The Secretary of State was entitled to exercise his discretion to determine policy in considering whether there was a necessary relationship between the proposed development and the benefit offered by the developer. Indirectly the case strengthens the policy role of the Secretary of State over local planning authorities. The future policy considerations of central government are likely to determine the shape of many planning decisions. Determining if such policies are in the public interest will excite a continuing debate about how environmental considerations should be considered in the formulation of policy.

Birtles and Stein have identified a number of matters that may be viewed as 'material considerations' and these include government policy (Birtles and Stein, 1994, pp. 71–2).

> Clearly a range of factors are always capable of being relevant, depending on the circumstances. These include the effect of the proposed development on local amenities and the local economy, road traffic and transport issues and safety. Environmental factors, including potential pollution emanating from the proposed development are frequently material, even though they may also be regulated under other statutory codes.

One of the most important qualities of the planning system is to adapt to change while advancing a planning strategy through carefully thought-out plans and policies. It remains to be seen if the development of government policy will deal adequately with the environment in the formulation of planning policy (see for example Planning Policy Guidance note 6, *Town Centres and Retail Developments,* and note 7, *The Countryside and the Rural Economy; Rural England* Cm 3016, HMSO, 1995, p. 88).

Procedural matters

The TCPA 1990 provides details of procedures including a timetable for drawing up plans. The timetable takes effect from the first stage, when a local authority decides to draw up a plan. There is a period for objections, representation and consultations (see: DoE Planning Policy Guidance note 12, HMSO). There are procedures for holding a local planning inquiry and for making representations to the Secretary of State. The validity of a development plan may be tested in the courts. A challenge may be made to the High Court under s. 287 of the TCPA 1990. In addition there is scope for judicial review (see Chapter 2) to test the validity of practices under the statutory arrangements for drawing up development plans.

The role of specialist information

Invariably development plans are drawn up through public consultation. Inputs into the planning process may be made from a wide variety of interested persons. The technical expertise involved in planning is usually widely drawn. Account is taken of government policy, the role of the European Community and other material considerations (see above) involved in arriving at the policy for the area. Planners, consultants and lawyers have a role in ensuring that plans are well prepared and follow the correct procedures laid down by statute (see addresses of experts on the environment at the end of this chapter).

Professionally qualified experts who give advice are under a general duty to exercise standards of professional care and skill in providing information and analysis (see: *Hedley Byrne & Co Ltd* v. *Heller & Partners Ltd* [1964] AC 465). The courts have a discretion when setting the standards of care that are expected. The principle developed by the courts of applying a high standard of care on professional advisers does not apply to any *informal* advice tendered by council officers to a member of the public (see: *Tidman* v. *Reading Borough Council, The Times,* 10 November 1994).

Planning agreements and undertakings

Section 106 of the Town and Country Planning Act 1990, as amended by the Planning and Compensation Act 1991, provides for planning obligations to be entered into with the local planning authority. The term 'planning obligations' refers to both agreements and undertakings. The essence of an agreement or obligation is that the legislation allows any person with an interest in land to make an agreement outside the normal planning procedures. The agreement in practice usually takes the form of allowing developers to obtain planning permission in circumstances where planning objections would have resulted in a refusal of planning permission. In return it is possible for the local planning authority to gain from the developer some concessions, for example to provide the planning authority with some additional land or to undertake major landscaping or road works at a site. The question of the use of agreements has significance for the environment. For example a developer may be encouraged to landscape the development site or plant with additional trees or provide resources to protect the environment as part of a planning bargain struck between the developer and the local planning authority (see: *Wimpey Homes Holdings Ltd* v. *Secretary of State for the Environment* [1993]; *R.* v. *Plymouth CC ex parte Plymouth and South Devon Co-operative Society Ltd* [1993] JPL 81; and (discussed above) *Tesco Stores Ltd* v. *Secretary of State for the Environment* [1995] 2 All ER 636).

The 1991 Act envisages the possibility that developers might enter a unilateral undertaking with the planning authority. In addition a new s. 278 of the Highways Act 1980 substituted by s. 23 of the New Roads and Street Works Act 1991 confers a broad power upon a highway authority to enter into agreements by which some other person will pay for the construction of roads or streets. Government policy therefore reflects a shift in attitude to the responsibilities between the public and private sectors. This might be open to the criticism that the developer may negotiate what in effect amounts to the purchase of planning permission. Planning permission, however, cannot be purchased (see: *Tesco Supermarkets* v. *Secretary of State* [1995] 2 All ER 636). There are additional provisions in the 1991 Act that provide for the modification or discharge of the agreement (see: the Town and Country Planning (Modification and Discharge of Planning Obligations) Regulations 1992, SI 1992 No. 2832).

Planning permission and nuisance

The grant of planning permission raises the question of whether a developer who is granted such permission may use it as a good defence for any subsequent action for nuisance (see Chapter 10). This question has been considered by the Court of Appeal in *Wheeler and Another* v. *JJ Saunders Ltd and Others* (*The Times*, 4 January 1995; see also: ENDS Report 240, January 1995). In general the Court of Appeal accepted that a grant of planning permission might change the character of a neighbourhood and subsequent nuisance action must be considered in all the circumstances. In the *Wheeler* case the facts concerned the grant of planning permission for two pig rearing houses. The plaintiffs brought an action in nuisance because of the smells from the pig units. The Court of Appeal upheld the action. The decision is significant because it clarifies an important principle. Developers who are granted planning permission must ensure that their operations comply with the additional statutory controls relating to those operations. A private action in nuisance is available to individuals to ensure that polluting activities are stopped. The courts are therefore slow to prevent the private individual from exercising rights in a nuisance action where it was in the public interest that the individual should succeed. The grant of planning permission is not a bar to such an action.

Planning and the environment: some conclusions

Only recently have environmental matters taken on prominence in the system of development plans. In 1990 the government's White Paper (see: *This Common Inheritance* Cm 1200 (1990)), acknowledged the importance of the environment in planning. The DoE has issued various guidances to take the environment into account and this is supported by parts of the Town and Country Planning Act 1990 (see: Planning Policy

Guidance note 12 and the *Environmental Appraisal of Development Plans – A Good Practice Guide* (DoE, 1994)). Environmental appraisal and assessment is also part of the planning process (see Chapter 6). However, it remains to be seen what effect techniques of assessment will have on the environment in the future.

▶ The meaning of development control

The scope of development control

There is a general principle defined in Part III and s. 55 of the Town and Country Planning Act 1990 (TCPA 1990) that any development land is subject to planning permission. The meaning and definition of development are contained in s. 55(1) of the TCPA 1990. Development is the carrying out of building, engineering, mining and other operations in, on, over or under land, or making any material change in the use of land or buildings (see: s. 55(1) of the Town and Country Planning Act 1990).

Demolition

Doubts about whether demolition or building operations require planning permission as falling under the definition of development have been settled by s. 55(1A) (see: The Planning and Compensation Act 1991 and also *Cambridge City Council* v. *Secretary of State for the Environment* [1991] EG 119). Demolition now requires planning permission (see: DoE *New Planning Controls over the Demolition of Buildings* (July 1991)) but this leaves the possibility of exemption by the Secretary of State (see: s. 55(2) of the Planning and Compensation Act 1991).

Recently certain categories of demolition are said not to constitute development. The details are contained in the Town and Country Planning (Demolition – Description of Buildings) (No. 2) Direction 1992 (Annex to DoE Circular 26/92).

Deemed planning permission and enterprise zones

There are a number of exceptions to the principle that planning permission is required. Exceptions are to be found in certain changes of use (see: Town and Country Planning (Use Classes) Order 1987, SI 1987 No. 764 as amended) and land which is subject to various Development Orders under the Town and Country Planning General Development Order 1988 (SI No. 1831). Deemed planning permission is provided under the Town and Country Planning General Development Order 1988 (SI 1988 No. 1831). There are also some special categories of exemption in areas where there are simplified planning zones or enterprise zones (see: Local Government Planning and Land Act 1990). Invariably such exceptions do not include circumstances where the land is subject to hazardous developments (see: Planning (Hazardous Substances) Act 1990).

There are also examples where the local authority or other statutory body such as a public utility has statutory powers which require authorisation from central government or a regulator. The grant of an authorisation, for example, to an electricity undertaker for the construction of a generating station under s. 36 of the Electricity Act 1989, may also in these circumstances carry the necessary planning permission (see: for example ss. 36 and 37 of the Electricity Act 1989). Indeed there are some circumstances where the grant of statutory powers, normally by Private Bill procedure, may be given specific authorisation by Order of the Secretary of State. For example major projects may be authorised for railways or canals under the Transport and Works Act 1992.

Change of use

The system of development control does have limitations. Once planning permission is secured there is no general requirement to seek further approval within the terms of the permission already granted. In cases where there is a change of existing use the planning authorities face difficult issues associated with the question of what comes within the definition of a material change of use. This question requires an evaluation of the facts of each case. Determining where to draw the line between what is or is not a change of use is often difficult. The approach adopted is to assess what is a primary function or use which may also be closely associated with an incidental or ancillary purpose. In many cases there may be a clear and natural connection between different uses that makes any planning application unnecessary.

The courts have adopted a strategic approach to the problem of what constitutes a change of use. That approach relies on determining what amounts to the planning unit under consideration. In *Burdle* v. *Secretary of State for the Environment* [1972] 3 All ER 240 the court adopted three ways to approach understanding what the use of land amounted to. First, in cases where the use of land can be identified as forming a single purpose, then ancillary or incidental activities may be treated as a whole planning unit. Second, even in cases where there are a variety of different uses over a period of time and where it is impossible to identify a single main purpose, the entire unit may form a single planning unit. Finally, within a single unit, if there are distinct and separate areas occupied for different and unrelated purposes, then each area may form a planning unit.

Excluded from planning permission are developments in continued use since 1 July 1948. The Crown does not require permission for its developments but there is a non-statutory consultation process (see: DOE Circular 18/84). Many environmentally harmful activities are not directly subject to planning controls, such as car pollution or agricultural activities (see: *This Common Inheritance*, Cm 1200 (1990).

Sections 191–4 of the TCPA 1990 may help to resolve problems over the existing use of land. These provisions permit any person who wishes to determine the lawfulness of any *existing* use of buildings or land or any operations to make application to the appropriate planning authority. The authority may issue a certificate setting out the legality of the existing scheme.

The planning application: procedures and principles

As part of the process of development control and in addition to the drawing up of the development plans, planning applications are an important means of protecting the environment. Over 600 000 applications are made each year for developments that require planning permission. Planning is open to the influences of many different groups and professions. It is possible to see the protection of the environment as a primary function of the planning system. On this view the local planning authority has to come to arrangements with developers that negotiate environmental concerns as part of the planning process.

However, it is a mistake to be misled into thinking that environmental concerns are the main focus of planning controls or indeed that planning may provide a means to protect the environment. Generally planning law has developed independently of environmental concerns (see: Tromans and Clarkson, 'The Environmental Protection Act 1990: its relevance to planning controls' [1991] JPL 507). Recent developments in the area of environmental impact assessment and integrated pollution control outlined in the previous chapter are likely to represent a formidable challenge to the future direction of the planning process. This will necessitate greater awareness of the environment in planning controls.

There are set procedures and prescribed forms as well as set fees for making a planning application (see s. 62 of the Town and Country Planning Act 1990 and in the General Development Order 1988, Town and Country Planning (Applications) Regulations, SI 1988 No. 1812). The local planning authority must determine a planning application within eight weeks of receipt of the application. Permission may be granted in full without any conditions attached. Permission may be granted with such conditions as the local authority 'may think fit'. Planning permission may be refused. In such cases of refusal there is a right of appeal, discussed in more detail below (see: s. 70(1)(a) of the Town and Country Planning Act 1990).

There are special procedures when the applicant for planning permission is the local authority itself. These are contained in the Town and Country Planning (General) Regulations 1992 (SI 1992 No. 1492) with amendments. As noted in Chapter 6 there are circumstances where applications for planning permission must be accompanied by an environmental assessment.

Applications for planning permission may be made for an existing site where there are substantial changes to be introduced. Evidence may be requested to assist in assessing the application and further information required for the purposes of clarification of points of detail. Outline planning permission may be sought setting out 'in principle' the purpose of the proposed development. Permission may be granted to include such matters as 'reserved matters' requiring specific conformity with design details or site access or landscaping.

One important aspect of the planning application is the requirement for publicity. Details of the planning proposal, a certificate confirming that the applicant is the owner of the land or that the owners have been notified or attempts made to notify the owner, must accompany the application. Publication of the planning application may be achieved through the use of a site notice, notification of the neighbours and publication in a local newspaper for larger developments with an impact on the environment.

The Secretary of State monitors the planning system. Section 78 of the Town and Country Planning Act 1990 provides a right of appeal to the Secretary of State against refusal of planning permission. Very often the appeal may be based on a procedural issue. For example, there is a statutory eight week period for a local planning authority to make a decision; if this has not been complied with or if an extension of time has not been sought, then an appeal may be lodged. Appeals may be made up to six months after the date of the non-determination. Birtles and Stein (1994, p. 79) note:

> One option used by developers, known as 'twin tracking', involves submitting two identical applications to the local planning authority and appealing one of them on the expiry of the period for determination. The developer can then continue to negotiate with the planning authority on the other one, in the knowledge that the impending appeal places an added pressure on the authority.

A right of appeal is limited to the applicant for planning permission. Objectors and landowners do not have a right of appeal.

Most appeals are heard and determined by an inspector from a team of inspectors appointed by the Department of the Environment for that purpose. A public inquiry becomes the focus of objectors. Such an inquiry must be held where either the applicant or the authority requests it. An inquiry or hearing may be held and there is the option for the matter to be settled by way of written representations (see: s. 320 of the Town and Country Planning Act 1990). Procedures at the inquiry are governed by rules of procedure and Codes of Practice (see: the *Code of Practice on Preparing for Major Planning Inquiries*, Annex 1 DoE Circular 10/88). In addition there are standards applied by the courts in cases of judicial review such as the rules of natural justice and that the conduct of the inquiry must be fair.

There are a number of distinctive features of the planning process that deserve particular mention as follows.

Secretary of State call-in powers

The Secretary of State has specific call-in powers under s. 77 of the Town and Country Planning Act 1990. This may include circumstances where the Secretary of State decides that it is preferable that applications for planning permission should be referred to him. Local authorities are under a duty to provide the Secretary of State with information and notification of certain types of planning permission where they do not propose to refuse the application (see: Town and Country Planning (Development Plans and Consultation), Direction 192, Annex 3, DoE Circular 19/92).

In practice call-in powers are seldom used. Their use is confined to those cases where national issues may appear to make the planning application go beyond matters raised at a local level. Once initiated the Secretary of State will determine the application after a public inquiry (see judicial review of call-in powers in: *Lakin Ltd* v. *Secretary of State for Scotland* [1989] JPL 339).

Planning conditions

Local planning authorities have wide powers under s. 70 to impose 'such conditions as they think fit' on the grant of planning permission. In addition s. 72 (1) provides that the local planning authority may impose conditions for regulating the use of any land under the applicant's control whether or not comprised in the application, so far as it is expedient in connection with the authorised development. Guidance on the use of conditions in planning permission has been issued by the DoE (see: DoE Circular 1/85). There are some restraints on the exercise of the discretion granted to the local planning authority: a condition must serve a planning purpose; the condition must fairly and reasonably relate to the permitted development; and the condition must not be unreasonable (see: *Newbury District Council* v. *The Secretary of State for the Environment* [1981] AC 578 [1980] 1 All ER 731). The courts exercise a review over conditions which may be regarded as unreasonable (see: *R.* v. *Hillingdon London Borough Council ex parte Royco Homes Ltd* [1974] QB 720).

Local planning authorities have powers under ss. 97–100 of the Town and Country Planning Act 1990 to revoke or modify planning permission. In the case of the revocation of planning permission s. 107 of the Town and Country Planning Act 1990 may provide compensation (see: *Canterbury City Council* v. *Colley* [1993] 1 All ER 591 on the question of how compensation is calculated). Discontinuance of any use or removal or alteration of any building is also within the powers of the local planning authority (see: ss. 102–4 of the Town and Country Planning Act 1990).

Enforcement

Unauthorised developments or a breach of planning control may be the subject of action by the planning authorities. Section 171A of the Planning and Compensation Act 1991 provides for new enforcement powers (Carnwarth, 1989). The 1991 Act introduces two new sections to the 1990 Town and Country Planning Act. There is a new s. 171A where the local planning authority may take action where there is a breach of planning control. This may arise where the development requiring permission takes place without permission, or where a planning condition attached to the development has not been complied with. Enforcement action may consist of issuing an enforcement notice or a breach of condition notice.

In cases where the local planning authority suspects that there is a breach of planning control it may serve a planning contravention notice. This may require specific action to be taken as to the nature of the operation or the conditions required. There are detailed procedural rules and appeal procedures contained in ss. 171D and 172 of the Act. In addition s. 187B provides for the issuing of a High Court injunction where the local planning authority considers it necessary or expedient for an actual or apprehended breach of planning control. There are powers to issue a stop notice under s. 183 of the Act (see Planning Policy Guidance (PPG) 18, December 1991). Local planning authorities may be liable to pay compensation under s. 186 in certain circumstances, such as when the stop notice is withdrawn or quashed or varies. Powers to issue stop notices are used sparingly, given the liability of the local planning authority for compensation.

▶ References and further reading

Alder, J. (1992) *Development Control,* 2nd edn. Sweet and Maxwell, London.
Ashworth, W. (1954) *The Genesis of Modern British Town Planning.* Routledge and Kegan Paul, London.
Ball, S. and Bell, S. (1995) *Environmental Law,* 3rd edn. Blackstone, London.

Birtles, W. and Stein, R. (1994) *Planning and Environmental Law.* Longman, Harlow.

Callies, R. and Grant, M. (1991) 'Paying for growth and planning gain: an Anglo-American comparison of development conditions, impact fees and development agreements'. *The Urban Lawyer,* **23**, 221.

Carnwarth, R. (1989) *Enforcing Planning Control.* HMSO, London.

Carnwarth, R. (1991) 'The planning lawyer and the environment'. *Journal of Environmental Law,* **3**, 57.

Department of the Environment (1994) *Environmental Appraisal of Development Plans – A Good Practice Guide.* DoE, London.

Gibson, J. and Warren, L. (1991) *Law, Policy and the Environment.* Blackwell, Oxford.

Grant, M. (1986) *Urban Planning Law.* Sweet and Maxwell, London.

Gray, K. (1994) 'Equitable property'. In Freeman, Oliver and Sanders (eds), *Current Legal Problems.* University College, London.

Heap, D. (1991) *An Outline of Planning Law,* 10th edn. Sweet and Maxwell, London.

Holder, J. *et al.* (eds) (1993) *Perspectives on the Environment.* Avebury, London.

Hughes, D. (1992) *Environmental Law.* Butterworths, London.

Lomas, O. and McEldowney, J.F. (eds) (1991) *Frontiers of Environmental Law.* John Wiley, London.

Malcolm, R. (1994) *A Guidebook to Environmental Law.* Sweet and Maxwell, London.

McAuslan, P. (1974) 'Planning Law's Contribution to the Problems of an Urban Society' 37 MLR 134.

McAuslan, P. (1980) *The Ideologies of Planning Law.* Pergamon Press, Oxford.

McLaren, J.P.S. (1983) 'Nuisance law and the industrial revolution – some lessons from social history'. *Oxford Journal Legal Studies,* **3**, 155.

Moore, *A Practical Approach to Planning Law,* 3rd edn. Blackstone Press, London.

Purdue, M., Young, E. and Robinson, R.J. (1989) *Planning Law and Procedure.* Butterworths, London.

Telling and Duxbury, (1990) *Planning Law and Procedure.* Butterworths, London.

Tromans, S. and Clarkson, M. (1991) 'The Environment Protection Act 1990: its relevance to planning controls' [1991] JPL 507.

▶ Reports

Monitoring Environmental Assessment and Planning (HMSO, 1991).

This Common Inheritance: Britain's Environmental Strategy, Cm 1200 (HMSO, 1990).

Biodiversity – The UK Action Plan, Cm 2428.

▶ Useful addresses

UK Register of Expert Witnesses, JS Publications, London.

Law Society, Legal Practice Experts, Law Society 50/51, Chancery Lane, London.

ENDS, Directory of Information on Environmental Information, Finsbury Business Centre, 40, Bowling Green Lane, London EC1R 0NE.

8 The countryside and the environment

The land that forms the countryside and coasts is an important part of the UK's heritage.

What we see today is the result of centuries of this interaction between man and nature. The countryside is also an integral part of the world's living environment: it is home for many wild species; its woodlands absorb carbon dioxide; and it is part of the natural cycle of water, carbon and nitrogen between air, land and sea. (*This Common Inheritance*, Cm 1200 (1990), para. 7.2.)

The countryside provides an important challenge for the development of the economy and the protection of the environment. Agriculture and forestry make up 90 per cent of land use in the United Kingdom. In the previous chapter we examined how planning developed as an essential tool in the built environment. In this chapter we examine how the countryside is affected by law and regulations. This covers the Common Agricultural Policy (CAP) of the European Union; agricultural land use, including the application of pesticides and fertilisers; National Parks; green belts; Areas of Outstanding Natural Beauty and areas of Special Scientific Interest; and forestry and woodlands.

There are competing demands on the rural environment. A healthy rural economy is an essential part of the country's economic development. Agricultural policy, whether under the Common Agricultural Policy (CAP) of the European Union or through the government's own policies, must ensure an adequate supply of food at a reasonable cost and at reasonable returns to the farmer. The rural environment is also exploited for a wide range of leisure interests and activities from rambling and hill walking to tourism and sports. Often the amenity of and access to the countryside are demanded by different groups and organisations with irreconcilable objectives. Not all activities are compatible with the protection of the environment. Deciding what is or is not in the interests of the environment may require reconciling differing objectives and goals in environmental policy. There are growing demands from pressure groups, such as the Council for the

Preservation of Rural England, for the greater protection of the environment and competing economic demands for employment and increased activity in rural areas. The government has published a Rural White Paper, *Rural England*, Cm 3016 (HMSO, 1995) for the future of the English countryside. In Scotland a separate but parallel exercise is under way building on the work contained in *Rural Framework* (Scottish Office, 1992).

Human activity in the countryside inevitably has an impact on the environment, influencing habitat stability and the maintenance of biological diversity. Kiss and Shelton (1993, p. 115) have noted the global significance of the protection of the environment:

> In recent centuries, the impact has been largely negative, with increased exploitation, pollution, and population growth leading to destruction and loss of habitat. It is estimated that in less than two hundred years, 128 species of birds and 95 species of mammals have disappeared from the globe. In some regions, over half the endemic species have become extinct since 1950. In others, large proportions of the remaining species, more than 50 per cent of all butterfly and freshwater species, plus two-thirds of the amphibian and all the reptile species reflect this trend. In France, more than 30 per cent of the species of flora are declining. Through Europe, large mammals, including the wolf, bear, lynx and other wildcats, face particular hostility and threats from competing land users, especially farmers and hunters.

In the United Kingdom information about the countryside and wildlife is provided in the *Countryside Survey 1990* (DoE, HMSO, 1993) containing a detailed satellite mapping of the whole country and detailed field studies. The survey provides information on the countryside and its habitats. The government intend to undertake a repeat survey for the year 2000.

▶ Agriculture

The Common Agricultural Policy (CAP)

The CAP was first formulated in the 1960s and rapidly became a means of integrating national agricultural policies into a common policy for the European Community. It has proved to be both controversial and contentious among Community members. It represents a substantial expenditure from the Community budget.

The Treaty of Rome provides, in Article 3a and Articles 38–47, the basis of the CAP. The main legal basis for most of the Common Agricultural Policy is to be found in Article 43(2) EEC and the main objectives of the policy are identified in Article 39 EEC. Taken together these Articles require the following (see Snyder, 1985):

- Increased agricultural productivity
- A stabilised market
- The availability of supplies
- A guarantee of reasonable prices to the consumer
- A fair standard of living for agricultural communities within the Community.

(For a critique of the CAP see House of Lords Select Committee on the European Communities: *20th Report on Agriculture and the Environment* 1993/94 247; also see The European Commission, *The Agricultural Situation in the European Union 1994 Report*, Luxembourg, 1995.)

The assumption underlining the CAP is that improvement in earnings may be achieved by a structural policy aimed at increasing productivity rather than control over market policy. In addition, it was hoped to overcome traditional difficulties over agricultural supplies by ensuring self-sufficiency within the Community. To ensure that the Community achieves these objectives protection is offered to the Community producers from competition outside the Community. Thus the CAP provides a common market in agricultural goods. The main means to achieve the regulation of the common market is through a central price support mechanism. This offers a guaranteed price to agricultural producers within the Community and protection against cheaper imports. Annually the Council of the Community sets target, intervention and threshold prices throughout the Community for agricultural products. A target price provides producers with an indication of the forthcoming price for the year ahead, giving producers an indication of production levels. The intervention price is set below the target price and is the figure that national authorities will pay to producers who are unable to sell their produce in the market. This provides a guarantee to producers. If the market in the Community for a given commodity falls below the intervention price, the producer may withdraw the product from the market and sell to an intervention agency. The intervention agency will pay the producer the equivalent of the intervention price. Finally, there is a threshold price which sets the lowest internal price for imports (Henderson, 1993).

There are a number of strategies which the intervention agency may adopt. It may store the commodity or sell it on the world market, usually at a price below the intervention price. Alternatively, it may sell the commodity to developing countries or to those in need. The financial implications of the CAP represent a considerable burden on Community resources. There is a European Agricultural Guidance and Guarantee Fund which provides financial support to the intervention agency. Over the period of the development of the CAP the intervention agency has been the subject of criticism. In the mid-1970s large surpluses in various commodities such as cereals, wine, milk, beef and other dairy produce resulted in the building and operation of large storage facilities. Such surpluses were a financial cost to the Community and a source of political embarrassment.

The cost of the CAP is a considerable burden on Community finances. In 1991 the Community spent well over ECUs 31 billion in guaranteeing prices to agricultural producers. This is over 53 per cent of the overall Community budget. The existence of large surpluses has required a number of reforms to the Community budget. Adjustments to price support in the event of over-production were attempted in the 1980s but had limited success. During the 1990s the Community has come under pressure to open up its market to external competition (see: the Uruguay Round of GATT and J. Marsh, 1992). Further reforms to the CAP were attempted in 1992.

The Commissioner responsible for agriculture (see: *European Commission Guidelines for the Reform of the Common Agricultural Policy*, COM(91) 100 final (1 February 1992)) introduced sharp reductions in the guaranteed intervention prices offered to cereal and beef suppliers. Subsidies for production were shifted to income support for agricultural producers and early retirement was encouraged. Land was designated to be set aside and thus taken out of agricultural production. Agricultural producers receive direct payment as compensation. Additional reforms were introduced to encourage environmentally friendly production and reductions in the intensity of farming methods.

Despite vocal opposition, the reforms were introduced in 1992 with the expectation that surpluses will be reduced. A more radical reform of the CAP, however, will be required if this ambition is to be realised. Radical reform appears unlikely given the complexity of negotiations between different Member States with influential farming interests.

The environment in the United Kingdom and other European countries continues to suffer from the excesses of the CAP (see below). The reforms are starting to address the considerable economic demands imposed by the CAP. If managed appropriately it may be possible to use some of the reforms to aid environmental protection. For example, at present set-aside has not necessarily resulted in any net benefits to the environment. It tends to have resulted simply in land being left fallow, perhaps as part of a rotation scheme. It may be environmentally desirable to use set-aside on a long-term or permanent basis, incorporating incentives to encourage the management of the set-aside land for habitat restoration. Alternatively, farmers could be given incentives to leave a buffer zone at the margins of fields (an area left unploughed and uncultivated), to encourage and protect wildlife. The landscape of the United Kingdom has been influenced throughout history by agricultural activities (Hoskins, 1955). The policies adopted as a result of the CAP have also left their mark on the countryside. It may be possible in future, however, with judicious management of the CAP, to ensure greater habitat conservation and reduce agricultural-based pollution.

Agriculture and the environment

The challenge that agriculture poses to the environment has proved controversial. Today agriculture is viewed as comparable to any other large industry. In the past, too often agriculture was treated as distinctive, mainly because of the misleading impression that agricultural activities naturally take care of the environment. In fact the intensive agricultural practices encouraged by the CAP have had several deleterious effects on the environment. There has been an expansion of the area of cultivated land involving the destruction of habitats such as hedgerows. The length of hedgerows in England and Wales has declined from 72 metres/hectare in the 1950s to 32 metres/hectare in the 1980s as a direct result of the CAP (Turner *et al.*, 1994). The *Countryside Survey 1990* (DoE, HMSO, 1993) presents evidence that this loss of hedgerows has continued into the 1990s: between 1984 and 1990 85 000 km of hedgerows were lost. There has been a tendency to monoculture and mechanisation on farms which has threatened a variety of species. In addition, in order to ensure high yields, intensive applications of fertilisers and pesticides have been necessary. These often spread beyond the agricultural environment into natural habitats, including aquatic habitats, as a result of run-off from agricultural land, and have had a range of detrimental effects (see below). Intensive husbandry techniques have resulted in the formation of large amounts of animal slurries, presenting major disposal problems and very real pollution and health risks. The conversion of large areas of land to monoculture, the extensive use of chemical fertilisers and overgrazing may all harm soil structure and potentially result in soil erosion. The drive for ever greater productivity means that agriculture can rarely now be considered to be in balance with the environment.

The agricultural industry makes widespread use of pesticides and fertilisers. Pesticides can be regarded as xenobiotic compounds. The term xenobiotic (foreign to life) was originally limited to compounds which were chemically synthesised by man including, of course, pesticides. In fact, this definition has been modified somewhat in recent years to include any toxic chemical, natural or chemically synthesised, which by some action of man, e.g. transportation or application, poses a threat to the environment (Leisinger, 1983). Pesticides rank among the most important xenobiotic compounds released to the environment primarily because they are used in large quantities, have a potentially deleterious effect on the environment and may be resistant to degradation. Biocides vary in the extent of recalcitrance, i.e. resistance to biodegradation, and therefore their stability and persistence in the environment. There are two interrelated reasons for recalcitrance:

1. *Environmental factors* (particularly in soils, a key site of xenobiotic degradation), e.g. pH, redox potential, temperature, etc. Pesticides which are chemically defined as biodegradable may in particular soil conditions be highly recalcitrant. For example, Paraquat, a bipyridilium herbicide, is degradable in laboratory systems. It is, however, highly cationic in aqueous conditions and binds strongly to humic substances and irreversibly to clays in soil, effectively becoming inaccessible for degradation and highly stable in the environment (McEldowney *et al.*, 1993).
2. *The chemical structure of the xenobiotic compound.* Biocides also vary in their environmental longevity and resistance to degradation due to their chemical structure. For example, dichlorodiphenyltrichloro-ethane (DDT) takes 3–15 years to degrade and be removed from the environment at recommended field application levels. Monuron takes between 22 and 100 weeks to degrade and the herbicide 2,4-D takes 2–4 weeks. The impact of environmental conditions on degradation can also vary with the chemical structure of the pesticide. In recent years there has been considerable interest in designing chemicals with pesticide activity which have limited longevity in the environment, i.e. are readily degraded. This type of molecular engineering is contributing to the development of clean technologies (see Chapter 14).

The physicochemical characteristics of the biocide and environmental conditions affect not only the recalcitrance of the biocide but also its mobility in the environment (Fig. 8.1). For example, the propensity of Paraquat to bind to clay domains means that this biocide will not be easily leached from soil into surface water and groundwater. Predicting the ultimate mobility and fate of biocides in soils is, however, very difficult. Soils are highly variable, e.g. clay, organic matter, sand content, pH, water capacity, etc., and this variation can be large even over small areas. Thus the mobility of a pesticide and the likelihood of it leaching into surface water or groundwater, even its availability for bioaccumu-lation (see below), cannot be predicted without consideration of local conditions and appropriate studies.

The impact of toxic substances such as pesticides on living organisms is related to the nature of the substance, its concentration, the time the organism is exposed to the toxicant (related in part to recalcitrance), the characteristics of the organism itself (Haslam, 1994) and environ-mental factors including the presence of other toxic substances (McEldowney *et al.*, 1993) (Fig. 8.2). Living organisms bioaccumulate

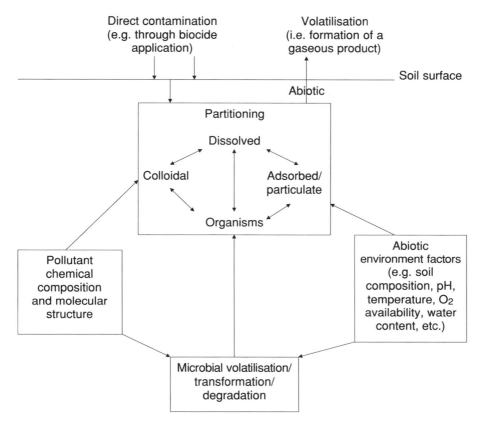

Fig. 8.1 Diagrammatic representation of factors affecting the mobility and fate of pollutants in soils.

and bioconcentrate pesticides to variable extents depending on the species, environmental conditions and the physical and chemical nature of the biocide, e.g. hydrophobicity, molecular size and structure, etc. Some of these factors affect the availability of the pesticide for uptake. For example, the irreversible adsorption of cationic pesticides to the surface of clay domains in soil or to sediment particles in aquatic systems may restrict their availability for biological accumulation (Fig. 8.2). Strictly speaking the terms bioaccumulation and bioconcentration are applicable only to aquatic environments. Bioaccumulation is the accumulation of pollutants by algae, plants, invertebrates and fish from both food and water, whereas bioconcentration is accumulation from water alone. Biomagnification, however, applies to both terrestrial and aquatic environments and is defined as the increases in pollutant concentration in the tissues of successive organisms along a food chain. Compounds particularly prone to bioaccumulation tend to be lipophilic

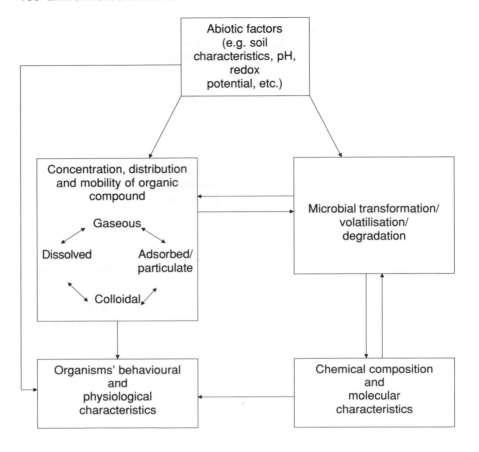

Fig. 8.2 Diagrammatic representation of factors affecting the bioavailability, toxicity and bioaccumulation potential of xenobiotic or recalcitrant organic compounds in the environment.

or analogues of essential nutrients, and include many pesticides (McEldowney *et al.*, 1993).

There have been many examples of the biomagnification of persistent xenobiotic compounds (Masson, 1991). One of the best known and often described is the biomagnification of the insecticide DDT (Fig. 8.3). The toxic effects of DDT were particularly acute in predators at the top of a food chain (see Chapter 1) owing to the biomagnification of the pesticide through the food chain. Eventually the impact of DDT was found to be so significant that its use was severely curtailed. The problem was increased by the relative recalcitrance of DDT (see above).

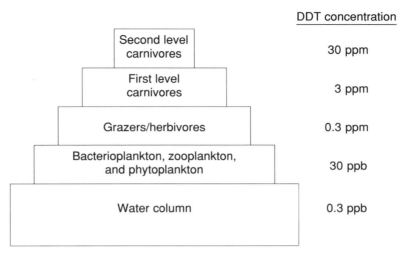

Fig. 8.3 Biomagnification of a pesticide such as DDT in an aquatic environment. The DDT concentrations are representative not actual measurements.

Consideration of this limited summary of the factors that affect the environmental persistence, mobility and impact of pesticides on living organisms suggests a key difficulty in the development of regulations to protect the environment from the use of pesticides. Predictions about the likely effects of pesticides, and other pollutants, in the environment require, at a minimum, an understanding of the probable (Moriarty, 1990):

● fate, distribution and concentration of the pollutant in the environment;
● relationship between pollutant environmental concentration and its uptake and accumulation by organisms;
● impact of accumulation on individual organisms;
● consequences of impacts on individual species for communities and the ecosystem as a whole.

Assessing these components and, therefore, the likely harm to the environment and individual ecosystems is exceptionally difficult and complex (see McEldowney *et al.*, 1993 for a discussion on predicting the environmental fate of pollutants). Indeed it is difficult to extrapolate beyond local environments. Even our understanding of the impact on humans is incomplete. It has only recently become clear that there appears to be a high risk of neurological damage associated with exposure to organophosphate sheep dips among farmers (*Lancet*, 1995).

There is a wide variety of pesticides used in farming (Table 8.1) including organohalogen and organophosphorus compounds which are among the EEC List I ('Black List') substances (Appendix A, EC

Table 8.1 Selected examples of commonly used biocides*

	Common name	Chemical formula
(a) Herbicides		
	Atrazine	2-chloro-4-ethylamino-6-isopropyl-amino-1,3,5-triazine
	2,4-D	2,4-dichlorophenoxyacetic acid, esters or salts especially amine salts
	2,4,-DB	4-(2,4-dichlorophenoxy) butyric acid, esters or salts
	Diquat	1,1'-ethylene-2,2'-bipyridyldiylium dibromide
	Glyphosate	N-(phosphoromethyl) glycine (isopropylamine salt)
	Paraquat	1,1'-dimethyl-4,4'-bipyridyldiylium dichloride
	2,4,5-T	(2,4,5-trichlorophenoxy) acetic acid
	Vernolate	δ-propyl dipropylthiolcarbame
(b) Insecticides		
(i) Carbamates		
	Aminocarb	4-dimethylamino-m-tolyl methyl carbamate
	Carbofuran	1-naphthl methylcarbamate 2,3-dihydro-2,2-dimethylbenzofuran-7-yl methylcarbamate
	Propoxur	2-isopropor oxyphenyl methyl carbamate
(ii) Organochlorines		
	Aldrin	(IR,4S,5S,8R)-1,2,3,4,10,10 hexachloro-1,4,4a,5,8,8a hexahydro-1,4:5,8-dimethanophthalene
	Chlordane	mixture of chlorinated camphenes 1,2,3,4,5,6,7,8 8-octochloro-2,3,3a,4,7,7a-hexahydro-4,7-methanoidene
	DDT	1,1,1,-trichloro-2-2-bis (4-chlorophenyl) ethane, formerly (dichlorodiphenyl-trichloroethane)
	Dieldrin	(IR,4S,5S,8R)-1,2,3,4,10,10-hexachloro-1,4,4a,5,6,7,8,8a-octahydro-6,7-expoxy 1,4:5,8-dimethano-naphthalene
	Endrin	(1R,4S,5R,8S)-1,2,3,4,10,10-hexachloro-1,4,4a,5,6,7,8,8a-octahydro-6,7-expoxy-1,4:5,8-dimethanonaphthalene
	HCH	1,2,3,4,5,6-hexachlorocyclohexane
	Lindane	γ-1,2,3,4,5,6-hexachlorocyclohexane
(iii) Organophosphorus		
	Chlorthion	O-(3-chloro-4-nitrophenyl O,O-dimethyl phosphorothioate
	Diazinon	O,O-diethyl-O-2-isopropyl-6-methyl-pyrimidin-4-yl phosphorothioate

Table 8.1 *continued*

Common name	Chemical formula
Disulfoton	*O,O*-diethyl *s*-2-ethylthioethyl phosphorodithioate
Parathion	*O,O*-diethyl-*O*-4-nitrophenyl phosphorothioate
Trichlorophon	dimethyl 2,2,2-trichloro-1-hydroxyethyl phosphate

* See Hellawell, 1986, for a more comprehensive list of biocides.

Groundwater Directive 80/68/EEC) (see Chapter 10). List I substances are those substances perceived as the most dangerously toxic. They tend also to be persistent and capable of bioaccumulation. Pollutants considered less dangerous are included on List II, the 'Grey List'. This list also includes biocides.

In their seventh report the Royal Commission on Environmental Pollution considered the problem of pesticide control. The European Community has taken action in a number of Directives. In Directive 76/895/EEC and Directive 86/362/EEC (as amended) the Community has attempted to protect consumers by setting limits on food pesticide residues (see: the Pesticides (Maximum Residue Levels in Food) Regulations 1988, SI 1988 No. 1378). In addition to setting limits to pesticide content in food, an increasingly large number of substances come within a list of prohibited substances or specific products containing prohibited substances. Detailed regulation of the food industry is provided in the Food and Environmental Protection Act 1985 and the Pesticides (Fees and Enforcement) Act 1989. Part III of the latter is concerned chiefly with pesticide control, regulation and enforcement.

Pesticides and other industrially produced chemicals undergo a hazard assessment before marketing. European Community Directive 79/831/EEC specifies the information required during product notification. The amount of information required increases with the expected amount of the compound to be marketed. Results from toxicological studies form an important part of the required data (Table 8.2). These are normally carried out using aquatic species on the assumption that water systems commonly receive chemical discharges either as industrial effluents or in discharges from sewage treatment works. The likely impact of the chemical on aquatic systems is assessed by comparing the predicted environmental concentrations of the compound with data on the lowest concentration of the chemical to cause the death of 50 per cent of the test population (LC_{50}). A 100- or 1000-fold difference between these concentrations is normally taken to indicate an insignificant environmental hazard to water systems, provided the predicted quantity of use of the chemical remains accurate.

Particularly relevant for applications of pesticides is consideration of the risk to terrestrial systems. Chemicals may present a particular risk to terrestrial systems either because of their mode of use (clearly important for pesticide sprays) or because of their physicochemical properties, e.g. soil binding characteristics (see above). In these cases information on selected species in addition to the aquatic organisms can be required. The Control of Pesticides Regulations (1986) require that if pesticides

Table 8.2. Information required within the EU for chemical hazard assessment*

(a) Levels and type of information required.

Base set
1. The identity of the chemical, e.g. structural formula, spectral data (impurities are normally ignored).
2. General information about the chemical, e.g. uses, amounts to be used and how to handle.
3. Physicochemical properties, e.g. partition coefficient between *n*-octanol and water.
4. Toxicology.
5. Ecotoxicology:
   (a) The acute toxicity (LC_{50}) for one fish species.
   (b) The acute toxicity (LC_{50}) for one species of *Daphnia*.
   (c) The rate of biotic and abiotic degradation processes, measured in standardised aerobic conditions. Anaerobic tests may be more appropriate for certain chemicals and may be stipulated by national authorities.

Level I tests (relate primarily to ecotoxicology tests)

1. A longer toxicity study (at least 14 days) for one fish species.
2. A longer toxicity study (at least 21 days) for one species of *Daphnia*.
3. A prolonged biodegradation study.
4. A test of 'growth inhibition', i.e. the effect on the rate of cellular division in one algal species.
5. A test of bioaccumulation normally on a single fish species.
6. A toxicity test with one species of earthworm.
7. A toxicity test with a 'higher' plant. A small free floating aquatic plant, *Lemna*, is commonly used.

Level II tests

The nature of additional tests is decided on the basis of results from Level I and base set tests. The aims are:

1. To assess the likelihood and extent of biomagnification along a food chain.
2. To determine the biological impact of prolonged exposure to the compound.
3. To assess the environmental fate of the compound if it is not easily degraded.

Table 8.2 *continued*

(b) Level of information required for market size of a given chemical

| Quantity marketed (tonnes) | | Amount of |
Per annum	Total	information needed
<1	—	Limited announcement
1 or more	<50	Base set
10 or more	50 or more	Base set or Level I
100 or more	500 or more	Level I
1000 or more	5000 or more	Level II

* Full notification is required for any chemical requiring base set information or above (McEldowney *et al.*, 1993).

are to be used during periods of crop, fruit tree or weed flowering then the acute oral toxicity of the pesticide to a bird species (not domestic hen) and the honey bee must be determined.

An unavoidable question relating to these hazard assessments is their reliability in predicting environmental harm. They clearly do not fulfil the criteria indicated by Moriarty (1990; see above) for predicting the environmental impact of pollutants. It is a challenge for the future to design improved and ideally relatively simple quantitative procedures to better establish and predict ecological and toxicological risks associated with the environmental release of xenobiotic chemicals.

According to the OECD (1991) Belgium, Germany, The Netherlands and the United Kingdom are among the largest users of fertilisers, in excess of 10 tonnes/km^2 over the OECD average. This large use of fertilisers has several implications, including cultural eutrophication; contamination of groundwater; and a contribution to the microbially catalysed production of ozone-depleting and greenhouse gases which can also contribute to the formation of acid rain (see Chapter 12). In reality the application of fertilisers is a relatively inefficient procedure to improve crop yields. Bremner and Blackmer (1981) estimated the nitrogen balances for Iowa, USA. One million tons of ammonium fertiliser were applied annually and were converted within 2–3 weeks after application to nitrate: 55 per cent of this nitrogen was lost either by leaching of the nitrate or denitrification (see below), 20–25 per cent remained in the soil, and only 20 per cent was removed in the harvest. These figures will of course vary with the soil type and other local conditions but they are indicative of the fate of nitrogen applied in fertilisers. Bacterial denitrification can result in the production of nitrogen oxides (Robertson and Kuenen, 1992). These gases contribute to ozone depletion in the stratosphere by competing for the free radicals which are needed for ozone formation. In addition, nitrite (formed in denitrification) reacts with ozone in the dark resulting in the production of nitrate and dinitrogen pentoxide (N_2O_5). Nitric acid is lost in rainfall contributing to acid rain (Rowland and Isaksen, 1988). The concentration of nitrous oxide (N_2O) in the atmosphere is thought to be rising. Although it is not a potent greenhouse gas it has an extensive lifetime of approximately 130 years compared to methane's 3–7 years (Wang *et al.*, 1976) (see Chapter 12).

Nitrogen- and phosphate-based fertilisers are significant contributors to cultural eutrophication of freshwater. Eutrophication also occurs as a natural process (Haslam, 1994), but the scale of eutrophication has been dramatically increased by man's activities. Fertilisers are not the only source of nitrogen inputs to water systems: a proportion of the nitrogen load is the result of atmospheric deposition. Fertilisers, however, make a major contribution to the process of cultural eutrophication. Nitrogen and phosphates are leached into inland waters after fertiliser application to agricultural land. The leaching of nitrate and nitrite into water systems often occurs after ammonium-nitrogen in fertilisers undergoes microbial nitrification. Phosphates tend to be bound more readily on soil particles although some leaching does occur. In response to the higher nutrient load in rivers caused by inputs of phosphates and nitrogen microbial growth increases. In particular there are often large phytoplankton blooms consisting primarily of cyanobacteria and dinoflagellates. These blooms occur predominantly in the spring when temperature, light intensity and water stratification conditions are appropriate for phytoplankton growth, and continue until nutrients become limiting. Phytoplankton species which dominate the blooms can be toxic to animals and man, presenting severe problems for the use of the water as a resource, e.g. amenity or drinking. When the bloom enters nutrient-deficient conditions high phytoplankton mortality results in rapid and substantial growth of other micro-organisms, which utilise the algae as a nutrient and energy source. The rapid rise in microbial activity can cause a rapid and major decline in the oxygen content of the water. This deoxygenation can be so severe that on occasions large fish kills occur. Eutrophication affects a number of other biological, chemical and physical factors (McEldowney *et al.*, 1993; see also Table 8.3 and Chapter 10). Interestingly, it is becoming evident that cultural eutrophication can also affect coastal waters. A number of algal blooms in coastal regions from the North Sea to the Baltic Sea to the Mediterranean are thought to have resulted in part from cultural eutrophication (GESAMP, 1990; Pearl, 1991) (see Chapter 11).

The problems arising from cultural eutrophication are considerable and have major economic and health implications. Drinking water extracted from eutrophic water may be difficult to treat and may be unpalatable. The water as a resource may be harmful to animals and

Table 8.3   Biological, chemical and physical effects of cultural eutrophication.

(a) Physical effects

1.   Average water depth decreases due to higher sedimentation rates. The lifespan of a lake may be decreased and waterways become shallower.
2.   Increased turbidity and reduced light penetration.

(b) Chemical effects

1.   Anaerobic conditions may develop, especially at night, in the absence of photosynthesis and after algal blooms.
2.   Chemical composition and pH of the water changes.

(c) Biological effects

1.   Higher plant productivity initially than water prior to nutrient input, algal blooms, initially higher plant and animal biomass.
2.   Green algae diversity may increase, but cyanobacteria dominate rapidly and diversity declines. Diversity of aquatic macrophytes also declines.
3.   Macro- and micro-invertebrate and fish diversity declines, and species which can tolerate the poor water quality dominate.

(*Source*: Adapted from McEldowney *et al.*, 1993)

humans because of the presence of toxins. Fish populations may be severely affected (see above) and amenity and commercial fishing detrimentally influenced. Indeed the amenity use of a water body in general may decline with eutrophication. In addition, water flow and navigation along waterways may be impeded by excessive growth of plants.

In recent years there has been growing concern about possible health risks associated with high nitrate levels in water. Freshwater and groundwater are major sources of drinking water and both may be heavily polluted by nitrates arising from agricultural land (WHO, 1985). Only drinking water containing nitrate levels below $10 \, \text{mg} \, l^{-1}$ is considered safe for consumption (WHO, 1984). In fact, the EC-imposed limit for potable water is $50 \, \text{mg} \, l^{-1}$ nitrate and evidence strongly indicates that only nitrate levels considerably in excess of this are problematic. Although nitrate itself does not pose a health risk, nitrite does. It causes methaemoglobinaemia (blue-baby syndrome) and at high pH may be converted to nitrosamines which may be carcinogens. Micro-organisms and plants are capable of reducing nitrate to nitrite (Glidewell, 1990) and may therefore contribute to production of nitrite in freshwater and groundwater which may be used for drinking water. In addition, nitrate is readily reduced to nitrite in the mouth and digestive tract. Water heavily contaminated by nitrate must, therefore, be treated before it is used as drinking water.

There are a number of Directives that apply to fertilisers. Directive 76/116/EEC (as amended) provides for the regulation, designation and labelling and packaging of fertilisers. There are rules which provide for available nitrogen content and the regulations lay down standards for the protection of the consumer and workers in the industry. Fertiliser use is also being controlled in nitrate-sensitive areas (see Chapter 10).

In recent years concerns have grown about other pollutant sources in agriculture. A report from the Department of the Environment in 1994 has noted the large and unregulated ammonia emissions from agriculture (see also: *Impacts of Nitrogen Deposition in Terrestrial Ecosystems* (DoE, 1994), ENDS Report 238, November 1994, pp. 6–7). These emissions arise primarily from animal wastes, a problem that has become particularly acute as a result of intensive 'factory' farming. A voluntary Code of Practice in 1993 warned farmers that animal houses and slurry spreads were the source of ammonia. Ammonia can be volatilised from animal slurries and their emissions, contribute to atmospheric nitrogen pollution. It has been estimated that UK emission of ammonia from agriculture is 372 000 tonnes annually (Kruse *et al.*, 1986). The wet and dry deposition of ammonia from the atmosphere contributes to cultural eutrophication (see above and Chapters 10 and 11) and also may cause major vegetation changes in normally nutrient-deficient terrestrial ecosystems because of the input of nitrogen (Robertson and Kuenen, 1993) (see Chapter 12). Ammonia deposition may also induce corrosion damage on buildings (Robertson and Kuenen, 1993). It is expected that controls on nitrogen in agricultural circumstances will be forthcoming in the future.

Animal slurries can have other pollution consequences. They can result in major and acute pollution incidents. Accidental slurry discharge into a freshwater system can cause a massive increase in microbial growth and activity. The resulting increased biological oxygen demand (BOD) together with the chemical oxygen demand (COD) associated with the slurries results in a rapid deoxygenation of water. This can give rise to major fish kills. Water pollution incidents arising from livestock farming are frequently reported (National Rivers Authority, 1990). Chronic pollution can also arise from slurry applications to farmland. Nutrient leaching from land-spread slurry will contribute to cultural eutrophication (see above).

Agriculture and nature conservation

Planning

The use of land for agricultural or forestry purposes was excluded from the definition of development control under s. 55(2)(e) of the Town and Country Planning Act 1990. Planning permission is not required to bring land into agricultural use. More importantly planning permission is not required for any agricultural changes of use, for example from non-agricultural *to* agricultural use. Section 336 (1) of the 1990 Act provides a full definition of agriculture that includes horticulture, fruit and seed growing, dairy farming, livestock breeding and various forms of market gardening, including fur and wool farming. It is therefore possible to make substantial and visible changes to the agricultural environment without interference from legal regulation. Hedgerows may be removed, stone ditches built or reallocated, ploughing and cultivation carried out remarkably free from intervention. The main planning limitations are in controlling the design and erection of new structures and buildings.

There are several reasons why agriculture is treated so beneficially in terms of the planning legislation. First the concept of planning controls developed in 1947 was focused on urban development with an emphasis on public health, sanitation, transportation, industrial location and infrastructure. Second, attitudes to the countryside have been ambiguous. As noted above, some view agriculture as a benevolent use of land for the benefit of the public; others view agriculture as a threat to the environment. Historically agricultural land use has been perceived as a 'stewardship' of trust over the land and therefore one of the least environmentally intrusive activities. During the second world war self-sufficiency in agricultural produce became an important goal in defeating the enemy. The goal of self-sufficiency has remained an influence today. As a result horticulture and intensive agriculture were encouraged. In contrast to this benevolent view it is possible to see agriculture as posing a threat to the environment. Agriculture is undoubtedly an important industry. Intensive agricultural practices have relied on the application of dangerous chemicals, including organophosphate pesticides, etc., and organic and inorganic fertilisers. In addition, they have resulted in the production of high BOD and COD organic waste (see above). Agriculture thus involves activities which are potentially polluting to both land and surface and groundwater.

Concerns about agricultural pollution are increasing and may cause a reassessment of agricultural practices. Perhaps in the future agriculture will be treated as equivalent to any other large industry. One example of a new approach to agriculture is the introduction of regulations to control straw and stubble burning to prevent atmospheric pollution (see: The Crop Residues (Restrictions on Burning) (No. 2) Regulations, 1991, SI 1991 No. 1590).

Permitted development rights on agricultural land are quite generous under the General Development Order 1988 (SI 1988 No. 1813 and amended by SI 1991 No. 2805). This is now replaced by Town and Country Planning (General Permitted Development) Order 1995, SI 1995 No. 418. There is scope within the above definition for carrying

out many activities such as building walls and engaging in the development of various sporting facilities with appropriate permissions. In
addition Schedule 2, Parts 6 and 7, of the General Development Order
provides for access roads, buildings, drainage and excavations connected
with permitted development rights. There are some technical limitations
such as the height of the buildings and the purpose for which buildings
may be erected. Up until 1992 the provisions of Part 6 applied to farms
over 0.4 hectares but after 1992 (see: SI 1991 No. 2805) the limit was
raised to 5 hectares. Limited permitted development rights are available
to farms that fall between 0.4 and 5 hectares. It is also stipulated that
the development has to be reasonably necessary for the purposes of
agriculture defined within the agricultural unit (see: Planning Policy
Guidance note 7, *The Countryside and Rural Economy*). The government
intends to issue a consultation paper on new business uses within rural
development and a guide for local planning authorities to promote
good practice in planning for rural diversification. A procedure for
planning appeals for small rural developments to be handled more
quickly was intended to be introduced at the end of 1995. Finally, the
government intends to publish a draft revision of Planning Policy
Guidance note 7, mentioned above (see: *Rural England* Cm 3016
(HMSO, 1995)).

▶ Protection of countryside and species

In addition to ethical arguments, there are three reasons commonly
used to support species and habitat conservation.

1. The maintenance of species diversity to retain useful traits in the
   gene pool. It is argued that species should be conserved in order to
   ensure the continued existence of useful substances, e.g. potential
   medicines and new pesticides, and characteristics, e.g. disease
   resistance or drought tolerance.
2. The maintenance of habitat and species as an amenity resource. This
   is certainly important in the United Kingdom where a range of
   different ecosystems are often used for recreational purposes, e.g.
   sailing, hill walking, bird watching, etc.
3. The maintenance of a stable and sustainable global habitat. The Gaia
   hypothesis, which maintains that the planet functions as an
   integrated living organism, raises the possibility that habitat loss may
   contribute to global instability (Lovelock, 1988). Although the
   extinction of individual species is unimportant here, the conservation of plant habitats is crucial. For example, in recent years it
   has become evident that there has been a major decline in
   temperate woodland in Europe. The lost trees are no longer able to

consume carbon dioxide and therefore their loss contributes to the greenhouse effect (see: the Conservation (Natural Habitats, etc.) Regulations 1994).

The Countryside Commission, National Parks and Areas of Outstanding Natural Beauty

Originally created in 1949 as the National Parks Commission, the Countryside Commission is an independent body with responsibility for the preservation and enhancement of natural beauty in England. It also oversees the amenities available for people to gain access to the country- side to enable them to enjoy it. Up until 1991 responsibility for nature conservation was found in a single body – the Nature Conservancy Council – and this was quite distinct from the Countryside Commission. Nature conservation included the conservation of flora and fauna. After 1991 this structure was changed on a geographical basis. In Scotland there is the Scottish Natural Heritage and in Wales the Countryside Council for Wales. These bodies exercise the functions of both the Countryside Commission and the Nature Conservancy Council. In England the Countryside Commission and the Nature Conservancy Council are retained, each with separate functions. The Countryside Commission has promoted discussion of how planning control should meet the needs of the countryside (see: *Planning for a Greener Countryside* (Countryside Commission, 1989)).

In addition to the work of the Countryside Commission there are a variety of legal responsibilities on government to conserve the natural beauty and amenities of the countryside (ss. 11 and 37 of the Country- side Act 1968). In addition there is a power for any local planning authority to enter into a management agreement with any owner of land to undertake conservation plans or to enhance the natural beauty of the amenity (s. 39 of the Wildlife and Countryside Act 1981). The Countryside Commission may make various grant-aided arrangements in England to assist in promoting these arrangements (currently 75 per cent in National Parks, 90 per cent in Exmoor and 50 per cent elsewhere).

The designation of National Parks was an important step first taken under the National Parks and Access to the Countryside Act 1949. Ball and Bell (1994, p. 431) note:

National Parks in Britain do not equate to the concept of a national park used in most other countries. Instead of being a wilderness area with few, if any, inhabitants they contain land on which large numbers of people live. They are effectively working environments. The aim of national park designation is to plan and manage the area so as to create a balance between recreation, amenity and economic development. Land ownership is unaffected by designation, although various public bodies are given powers to purchase land, and in practice much of some parks is in the ownership of a public body, or of the National Trust.

Section 5 of the 1949 Act contains the basis of the National Parks policy. Part III and s. 61 of the Environment Act 1995 has amended s. 5 of the 1949 Act. The 1995 Act provides that the existing National Park Boards and Committees in England and Wales are to be wound up and replaced by new National Park Authorities which will continue as part of local government but independent of any county council control. Taken together the following objectives and roles are set out for the National Parks:

● The preservation and maintenance of the countryside.
● The enhancement of natural beauty, wildlife and cultural heritage.
● Promoting opportunities for the understanding and enjoyment of the special qualities of the National Park areas by the public.

The designation, management, organisation and structure of the National Parks are intended to facilitate these aims and objectives. In addition s. 62 of the Environment Act 1995 inserts a new s. 11A into the National Parks and Access to the Countryside Act 1949. A National Park Authority 'shall seek to foster the economic and social well-being of local communities within the National Park'. This objective is to be secured without significant expenditure. It represents the Government's intention to bring National Parks into line with current public sector and local authority activities (see: *Fit for the Future: A Statement by the Government on Policies for National Parks*, Department of the Environment, January 1992). There is also an important duty under s. 62 of the Environment Act 1995 on government departments and other public bodies to have regard to National Park purposes in carrying out their functions in respect of National Parks.

There are 10 national parks: the Peak District (1404 km^2); the Lake District (2243 km^2); the Yorkshire Dales (1761 km^2); North York Moors (1432 km^2); Northumberland (1031 km^2); Snowdonia (2171 km^2); the Brecon Beacons (1344 km^2); the Pembrokeshire Coast (583 km^2) ; Exmoor (686 km^2); and Dartmoor (945 km^2) (Reid, 1994, pp. 177–86). Since 1949 this designation has attempted to integrate the conservation and enjoyment of the country with agriculture and forestry as well as the social and economic needs of the area. Designation is vested in England in the Countryside Commission and in Wales in the Countryside Council. Such designation is subject to confirmation by the Secretary of State and subject to objections or representations being raised. A local inquiry may be held to hear representations and the Secretary of State or the Commission or the Council may modify the designation.

Additional powers have been granted to the Secretary of State under s. 63 of the Environment Act 1995 in respect of establishing National Parks and setting out their functions. There are specific powers under s. 64 of the Environment Act 1995 that apply to National Park Authorities in Wales.

The organisation and structure of each of the National Parks is devolved to a local level. There is a National Park Authority for each National Park and under the Environment Act 1995 members for England *only* (these provisions over membership do not apply to Wales) will be appointed as follows. One-half of the members *plus one* will be appointed by local authorities with land in the parks. The remaining members will be appointed by the Secretary of State, of whom one-half *minus one* will be drawn from the relevant parishes. The new system of appointment gives parishes a much greater role in National Parks. This replaces the system under the 1949 Act where the authority was either a committee of the relevant local authority or a separate board. One-third of the members were appointed by the Secretary of State, on the recommendations of the Countryside Commission, and one seventh of members were appointed by the constituent district councils (see Schedules 7–10 of the Environment Act 1995 which provide further detailed and comprehensive rules for the organisation, status and composition of National Parks).

The National Park Authority must prepare a National Park Management Plan, subject to five yearly revision, and containing the formulation of the policy for the management of the Park. The ordinary planning controls apply, but are strengthened by restrictions on what qualifies as 'permitted development' (see: Town and Country Planning General Development Order 1988, SI 1988 No. 1813, Schedules 1 and 2; now see: SI 1995 No. 418). A map of each Park, available to the general public, must be drawn up showing the designation of the important areas of the Park whose natural beauty is important to conserve (see: ss. 42–4 of the Wildlife and Countryside Act 1981 as amended). There are areas that may be given special protection in the form of pro-hibitions on ploughing the land or the carrying out of activities that may interfere with the quality of the land. In addition, there are extensive powers available to the planning authorities in National Parks to restrict the use of roads or to regulate the use of waterways for boating, bathing, fishing and other forms of recreation. There are by-law powers available to the planning authorities to regulate the National Park and financial grant aid powers to facilitate the carrying out of particular projects to enhance the development of the National Parks. Invariably such powers require a careful judgement in balancing the interest of conservation and the promotion of recreation. In fact this conflict is nowhere more apparent than in areas where popular access from the public is in danger of putting in jeopardy the conservation of an area. One example is the Pembroke Coast, which attracts large numbers of visitors mainly because of its intrinsic beauty and ease of access from high-population centres. There may be a need for conservation to be given priority over the other objectives included in the protection of National Parks (see: *Fit for the Future.* Report of the National Parks Review Panel, 1991).

Section 65 of the Environment Act 1995 contains additional general purposes and powers for National Park authorities. This includes the extension of ss. 37 and 38 of the Countryside Act 1968 which provides general duties as to the protection of the interests of the countryside and the avoidance of pollution. Section 66 of the 1995 Act provides powers for National Park management plans and ss. 67–70 powers for planning matters. The finances of National Parks are provided under ss. 71–4 of the Environment Act 1995. This covers the levying of money, the making of grants by the Secretary of State and controls on capital finance and borrowing. The impact of the Environment Act 1995 will be to grant some autonomy to the organisation of National Parks from local authority influence. At the same time National Parks will be subject to competitive tendering and financial controls.

In conclusion major industrial or commercial developments are not normally permitted in National Parks. On a case-by-case basis new areas may be considered for designation as a National Park. The Government generally provides 75 per cent of their funds and through the preparation of development plans for the Parks the quality of the environment is intended to be protected.

In addition to National Parks there are Areas of Outstanding Natural Beauty (AONB). There are 38 AONBs in England and Wales covering 20 000 km^2 or over 13 per cent of the total land area of England and Wales. AONBs are designated by the Countryside Commission in England and the Countryside Council in Wales under s. 87 of the Countryside Act 1949. There is an extensive consultation process prior to designation. The relevant planning authority in the area where there is an AONB has powers under ss. 11 and 88(2) of the 1949 Act to preserve and enhance natural beauty in the area. In general the planning arrangements must take account of AONBs. Thus planning permission is normally refused for major developments, including roads or industrial or commercial building. However, it is important to stress that refusal of planning permission is not automatic. Each application must be examined on its own merits and account taken of the AONB. Planning regulations may be imposed (see: s. 106 of the Town and Country Planning Act 1990). Extensive regulations may be made under s. 22 of the Road Traffic Regulation Act 1984 for roads adjacent to or on land close to an AONB.

In addition to AONBs there are Environmentally Sensitive Areas (ESAs) set up under EC Regulations 797/85 on Improving the Efficiency of Agricultural Structures. Such areas may be found within

National Parks or AONBs and contain important wildlife sites. The main mechanism for their protection is that the government, through the Ministry of Agriculture Fisheries and Food, provides incentive payments to farmers that provide for the sites' upkeep and maintenance (see s. 18 of the Agriculture Act 1986). There is no formal enforcement mechanism; the farmer enters into a voluntary agreement.

There are other designations – Sites of Special Scientific Interest (SSSIs). Such sites are protected because of their scientific interest. Designation may be given to sites where the flora or fauna, or geological or biological interest, requires protection. The Nature Conservancy Council (see: s. 28 of the Wildlife and Countryside Act 1981), informs the owners of the site and classifies the activities which may be carried out that are compatible with the protection necessary for the site. There is an important period of four months which allows the Nature Conservancy Council to negotiate with the site owner. In cases where the site is deemed to be of national importance or where there is a threat to a species then a nature conservation order may be made under s. 29 of the Wildlife and Countryside Act 1981. A possible lacuna in these arrangements is in the definition of an occupier within s. 28 of the Wildlife and Countryside Act 1981. In *Southern Water Authority* v. *Nature Conservancy Council* (1993) 5 *Journal of Environmental Law* 109, the House of Lords accepted that a person who has no connection with the land prior to commencing a proscribed activity is not an occupier within the meaning of s. 28 of the Act. In practical terms someone who dumps rubbish on land within an SSSI and then departs does not commit any offence under the 1981 Act.

Finally there are designated Special Protection Areas under the EC Birds Directive and Ramsar Convention. The United Kingdom has currently 77 Special Protection Areas and 70 Ramsar sites.

Development in rural areas: green belt land

One of the most important aspects of planning law is the creation of green belts as a means of limiting urban growth (Mandelker, 1962; *Second Report of the Greater London Regional Planning Committee*, 1933) (see also Chapter 7). The green belt system is simple in outline: an area of open space around towns, villages and cities is designated with powers granted to the local authority to ensure that no development takes place (see: the Green Belt (London and Home Counties) Act 1938 as a model of its kind). Originally intended for the specific problems of London, it was hoped that strict adherence to development control in other parts of the country would make extension of the green belt idea unnecessary. Ten years after the Second World War Circular 42/1955 was issued urging authorities to establish green belt areas. The aim was not to make green belts independent of development control but to offer an additional form of protection against the encroachment of urban development. The 1955 Circular contained details of how sketch plans should be drawn up and green belt areas designated. Planning within the green belt was to be tightly controlled and it was assumed that agriculture would occupy the areas of land not subject to urban control. By 1988 it was estimated that green belts covered 4.5 million acres (1.8 million hectares) or 14 per cent of England. Today green belt areas are designated within the Development Plan (see: Planning Policy Guidance note 2, January 1988). In general, countryside development policies apply within the green belt area. A number of circulars provide general policy guidance on the needs of nature conservation and the consultations necessary to achieve these aims (see: DoE Circulars 16/87 and 27/87).

Green belts are today an intrinsic part of the environment in Britain. The main challenge to their existence comes from the increase in new house building schemes and out-of-town shopping sites around the outskirts of our villages, towns and cities. The policy on house building (see: Planning Policy Guidance note 3, *Land for Housing*, January 1988) sets out the requirements of a healthy building industry and the need for conservation of green belt land.

Transport policy

An important part of the rural environment is the road system which connects major urban conurbations. Since 1970 road traffic in the United Kingdom has doubled and it is estimated that air travel undertaken by UK passengers has risen three-fold. In a recent report the Royal Commission on Environmental Pollution has noted how growth in traffic is not easily accommodated within the existing road system (see Royal Commission on Environmental Pollution 18th Report, *Transport and the Environment* (HMSO, 1994)). The report has also warned of the environmental consequences of the forecast increase in traffic in terms of air quality, noise, global warming, the effect on natural landscapes and on the consumption of natural resources. Approximately 35 per cent of UK atmospheric emissions arise from the internal combustion engine. The emissions are composed of 92 per cent carbon monoxide, 4.5 per cent hydrocarbons, 3 per cent nitrous oxides and 0.5 per cent sulphur oxides. They are not only gaseous, but also include liquid and particulate emissions (see Chapter 12 for a discussion on the health and environmental impact of traffic emissions).

The Royal Commission report recommends eight key objectives which should inform government policy on the environment:

- To ensure that an effective transport policy is part of an integrated land use policy.
- To achieve standards of air quality to prevent damage to health and the environment.
- To improve the quality of life particularly in towns and cities.
- To encourage and increase modes of personal transport less damaging to the environment.
- To halt loss of land to transport infrastructure in areas of conservation, cultural or scenic or amenity value.
- To reduce carbon dioxide emissions from transport.
- To reduce noise nuisance from transport.
- To reduce substantially the demands which transport, infrastructure and the vehicle industry place on non-renewable materials (see: ENDS Report 237, October, 1994, p. 14).

Looking towards the beginning of the next century, the report provides an important challenge to government policy and the development and conservation of the rural environment.

There are also important issues raised about charging for the use of motorways as a possible solution to the environmental and congestion problems caused by road traffic in urban areas (see: *Third Report Transport Committee: Urban Road Pricing* HC 104-1, 22 March 1995). It remains to be seen whether proposals for road pricing will meet the current political agenda.

Species protection

We are primarily concerned here with the law that protects plants, animals and habitat. Historically protection was achieved by the law prohibiting a range of specific activities on the basis of a case-by-case approach. Once a problem was recognised attempts were made to deal with it, usually by prohibiting some cruelty. A more systematic approach has been adopted in the modern attitudes to nature conservation. It is now accepted that the protection of endangered species requires active steps to prevent their extinction. For example various attempts to protect birds resulted in a number of Birds Protection Acts in the nineteenth century, and even in the Protection of Birds Act 1954 this *ad hoc* approach has persisted. Very often the initiative has not been taken by the government but through a mixture of voluntary organisations and protection groups, e.g. the Royal Society for the Protection of Birds.

The Nature Conservancy Council for England advises the Government on nature conservation and Sites of Special Scientific Interest and manages National Nature Reserves. There are similar organisations for Scotland and Wales (see above). The involvement of a number of different agencies inevitably leads to a somewhat mixed approach to nature and habitat conservation. The protection of the natural habitats is also a focus of Community law.

In the United Kingdom the main legislation for the protection of habitats and species is the Wildlife and Countryside Act 1981. Among the habitats that may be protected under national law are wetlands such as areas of marsh, peat, bog and water. The Halvergate Marshes in the Norfolk Broads are a good example of a wetland area that has been protected and of the conflicts that can arise during habitat protection. There was a dispute during the 1980s between those who wished to conserve the marshes for grazing and those who wished to drain the land for subsequent cereal cultivation. There were considerable incentives to encourage drainage. The Ministry of Agriculture offered funding for drainage and the CAP offered incentives to convert from livestock to arable farming. The Internal Drainage Board (IDB) proposed a number of drainage schemes for the marshes. In 1982 the Ministry of Agriculture, Fisheries and Food and the Department of the Environment accepted a compromise solution, avoiding a public inquiry and restricting the capacity of the drainage pumps. In effect a planning restraint had been placed on an agricultural practice (see above for a discussion of planning and agriculture). Under the 1981 Wildlife and Countryside Act the compensation payments for conservation of the marsh were excessive (approximately £1 million annually). In the end an exceptional Planning Direction was placed on the farmers to prevent drainage and in 1985 the Broads Grazing Conservation Scheme was set up. A fee of £50 per acre was offered to farmers to retain livestock grazing. The Broads were designated an Environmentally Sensitive Area in 1987 (see Hughes, 1992, for a more detailed discussion of this case and of wetland conservation).

The habitats of wild birds are regulated under Directive 79/409/EEC. This provides for specially protected areas to be designated by Member States for the protection of birds. It is expected that such protection will be extended in the coming years.

There are other examples of specific legislation to protect particular species, for example, the Conservation of Seals Act 1970 and the Badgers (Protection) Act 1992. In the case of other animals there is a list contained in Schedule 5 of the Wildlife and Countryside Act 1981 which affords protection to bats, reptiles, amphibians and various rare fish, butterflies and other animals. In October 1992 protection was extended to include the Lagoon sea slug, 23 species of moss and 10 lichens (see: *This Common Inheritance Third Report,* Cm 2549 (HMSO, 1994), para. 8.10).

Finally, on 21 June 1994 the Secretary of State for the Environment announced the future of the Countryside Stewardship Scheme, which is to be transferred from the Countryside Commission to the Ministry of Agriculture, Fisheries and Food from April 1996. Under the

Environment Act 1995 environmental grants will be available for a wide variety of purposes including species conservation and public access conducive to conservation.

▶ Trees and woodland

Agriculture and forestry take up 90 per cent of the land (see: *This Common Inheritance*, Cm 1200 (HMSO, 1990), para. 7.5) and provide a significant impact on the environment. Forests and woodlands have an important role in the control of carbon dioxide levels in the atmosphere. They act as carbon sinks during photosynthesis. Deforestation and the destruction of woodlands, therefore, cause a decline in the capacity of plant biomass to remove carbon dioxide, a greenhouse gas (see Chapter 12), from the atmosphere. This results in increased concentrations of this greenhouse gas in the atmosphere. Forests are also a resource of considerable economic importance supporting a range of industries, e.g. timber, paper, etc. In the present day only 10 per cent of the land in Britain is occupied by forest.

In recent years, the destruction of native woodland in the United Kingdom has primarily been a result of the extension of forestry and the expansion of agriculture. Woods are traditionally described in terms of the 'dominant' tree, e.g. oak woodland, deciduous lime woodland and beech woodland. This species (one or a few together), because of its abundance or size, determines the characteristics of a particular woodland. These woods, of course, provide habitats for a great diversity of plants and animals. For example, oak woodland is the major wood type throughout England and is common in Wales and southern Scotland. Oak woodland, either predominantly pendunculate oak (*Quercus robur*) or sessile oak (*Quercus petraea*), contains a variety of other tree types including ash (*Fraxinus excelsior*), elm (*Ulmus* spp.), maple (*Acer campestre*), hornbeam (*Carpinus betilus*) and lime (*Tilia cordata*). Beneath these are a number of shorter trees such as holly (*Ilex aquefolium*), and beneath these are the shrub layer including roses (*Rosa* spp.), hawthorn (*Crataegus laevigata*) and hazel (*Corylus avellana*). The ground layer consists of a wide variety of flora, e.g. bluebells (*Scilla non-scipta*) and brambles (*Rubus fruticosa* agg.) (see Tansley, 1949 for a complete list of flora). Associated with these plants are a vast diversity of fauna. The transformation of woods into plantations for forestry or the planting of trees for forestry has tended to reduce the diversity of woodlands and diversity within woodlands. For example, the often dense single planting of conifers, a relatively common practice in forestry, results in a dense canopy limiting light penetration to lower layers of the forest. This together with the increased soil acidity induced by many conifers offers a suitable habitat to only a limited range of other plants and ultimately, therefore, animals. Mixed planting and the planting of deciduous trees is now being encouraged (see below).

The Forestry Commission is the government department responsible for the forestry policy in Britain. It has a statutory appointed Chairman and Board of Commissioners. There is a Policy and Resources Group responsible for the Parliamentary and policy aspects of the Commission's tasks. The main legislation is the Forestry Act 1967 (but also see the Forestry Acts 1919 to 1944). The Commission is primarily concerned with nature conservation and management but it has also a commercial function. It invariably consults with the Countryside Commission over matters of common interest such as afforestation. In cases of dispute the matter is referred to ministers. Section 4 of the Wildlife and Countryside (Amendment) Act 1985 provides a new duty to achieve a balance between afforestation, the management of the forest and the conservation of natural beauty and of flora and fauna. There are various grants available such as an initiative under the Broadleaved and Woodland Grants scheme. This scheme is intended to improve the visual and recreational potential of the countryside.

Currently there are proposals, launched in October 1993, to create a New National Forest in the Midlands. Government policy on forests and woodlands is contained in *Sustainable Forestry: The UK Programme* (HMSO, 1994). Grant aids may be provided to encourage native species of trees and this has included 'some 15 500 hectares of broadleaves, mainly native species, and over 25 000 hectares of native pinewoods' (see: *This Common Inheritance The Third Report*, Cm 2549 (HMSO, 1994), para. 8. 27).

There are a wide variety of privately owned woodlands that are subject to few legislative controls. Since 1985 the proportion of private broadleaved planting has increased from around 9 per cent to 17 per cent of the total. Tax incentives exist to encourage and promote afforestation. The Forestry Commission provides general advice and pro-motes schemes for the forestry industry. It also sets standards and carries out regulatory functions to oversee the health of plants and undertakes research into forests. The Commission may also adopt a felling policy for the careful management of woodlands. It may also provide grants for woodland management. For example, since April 1992 grants have been available for the management of all types of woodlands based on a strong emphasis on maintaining and improving their environmental value.

In terms of planning permission, local planning authorities have limited powers under s. 197 of the Town and Country Planning Act 1990 to preserve trees and woodland. There are powers to make tree preservation orders and where felling is permitted conditions such as replanting may be imposed. The procedure for making a tree preservation order is contained in SI 1969/17. There are certain procedural requirements, such as placing a copy of the order for inspection near the locality of the trees and with certain occupiers of land adjacent to the trees. Once an order is made it is subject to a six weeks' challenge to the High Court. Trees that are dangerous through disease, damage or size are not subject to an order (see: *R.* v *Brightman* [1990] 1 WLR 1255). Section 206 of the 1990 Act provides that landowners have a duty to replace trees that come within an order and are unlawfully removed. Powers of enforcement are granted to the local planning authority. In appropriate circumstances orders may result in criminal proceedings.

In addition to the protection afforded to trees under the 1990 Act there are protections granted under the Forestry Act 1967 that apply only to those trees that are not subject to a tree preservation order. This may be because no order has been made or there is limited jurisdiction to make an order. In cases where trees fall under the jurisdiction of both the Forestry Commission and the local authority the rule is that applications to fell any tree must be made to the Forestry Commission (see ss. 10 and 15 of the Forestry Act 1967). The Forestry Commissioners may issue a licence for tree felling and the failure to have a licence may result in a prosecution under s. 17 of the 1967 Act.

Finally, ss. 97–9 of the Environment Act 1995 contain powers for the government to introduce regulations to protect hedgerows and to make grants for conservation purposes.

▶ References and further reading

Ball, S. and Bell, S. (1995) *Environmental Law*, 3rd edn. Blackstone Press, London.

Bremner, J.M. and Blackmer, A.M. (1981) 'Terrestrial nitrification as a source of atmospheric nitrous oxide'. In C.C. Delwiche (ed.), *Denitrification, Nitrification and Atmospheric Nitrous Oxide*. John Wiley, New York, pp. 151–70.

Church, C. and Phinnemore, D. (1994), *European Union and European Community*. Harvester, Sussex.

GESAMP (Group of Experts on the Scientific Aspects of Marine Pollution) (1990) *The State of the Marine Environment*. (Joint Group of Experts on Scientific Aspects of Marine Pollution.) Blackwell Scientific Publications, Oxford.

Gibbons, J. (1992) 'The Common Agricultural policy' in F.McDonald and S.Dearden (eds) *European Economic Integration*. Longman, Essex, pp. 131–45.

Glidewell, C. (1990) 'The nitrate/nitrite controversy'. *Chem. Brit.*, **26**, 137–40.

Haslam, S.M. (1994) *River Pollution an Ecological Perspective*. John Wiley & Sons, Chichester.

Henderson, R. (1993) *European Finance*. McGraw-Hill, Maidenhead.

HMSO (1994) *Sustainable Forestry: The UK Programme*. HMSO, London.

Hoskins, W.G. (1995) *The Making of the English Landscape*. Morrison & Gibb, London.

Hughes, J.M.R. (1992) 'Use and aduse of wetlands'. In A.M. Mannion and S.R. Bowlby (eds). *Environmental Issues in the 1990s*. John Wiley & Sons, Chichester, pp. 211–26.

Kapteyn, P.J.G. and Verloren Van Themaat, P. (1990) *Introduction to the Law of the European Communities*. Kluwer, Dedeuter, The Netherlands.

Kiss and Shelton (1993) *Manual of European Environmental Law*. Cambridge University Press, Cambridge.

Kramer, L. (1993) *European Environmental Law Casebook*. Sweet and Maxwell, London.

Kruse, M., Simon, A.P. and Bell, J.N.B. (1986) *An Emissions Inventory for Ammonia Arising from Agriculture in Great Britain*. Report, Imperial College Centre for Environmental Technology, University of London.

Leisinger, T. (1983) 'Microorganisms and xenobiotic compounds'. *Experientia*, **39**, 1183–220.

Lovelock, J. (1988) *The Ages of Gaia*. Oxford University Press, Oxford.

Malcolm, R. (1994) *A Guidebook to Environmental Law*. Sweet and Maxwell, London.

MacEwan, A. and MacEwan, M. (1982) *National Parks: Conservation or Cosmetics?* George Allen & Unwin, London.

MacEwen, A. and MacEwan, M. (1987) *Greenprints for the Countryside*. George Allen & Unwin, London.

McEldowney, S., Hardman, D.J. and Waite, S. (1993) *Pollution: Ecology and Biotreatment*. Longman, Essex.

Mandelker, D.R. (1962) *Green Belts and Urban Growth*. University of Winconsin Press, Winconsin.

Marsh, J. (ed.) (1992) *The Changing Role of the Common Agricultural Policy: The Future of Farming in Europe*. Pinter, London.

Mason, C.F. (1995) *Biology of Freshwater Pollution*, 3rd edn. Longman, Essex.

Moriarty, F. (1990) *Ecotoxicology, The Study of Pollutants in Ecosystems*, 2nd edn. Academic Press, London.

Mostafa K. Tolba and others (eds) (1993) *The World Environment 1972–1992 Two Decades of Challenge*. Chapman & Hall, UNEP.

National Rivers Authority (1990) *Water Pollution from Farm Waste 1989*. National Rivers Authority South West Region. Manely House, Kestral Way, Exeter.

Pearl, H.W. (1991) 'Nuisance phytoplankton blooms in coastal, estuarine, and inland waters'. *Limnol. Oceanogr.*, **33**, 823–47.

Reid, C. (1994) *Nature Conservation Law.* Sweet and Maxwell, London.

Robertson, L.A. and Kuenen, G. (1992) Nitrogen removal from water and waste. In J.C. Fry, G.M. Gadd, R.A.Herbert, C.W. Jones and I.A. Watson-Craik. *Microbial Control of Pollution.* Cambridge University Press, Cambridge.

Rowland, F.W. and Isaksen, I.S.A. (eds) (1988) *The Changing Atmosphere.* John Wiley & Sons, Chichester.

Schama, S. (1995) *Landscape and Memory.* Fontana Press, London.

Shoard, M. (1981) *The Theft of the Countryside.*

Snyder, F. (1985) *Law of the Common Agricultural Policy.* Sweet and Maxwell, London.

Stevens, R., Spurgeon, A., Calvert, I.A., Beach, J., Levy, L.S., Berry, H., Harrington, S.M. (1995) 'Neurophysiological effects of long-term exposure to organophosphate in sheep dip.' *Lancet,* **345**, 1135.

Tansley, A.G. (1949) *The British Islands and their Vegetation.* Cambridge University Press, Cambridge.

Turner, R. K., Pearce, O., Bateman, I. (eds) (1994) *Environmental Economics.* Harvester Wheatsheaf, London.

Wang, W.C., Yung, Y.L., Lacis, A.A., Mo, T. and Hansen, J.E. (1976) 'Greenhouse effects due to man-made perturbations of trace gases'. *Science,* **194**, 685–90.

WHO (1984) *Guidelines for Drinking-Water Quality,* Vol 2. World Health Organisation, Geneva, pp. 290–2.

WHO (1985) *Health Hazards from Nitrates in Drinking-Water.* World Health Organisation, Copenhagen.

▶ Reports

Countryside Survey 1990: Main Report. (DoE, 1993).

Hobhouse Report: *National Parks in England and Wales,* 1947.

House of Lords Select Committee on the European Communities: *20th Report on Agriculture and the Environment Session* 1993/94 HL 247.

Rural England, Cm 3016 (HMSO, 1995).

This Common Inheritance, Cm 1200 (HMSO, 1990) and *The Third Year Report* Cm2549 (HMSO, 1994).

UK Annual Report: This Common Inheritance, Cm 2822 (HMSO, 1995).

Land use and waste

The generation and disposal of waste is an intrinsic part of any developing or industrial society. Waste, from both domestic and commercial sources, has grown significantly in the United Kingdom over the past decade. Commercial and industrial waste comprises by far the largest proportion of the estimated 435 million tonnes of waste produced annually in Britain. Waste disposal sets enormous challenges for the protection of the environment and for the safe monitoring of waste disposal sites. Government policy consists of a number of elements including waste reduction through processes such as recycling and energy recovery. The government has developed a hierarchy of waste reduction, reuse, recovery and disposal. There is a general commitment to waste minimisation and Part V of the Environment Act 1995 provides for a National Waste Strategy for England and Wales and Scotland. In preparing such a strategy the Secretary of State is obliged to consult the newly created Environment Agency for England and Wales and the Scottish Environment Agency.

To many environmentalists waste recycling and reduction is a preferred option to disposal. Disposal of waste and the regulation of waste disposal sites, however, are also an important part of government policy. Current legislation on waste in the United Kingdom is contained in the Control of Pollution Act 1974, a piecemeal enactment brought into force over a period of years. Part II of the Environmental Protection Act 1990 (hereinafter the EPA) contains provisions for the collection and disposal of waste. The 1990 Act created a number of regulatory bodies with responsibilities over the regulation of waste collection: waste regulation authorities (WRAs), waste collection authorities (WCAs) and waste disposal authorities (WDAs). The 1990 Act has been further amended by the Environment Act 1995.

Waste disposal usually takes place in large landfill sites and various legal controls are in place to ensure that disposal is safe and carefully monitored. The law in this area is influenced by a number of EC Directives and international agreements. The legal protections explained in Chapter 6 detailing Integrated Pollution Control are relevant to the regulation of waste. The disposal of waste raises issues about land and water contamination, air pollution through emissions caused by incineration and noise pollution through recycling plants. It is therefore essential to consider waste in the context of the whole biosphere.

▶ The legislative framework

Waste is widely defined under s. 75 (2) of the Environmental Protection Act 1990 to include:

(a) any substance which constitutes a scrap material or an effluent or other unwanted surplus substance from the application of any process; and

(b) any substance or article which requires to be disposed of as being broken, worn out, contaminated or otherwise spoiled.

Waste also includes 'any thing which is discarded or otherwise dealt with as if it were waste shall be presumed to be waste unless the contrary is proved'. There are various types of controlled waste (see: Controlled Waste Regulations 1992, SI 1992 No. 588) which fall into three categories: industrial, commercial or household waste (Table 9. 1). The three categories of waste only appear relevant to whether a waste collection authority must collect the waste and what charges may be made. One notable exclusion from the three categories is agricultural waste and this means that agricultural waste is exempt from the licensing requirements of the Act. However, agricultural waste appears to come within EC Directive 91/156. This Directive narrowly defines certain categories of waste, such as animal carcasses, that may be exempt from licensing. Thus fertiliser bags, discarded plastic containers and fencing ought to come within the licensing controls under the Act. In fact agriculture is one of the largest producers of waste (see Chapter 8). Only the waste produced during a variety of mining and quarrying operations exceeds it in quantity (Table 9. 1). There are a variety of commercial and industrial wastes produced, but among the most varied is domestic, i.e. household waste (Table 9. 2).

There is considerable difficulty in incorporating the EC Directive 91/156 into the UK's law. The Directive defined waste differently than existing UK law. Article 4 of the Directive obliges Member States to ensure that waste is recovered or disposed of without endangering human health and without using processes or methods which could harm the environment (see ENDS Report 231, April 1994, pp. 15–16). The Directive is now part of the UK's law under the Waste Management Licensing Regulations SI 1994 No. 1056.

Section 33(1) of the Environmental Protection Act 1990 makes it an

Table 9.1. Approximate annual amount of controlled and other wastes arising in the United Kingdom

Waste type	Annual production (Mt)
(a) Controlled waste	
Household	20
Commercial	15
Demolition and	
construction	32
Dredged spoils*	43
Industrial	
Blast furnace and	
steel slag	6
Power station ash	13
Other	50
Sewage sludge[†]	36
(b) Not controlled waste	
Agriculture	80
Mining and quarrying	
Colliery and slate	51
China clay	27
Quarrying	30

(*Source*: Adapted from Gascoigne and Ogilvie, 1995)
* Dredged spoils are a controlled waste when licensed under the Food and Environmental Protection Act (see Sch. 6 of Collection and Disposal of Waste Regulations, 1988).
[†] Sewage is not a controlled waste when disposed of on agricultural land or within a sewage works.

Table 9.2 Composition of domestic waste in the United Kingdom

Substance	Per cent of total domestic waste
Paper and card	33.2
Degradable kitchen and	
garden waste	20.2
Glass	9.3
Miscellaneous combustibles	8.1
Fines	6.8
Dense plastic	5.9
Ferrous metal	5.7
Plastic film	5.3
Textiles	2.1
Miscellaneous non-combustibles	1.8
Non-ferrous metals	1.6

(*Source*: Adapted from Gascoigne and Ogilvie, 1995)

offence to unlawfully deposit or deal with controlled waste. There are various defences to the criminal offence:

- The offence must be done 'knowingly'.
- The offence does not apply to household waste from a domestic property.
- The person acted with due diligence and took all reasonable precautions.
- The acts done were as a result of an emergency or to avoid danger to the public.
- The person acted under instructions from his or her employer and neither had any reason to suppose that the acts done were in contravention of the Act.

There are exemptions contained in the Controlled Waste Regulations 1992 (SI 1992 No. 588). The offences are triable either summarily or on indictment (see Chapter 2) with penalties of, respectively, a maximum six months' imprisonment or a fine not exceeding £20,000 or both, or a maximum of five years' imprisonment if the offence relates to special waste (see below).

There are certain categories of waste that merit separate consideration, namely: radioactive waste (see: Radioactive Substances Act 1993); explosives (see: Explosives Act 1875); and mineral wastes which fall under the planning legislation. The provisions on waste also apply to waste that is intended to be recycled (see: *R.* v. *Rotherham MBC ex parte Rankin* [1990] JEL 503).

The regulation of waste in the United Kingdom takes account of European (see: the framework Directive 75/442/EEC) and inter-national (see: Basle Convention on the Control of Transboundary Movement of Hazardous Wastes and their Disposal, 1989) obligations.

There are three types of regulatory authority. Recent changes introduced by Part I of the Environment Act 1995 ensure that the new Environment Agency will take over the role of the waste regulation authorities. In addition Part V of the 1995 Act provides that the Secretary of State is to be given a new duty to prepare a waste strategy. The Environment Agency will have a role in giving strategy advice. The following sets out the arrangements in place taking account of the Environment Agency.

Waste Regulation Authority (WRA)

The Waste Regulation Authority (WRA) administers waste management licensing requirements in the Control of Pollution Act 1974 and under the 1990 Act. The Environment Agency under the Environment Act 1995 is set to take over responsibilities for all the Waste Regulation Authorities. The WRA acts as a pollution control regulator responsible for the operation of the system of licensing of waste carriers, the enforcement of any special provisions and legal controls including the operation of a duty of care. The WRA in English non-metropolitan areas is the county council and in Wales the district councils. In metropolitan areas it is the district council or London borough council. In areas such as Greater London, Greater Manchester and Merseyside a joint body has been established. There are powers for the Secretary of State to alter these arrangements, as in South Yorkshire. Each WRA must produce a plan for the treatment and disposal of controlled waste (Table 9. 1). The plan should include the kinds and quantities of controlled waste expected to be produced and the preferred method of treatment. Also included must be the authority's waste policy in respect of its licensing obligations. An important part of the plan must be the costs and benefits of the likely effects of the arrangements. The WRA is required to consult with the Waste Collection Authority (see below) in its area and any representative of persons likely to be engaged in disposal or treatment of controlled waste. Before the plan may be adopted it must be approved by the Secretary of State and it must conform to statutory requirements for information and consultation.

Under s. 64 of the EPA, WRAs are required to maintain a public register. This includes details of all current or recently current licences. Details of applicants and matters relevant to their application are also included on the register. Convictions and any action taken by the authority using its legal powers must also be included on the register. There is a specific 'confidentiality' clause. Under s. 66 of the EPA any person who considers the information is commercially confidential may apply to have it excluded from the register. Section 66(11) provides that if the information on the register would 'prejudice to an unreasonable degree the commercial interests' of the individual then it may be deemed confidential and not disclosed. There is a system of appeals to the Secretary of State in matters of dispute.

The Waste Collection Authority (WCA)

The Waste Collection Authority (WCA) is the district council or London borough council. It has the duty to arrange for the collection of household waste and if requested by the occupier of premises in its area to collect any commercial waste from the premises or to arrange for the collection of waste (see: s. 45 of the EPA 1990). The definition of household waste is left largely to the discretion of the occupier of premises. There is a duty on the WCA to arrange for the collection of waste except waste which is situated at a place which in the opinion of the authority 'is so isolated or inaccessible' that the cost of collecting it would be unreasonably high.

Generally household waste is to be collected free of charge but the

Controlled Waste Regulations 1992 may provide for charges to be levied for large items such as garden waste or commercial waste products from residential premises. For waste other than household waste a 'reasonable' charge may be made for collection and disposal. Receptacles may be provided at reasonable charge for the disposal of waste. The collection of waste is therefore tightly regulated. Similarly the disposal of the waste must be made only to such places as the Waste Disposal Authority directs.

Waste Disposal Authority (WDA)

The Waste Disposal Authority (WDA) is the same body as the WRA. However, s. 30 and Schedule 2 of the Environmental Protection Act 1990 provide for an organisational separation of the regulatory functions of the WRA and the WDA. The WDA has two main functions. First, as noted above, it must arrange for the disposal of controlled waste in its area and liaise closely with the WCA to provide suitable sites for the disposal of waste collected by the WCA. Second, the WDA must provide suitable sites for residential disposal of household waste. Such sites must be open at reasonable times and at least one period during the weekend. Different types of waste may be disposed of at different locations. In recent years there has been a trend towards setting up local authority waste disposal companies (see s. 32 and Schedule 2 of the Environmental Protection Act 1990).

▶ Waste disposal and management

The Environment Act 1995

The arrangements for the management and disposal of waste are under continuous review. The government's latest strategic plan (*Sustainable Waste Management: A Waste Strategy for England and Wales*, DoE, January 1995) continues a general trend towards encouraging 'waste reduction, reuse and recovery (including recycling) and the safe disposal of remaining wastes' (see: *This Common Inheritance, The Third Report 1995*). This strategy for waste is further reinforced by Part V of the Environment Act 1995 in the development of a National Waste Strategy (discussed below). It is expected that the Government will implement the EU Packaging and Packaging Waste Directive through the regulations under the provisions of the 1995 Act.

Section 93 of the 1995 Act allows the Secretary of State to make regulations imposing producer responsibility obligations. These obligations may be in respect of products or materials. The obligations may insist on reuse, recovery, or recycling of products or materials. The obligations must take account of the following:

- The proposed exercise of the power would be likely to result in an increase in the reuse, recovery or recycling of the products or materials in question.
- Any such increase would produce environmental or economic benefits.
- The benefits are significant as against the likely costs resulting from the imposition of the proposed producer responsibility obligation.
- The burdens imposed on businesses by the regulations are the minimum necessary to secure those benefits.
- The burdens are imposed on persons most able to make a contribution to the achievement of the relevant targets:
  - having regard to the desirability of acting fairly between persons who manufacture, process, distribute or supply products or materials; and
  - taking account of the need to ensure that the proposed producer responsibility obligation is so framed as to be effective in achieving the purposes for which it is to be imposed.

Section 94 of the Environment Act 1995 further provides additional procedural requirements as to how such obligations may be made and enforced with an appeal structure against any order. Section 95 of the 1995 Act creates a new offence of breaching a producer responsibility.

It is also intended that under the Environment Act 1995 the new Environment Agencies will benefit from the development of a *statutory* strategy for waste management to be undertaken by the new Agencies. Section 92 of the Environment Act 1995 gives responsibilities to both the new Environment Agency for England and Wales and the Scottish Environment Protection Agency.

Schedule 12 and s. 92 of the Environment Act 1995 provide that the objectives of the National Waste Strategy shall include:

- Ensuring that waste is recovered or disposed of without endangering human health and without using processes or methods which could harm the environment and without risk to water, air, soil, plants or animals; causing nuisance through noise or odours or adversely affecting the countryside or places of special interest.
- Establishing an integrated and adequate network of waste disposal installations, taking account of the best available technology not involving excessive costs.

It is expected that the objectives of the National Waste Strategy will not be issued until 1997 at the earliest. The Strategy will take account of sustainable development and involve the best possible use of unavoidable waste, while minimising the risk of pollution or harm to human health from waste disposal or recovery.

Schedule 12 provides an important link between the development of clean technologies that are sparing in their use of natural resources and the use of the nearest appropriate installations for waste disposal. The overall objective of Schedule 12 is to ensure that the European Community as a whole is to become self-sufficient in waste disposal. Member states of the Community are expected to move towards that goal. It is hoped that the Environment Act 1995 will contribute to the effectiveness of the government's waste management hierarchy of waste reduction, reuse, recovery and disposal. It remains to be seen how effective these sections of the 1995 Act will be in providing implementation mechanisms for the national waste strategy.

Waste strategies: reuse, recovery and recycling

The development of clean technology and waste minimisation procedures is encouraged. A variety of techniques contribute to these developments including internal alterations to operating plants' design and processes, reuse and recycling of material and energy within a plant, and the redesign and modification of products, producing 'environmentally sound products'. Care must be taken in the development of such techniques to ensure that environmental harm actually decreases. The environmental risk associated with the plant and product may simply change. Ultimately it may be the case that those products that give rise to highly toxic and recalcitrant waste (see Chapter 8) will no longer be produced and marketed.

The safe disposal of waste has proved problematic. In the United Kingdom, at present, two technologies are routinely employed for the disposal of waste: incineration (9.5×10^4 tonnes annually) and physical containment, e.g. in landfills (1.3×10^6 tonnes annually). A relatively small proportion (approximately 0.01 per cent) of the landfill waste is imported.

There are several types of landfill used for the disposal of waste. Class I landfills are engineered, e.g. by incorporation of a liner of either clay or plastic, and managed to ensure that the release of leachate (see below) to the environment is extremely low (NRA, 1992). Gas (see below) migration may also be reduced. An extension of the containment landfill is found in the entombment landfill. In these landfills not only is the waste contained, but the landfill is engineered to prevent the infiltration of liquids. Essentially the waste is stored in dry conditions indefinitely. It was initially proposed in the United Kingdom, by NIREX UK Ltd, to dispose of low-level radioactive waste in entombment type systems. Class II landfills are characterised by an unsaturated zone through which leachate can percolate to the water table. These landfills work on the principle of dilute and disperse. The leachate is attenuated and diluted in the waste and the surrounding soil and rock strata (see Westlake, 1995, for further discussion of landfill development and management and Watson-Craik *et al.*, 1993, for a discussion of the physicochemistry and microbiology of co-disposal landfills).

United Kingdom landfills may also be classified in terms of the waste they contain: *mono-disposal* sites contain one homogeneous waste; *multi-disposal* sites contain a heterogeneous mixture of wastes; and *co-disposal* landfills contain industrial wastewaters and sludges, mixed with sewage sludge and degradable commercial, industrial and domestic waste. Some industrial wastes consist of, or contain, substances which are toxic or hazardous, i.e. capable of harming living organisms or the environment. Co-disposal has gained prominence as a waste disposal procedure primarily because of cost considerations and because the dumping of sewage sludge at sea is to be curtailed (see Chapter 11). Waste disposal costs for landfill range from £2. 50 to £35 per tonne compared to £20 to £900 for incineration (Porteus, 1985).

The history of landfill has not been without controversy and problems. Much of the waste in landfills is biodegradable. The predominantly anaerobic degradation of the waste produces a range of leachate components, e.g. fatty acids, and gas products, e.g. methane, in the short and long term (Table 9.3). In the case of Class II landfills it is now becoming apparent that leachates from landfills are not necessarily attenuated in the surrounding geology and that groundwater and surface water can become contaminated (see ENDS Report 229, February 1994, p. 12). Pollutants known to arise from landfills include gases, e.g. carbon dioxide and methane (both greenhouse gases); volatile fatty acids, e.g. acetate, propionate, butyrate; and heavy metals, e.g. zinc, cadmium, chromium and iron. In addition to this it is possible for relatively recalcitrant and perhaps toxic chemicals disposed of in landfill to leach, depending on the physicochemical and environmental conditions within the landfill and the chemistry of the substance. There are notorious cases where landfill leachate has caused major health problems in people exposed to the leachate, e.g. Love Canal (Niagara Falls, New York State) (Watson-Craik *et al.*, 1993). Many of the substances defined by the EC Groundwater Directive (80/68/EEC) List I and List II compounds (Appendix A) can be identified in leachates from Class II landfills. This in part has been responsible for the development of the UK policy to encourage the use of Class I, i.e. containment landfills (Westlake, 1995).

The concerns about the environmental problems that may arise from landfill, in particular those with regard to the production of greenhouse gases (see Chapters 6 and 12) and the risks of surface water and groundwater contamination, have led to incineration being a favoured waste disposal technology (Royal Commission on Environmental Pollution, 1993).

Table 9.3 Examples of typical landfill gas and leachate composition of fresh and aged domestic waste

	Fresh wastes	Aged wastes
Leachates (img l^{-1})		
TOC	8000	465
Volatile acids (as C)	5688	5
NH_3–N	790	370
NO_3–N	3	1
Ortho–P	0.13	1.4
Cl	1315	2080
Na	9601	300
Mg	252	185
K	780	590
Ca	1820	250
Mn	27	2.1
Fe	540	23
Cu	0.12	0.03
Zn	21.5	0.4
Pb	0.4	0.14
Gases (% vol.)		
Methane	–	63.8
Saturated hydrocarbons	0.074	0.005
Alcohols	0.127	<0.00001
Hydrogen sulphide	0.0014	0.00002

(*Source*: Adapted from Westlake, 1995)

There is no doubt that incineration is a highly efficient method of waste destruction. In addition, only non-combustible materials remain after incineration and there is a considerable reduction in the volume of waste that must be disposed to landfill. The operating conditions necessary to achieve full incineration are, however, tightly specified. Temperatures of 850 °C and 1200 °C must be achieved for municipal waste and chemical waste incineration, respectively, with sufficient contact time (usually seconds) and mixing to ensure total combustion of the waste. It is now recognised that because of operational deficiencies at some plants these conditions may not be met, resulting in incomplete combustion of waste and emission of pollutants from smoke-stacks (Gerrard, 1995). These emissions have been found to include polychlorinated biphenyls, dioxins, dibenzofurans, polyaromatic hydrocarbons and heavy metals. Many of the compounds are toxic, relatively or very recalcitrant, bioaccumulate (see Chapter 8) and may potentially contribute to environmental and health problems in the locality of incineration plants. In particular, dioxins are among the most toxic and recalcitrant chemicals known to man (see Chapter 8). New integrated pollution control (IPC) regulations (see Chapter 6) will require the upgrading of municipal solid waste (MSW) incinerators and will substanially reduce dioxin and other emissions as a result. Most MSWs are 20–30 years old and are currently responsible for 70 per cent of the 560–1100 g of dioxin released in the United Kingdom annually. IPC regulations will also reduce dioxin emissions from clinical and chemical incinerators (and from metal works). It is intended to cut dioxin emissions in the United Kingdom by 90 per cent through these IPC measures to below 350 g annually (*Chemistry & Industry*, 2 October 1995). Even given these measures, environmentalists would prefer to give recycling priority over incineration (see: ENDS Report 240, January 1995, p. 34).

One aspect of the government's strategy is that waste recovery includes three elements – recycling, composting and energy from waste – which receive equivalent status. The reuse and recycling of material and the recovery of energy from waste must inevitably contribute to sustainable development.

The initial stage of recycling is the segregation of waste materials separating out the recyclables, e.g. clean paper products, glass, metals and plastic. This may occur at home, in kerbside schemes, e.g. bottle banks, but more importantly in the United Kingdom at present, in treatment plant facilities or prior to landfilling. There are a number of technical constraints on the recycling of materials, for example contaminants in the material may be above the standards set by individual industries for primary raw materials (Gascoigne and Ogilvie, 1995). Biodegradable substances and materials which cannot be recycled are commonly put to landfill; however, they can be recycled through processes such as composting and used in energy recovery.

Composting is an aerobic microbial process involving a community of micro-organisms (Finstein, 1993). Composting reduces the volume of waste through its degradation and mineralisation. There are several problems associated with composting organic waste. These in part relate to technical difficulties since the feedstock is likely to be highly variable and the product may therefore be of variable quality. Any composted material may be difficult to utilise in horticulture owing to the potential contamination of urban waste with toxic organics and heavy metals. It may be possible to remove contaminating materials prior to composting or find alternative uses for the compost, e.g. infill in construction projects (Gascoigne and Ogilvie, 1995). Considerable heat is generated during composting. Although thermophilic micro-organisms are involved in composting, the self-heating must be controlled in order to achieve optimum conditions for rapid efficient composting. The excess heat can be used as energy to power the composting plant.

Alternative microbially based procedures for waste degradation are under development; although as yet not adopted into UK policy, both Denmark and Holland are investing extensively in the technology. For example, in Denmark, large-scale anaerobic digestion or biogas plants for the digestion of agricultural waste mixed with organic industrial and municipal waste are in operation in several regions. At Fangel in the municipality of Odense a biogas plant treats industrial wastes, e.g. from slaughterhouses and the food industry, mixed with source-sorted household waste and animal manures. Following sanitisation of the animal and slaughterhouse wastes, biodegradation occurs in an anaerobic digester. The effluent from the degradation is separated into a fibrous fraction which is composted and marketed, and a liquid fraction which is returned to farms for land-spreading as fertiliser. The anaerobic digestion process produces methane, i.e. biogas. This biogas is burnt in a gas furnace generating heat for the plant's operation and surplus heat is fed into the district heating for Odense (Colleran, 1993) (Fig. 9.1).

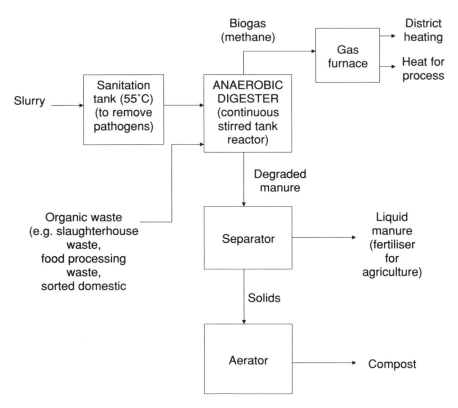

Fig. 9.1 Simplified schematic diagram of a biogas plant based on the Fangel plant (Odense, Denmark). (For full detials of the plant see Colleran, 1993.)

It is possible to recover energy in the form of biogas from landfill sites. Microbial degradation of organic waste in landfills is primarily under anaerobic conditions and therefore methane is one of the gases produced. It is technically possible to abstract biogas from a landfill which has been specifically designed on this basis. Energy can also be recovered from some waste materials by physicochemical processes, e.g. energy recovery from scrap tyres (Gascoigne and Ogilvie, 1995).

The existing framework of waste management will be explained in outline below. Clearly the work of the new Environment Agency will be significant in the future development of this area.

▶ Procedures and powers

Licensing arrangements

The system of waste management licensing contained in Part II of the EPA (Environmental Protection Act 1990) builds on the Control of Pollution Act 1974 by extending licensing from the regulated disposal sites to the entire process of waste management (see: SI 1994 No. 1096, The Environmental Protection Act 1990 (Commencement No. 15) Order 1994 and SI 1994 No. 1056, The Waste Management Licensing Regulations 1994). The legal regulations under the EPA are also supported by a comprehensive circular and various papers issued by the Department of the Environment (see: DoE Circular 11/94 Environmental Protection Act 1990 Part II; Waste Management Licensing: the Framework Directive on Waste; Waste Management Paper No. 4, Licensing of Waste Management Facilities; and Waste Management Paper No. 26A, Landfill Completion, HMSO, 1994). Provisions of the Environment Act 1995 will also apply.

It has already been noted above, that s. 35(1) of the EPA provides a broad definition of waste. Section 33 of the EPA prohibits anyone from depositing controlled waste (Table 9. 1) or knowingly causing or permitting its deposit in or under land unless a waste management licence is in force and the deposit of the waste is in accordance with the licence (see: *Ashcroft* v *Cambro Waste Products* [1981] 3 All ER 699). A licence may only be issued to an applicant that the authority deems to be 'a fit and proper person' and the licensed activity must be in the hands of a technically competent person (see s. 74(3) of the EPA). There is likely to be a requirement that the a licensee should be a holder of a certificate of competence from the Waste Management Industry Training and Advisory Board (under the new Environment Act). A site licence may be granted to the occupier of land or, where appropriate, a mobile plant licence may be granted. Applications must be in writing to the relevant WRA. A licence may only be issued in respect of land in which planning permission exists for that use or where there is a certificate of lawfulness under s. 191 of the Town and Country Planning Act 1990. Consultations must take place between the WRA and the National Rivers Authority (now the Environment Agency) (see Chapter 10) and the Health and Safety Executive may make representations. In cases of dispute, where for example the NRA objects to an application, the matter may be referred by either the WRA or the NRA to the Secretary of State. Where the land is on a site of Special Scientific Interest (see Chapter 8) then English Nature or the Countryside Council for Wales must be consulted.

In cases where the application for a licence is properly made and the applicant is deemed to be 'a fit and proper person' the WRA is restricted in rejecting the applicant. In these circumstances rejection may only come about if the WRA regards it necessary for the prevention of pollution of the environment, harm to human health or serious detriment to the amenities of the locality. The latter ground does not apply where the land that is the subject of the application has planning permission. There is a procedure of appeal to the Secretary of State within six months of a refusal or deemed refusal of a licence.

The licensing arrangements also contain provisions for setting out conditions to be attached to the licence. Section 35(3) of the EPA provides that the WRA may grant a licence subject to such conditions that appear to the authority 'to be appropriate'. Such conditions may relate to the activities which the licence authorises and to the precautions to be taken and the works to be carried out in connection with those activities. As s. 35(3) is broadly defined, the courts have a wide discretion as to how to interpret the general purpose of the legislation (see: *AG's Reference (No. 2 of 1988)* [1990] 1 QB 77). In legal terms, conditions must not be unreasonable and must not be too widely drawn. They must relate to the specific nature of the proposal and not go beyond the nature of the operation. Conditions cannot be used for an ulterior purpose or as a substitute for rejecting a licence. There are also powers under s. 35(3) to impose on the licence holder obligations that extend beyond the period of the activities undertaken under the licence. In addition the licence conditions may include conditions relating to other types of waste that are not controlled waste. Licence holders may be expressly provided with powers under the licence to carry out work that is not previously authorised.

The monitoring and enforcement of licence conditions is also regulated under the EPA. Under s. 42(1) the WRA has a duty to monitor the operation of the licence and any conditions imposed on the licence holder. The obligations arising out of s. 42(1) appear strict. The WRA has a duty to monitor the operation of the licence to ensure that the conditions are complied with and that the activities covered by the licence do not cause pollution of the environment or harm to human health or become seriously detrimental to the amenities of the locality (see above for potential risks). There is a duty on the WRA to consult with the NRA (now the Environment Agency) should there be any pollution of water caused by the activities under the licence. There are powers to ensure that emergency work is carried out (see: ss. 42(2) and 42(3)). The WRA may serve notice on a licence holder to comply with the licence conditions and if necessary take steps to prosecute the offender. A licence may be revoked or suspended in whole or in part. The latter applies mainly to the case where the person is no longer deemed by the WRA to be 'fit and proper' or technically competent in the definition set out above in s. 33. Any partial revocation still permits the continuation of any licence conditions although the site may not be operating. The WRA has powers to suspend activities authorised in the licence but continue to enforce any conditions on the site. This may occur where the holder of the licence is no longer deemed by the WRA to be 'fit and proper' or technically competent. It may arise where there is serious pollution of the environment or serious harm to human health has resulted from the activities to which the licence relates and that carrying on those activities may cause such serious harm to the environment or to human health. There are penalties in criminal law for licence holders in the event of breaches of the sections of the EPA outlined above. There are some statutory defences available to operators under s. 33(7) (a) where the defendant took all reasonable precautions and exercised due diligence (see: *Durham CC* v *Peter Connors Industrial Services Ltd* [1993] Env LR 197).

The EPA provides for modification, transfer or surrender of licences. There are extensive rights of appeal to the Secretary of State when dealing with disputes arising out of the exercise of licensing or modification powers. The Secretary of State may appoint individuals to carry out the appeal procedure which is also detailed in the legislation. This includes various procedural requirements on making a case out in writing or on the conduct of a hearing either in public or in private.

Section 34 of the Environmental Protection Act 1990: Duty of Care

The introduction of a duty of care on those who deal with waste giving rise to criminal liability followed from the recommendations of the Eleventh Report of the Royal Commission on Pollution (see: Cmnd 9675 (HMSO, 1985)). Persons who deal with controlled waste are required to take reasonable measures to prevent any unauthorised or harmful deposit, treatment or disposal of the waste. This includes the prevention of the escape of waste from their control or that of any other person. Under the statutory defence a disposal operator cannot be held liable for the escape of the waste or products arising from the waste if the best practice available at the time was employed. The duty of care does not apply to domestic occupiers in respect of household waste. However, there are important rules about the proper transfer of waste and procedures set out for the documentation and details of the transfer, such as the containers to be used and their contents (see: the Environmental Protection (Duty of Care) Regulations 1991, SI 1991 No. 2839). There is a statutory code made by the Secretary of State under s. 34(7) of the EPA (see: *Waste Management: the Duty of Care, A Code of Practice*, DoE, 1991). It is a criminal offence to breach the duty of care. Penalties are provided under s. 34(6) of the EPA. The provisions of the Code are admitted in evidence. It is also clear that breach of the duty of care does not require proof of harm. The scope of the duty of care is exceedingly wide as everyone engaged in the waste chain, from production of the waste to ultimate disposal, including those responsible for the carriage of waste, comes within the scope of the duty.

Carriers of waste

Carriers of waste must be registered with the WRA. In addition to the duty of care there are specific duties set out in the Control of Pollution (Amendment) Act 1989 and supplementary regulations (see: the Controlled Waste (Registration of Carriers and Seizure of Vehicles) Regulations 1991, SI 1991 No. 1624). There are certain exempted groups from the requirement to register, such as local authorities, British Rail and various charities. WRAs, WCAs and WDAs are also exempt, as are certain persons who satisfy prescribed requirements under the law of any other EC Member State. Applications for registration must be made to the WRA. There are powers to refuse registration, for example if it is held that the applicant is not a desirable carrier. Also there are powers to revoke registration. A right of appeal to the Secretary of State exists.

Enforcement of the above controls is devolved to a police constable or an authorised officer of a WRA. There are powers to stop a vehicle where there is reasonable suspicion that there is unlawful transportation of controlled waste. In the event of this being proved, there are powers for the disposal of vehicles used for the illegal disposal of waste.

Planning

Waste disposal in England is treated as a matter of planning law. The Town and Country Planning Act 1947 provided that waste disposal amounted to a material change of use and therefore required planning permission. In the early stages of planning law the conditions attached to planning permission constituted the earliest form of site licence. Section 38 of the Town and Country Planning Act 1990 as amended by

Schedule 4 of the Planning and Compensation Act 1991 requires planning authorities (normally at the county level) to prepare waste policies and mineral extraction policies for their area. Such plans must be approved by the Secretary of State and conform to the relevant structure plans (see Chapter 7). Indeed even existing waste sites may be deemed to undergo a material change of use when the superficial area of the deposit is extended or its height is raised and this exceeds the height of the adjoining land. There are some exemptions granted under the Town and Country Planning (General Development) Order 1988 (now see: [1995] JPL 373).

There is extensive guidance issued by the Department of Environment on the disposal of waste in the government's Sustainable Development Strategy (see: *Sustainable Waste Management: A Waste Strategy for England and Wales*, Consultation Draft, Department of the Environment, January 1995).

▶ Contaminated land and special waste

Contaminated land

Contaminated land has proved problematical and not susceptible to easy solution. The estimate is that 27 000 hectares of land fall within the category of contaminated land, that is land contaminated with noxious substances. Contaminated land has historically arisen from a variety of activities including mining and smelting, town gas works, steelworks and foundries, and railway goods yards. These types of operations are the origin of a large proportion of the contaminated land in the United Kingdom. In the present day contamination of land may arise from a variety of commercial and industrial sources either as a result of accidents or through the activity itself, e.g. landfills and scrapyards. Contaminated sites commonly have a large number of potentially harmful substances present which may be solids, in solution, liquids or gases. Substances such as heavy metals, e.g. cadmium, lead and copper; inorganic compounds, e.g. asbestos and sulphate; organic compounds, e.g. PCBs, dioxins, chlorinated hydrocarbons, polyaromatic hydrocarbons, phenolic compounds; and gases, e.g. methane, are relatively common contaminants. A number of hazards may arise from contaminated land including:

● Prevention and inhibition of plant growth and toxic effects on invertebrates and vertebrates
● Contamination of surface water and groundwater
● Uptake of contaminants by food crops and entry into the human food chain
● Human ingestion, inhalation or skin contact with the contaminants

● Chemical degradation of building materials
● Fire and explosion.

The extent of the ecological impact depends on the ecotoxicity and toxicity characteristics of the substances, their physicochemistry and concentration, and site environmental conditions (see Chapter 8). Heavily contaminated sites are often associated with severe disruption of ecosystem function. Plant species diversity and abundance is often low, i.e. the species are restricted to those tolerant of the contaminating substances. Other components of the ecosystem, e.g. micro-organisms and invertebrates, are also adversely affected showing low abundance often linked to low activity (McEldowney *et al.*, 1993). The impact of the contaminating substances on the microbial community may have a deleterious effect on the cycling of nutrients, i.e. the biogeochemical cycles, in the ecosystem, causing further degeneration of the eco- system (Harris and Birch, 1992).

The first attempt to legislate on contaminated land may be found in s. 143 of the EPA. That section requires that a register of contaminated land should be maintained by each district council or London borough. This was regarded as a first step to enable the land to be cleaned up. However, this left a number of questions unanswered. Who is responsible for paying the costs of any clean-up? Once land is identified as being contaminated what are the implications for its future use? Such questions remain to be answered. In July 1992 a consultation paper and draft regulations were published but further progress was delayed. In 1994 *A Framework for Contaminated Land* was published and after consultation draft legislation was prepared.

Contaminated land and the Environment Act 1995

The new Environment Act 1995 contains important provisions on contaminated land which occupied a major part of the time spent in debate on the Bill. The policy on contaminated land contained in the 1995 Act is set out in a *Framework for Contaminated Land* (DoE, November 1994). Section 57 of the Environment Act 1995 inserts 28 new sections after s. 78 of the Environment Protection Act 1990. There is a statutory definition of contaminated land and there are regulatory procedures for the control of contaminated land which follow the scheme for statutory nuisances contained in the Environment Protection Act 1990.

Contaminated land is defined as land which appears to the relevant local authority to be causing or to have a significant possibility of causing significant harm. Harm is defined as: 'harm to the health of living organisms or other interference with the ecological systems of which they form part and in the case of man, includes harm to his property'. It is envisaged that the Secretary of State will provide detailed guidance and regulations after a period of consultation and advice. Mortgage lenders will have noted that the definition of owner specifically excludes a mortgagee not in possession but includes a mortgagee in possession. Some legal protection is offered to lenders from liability if they are forced to take possession of a mortgaged property.

Under the 1995 Act new duties are placed on local authorities to act in accordance with the Secretary of State's guidance. Local authorities will have to inspect their areas to identify contaminated land and to decide whether any such land should be designated a special site, which makes the new Environment Agency the enforcing authority. A critical part of the new legislation is an attempt to distinguish between degrees of contamination. The main tool for the securing of assessment and the clean-up of a site will be the issuing of a remediation notice (see: ENDS Report 243, April 1995, p. 27). Failure to comply with the remediation notice is an offence and there are appeal procedures. Remedial works may be carried out in certain cases and the enforcement authorities will be able to recover costs from the polluter including the power of sale of the land in appropriate circumstances. There will be a register of remediation notices maintained by the enforcement authorities.

The new arrangements under the 1995 Act implement the 'polluter pays' principle and occupiers of land are responsible for certain aspects of its condition if the original polluters cannot be found. In general terms the new provisions do not appear to create new liabilities but serve to clarify existing arrangements. The new Environment Agency will make regular reports on contaminated land and may give guidance to local authorities on specific sites.

The new arrangements on contaminated land under the Environment Act 1995 leave some uncertainty as to how tough the regulatory controls over contaminated land will be. The answer will largely depend on the guidance and the regulations to be issued by the Secretary of State. In arriving at the guidance it is clear that delicate balances between protecting land values and improving the environment will have to be drawn.

The contaminated land provisions of the 1995 Act attempt to settle liability of polluters and landowners, waste producers and carriers. It should not be overlooked that the normal process of development and redevelopment of land will continue to afford one of the best means of clearing up contaminated land. Contamination is a material consideration for planning authorities (see Chapter 7) in the grant of planning permission. Registers of contaminated land under s. 143 of the Environmental Protection Act 1990 will remain a valuable guide for the planning authorities. Will there be a different standard for contaminated land applied by the planning authorities from the standard applied by the enforcement authorities under the 1995 Act? This may prove to be one of the major controversial issues left unresolved by the 1995 Act.

Remedial treatment of contaminated land

In addition to the remediation notices that can be issued under the Environment Act 1995 there are planning powers under s. 215 of the Town and Country Planning Act 1990 which allow planning authorities to require owners or occupiers of land to remedy the condition of their land so as not to affect adversely the amenity of other neighbouring land. At first glance this may appear to be a valuable power. However, its effectiveness is diminished by a number of factors. An appeal against a notice under s. 215 is possible on the basis that even if the condition of the land does adversely affect the amenity of the neighbouring land, provided it is attributable to the ordinary course of events and is not in breach of planning control, then the notice must be quashed. Even if there is non-compliance with the notice, the penalty is set at a level 3 summary offence. Given the limitations of the section and the low penalty, it is unlikely to provide a realistic means of enforcing the notice.

Remedial treatment may take several forms and involves the removal or treatment of the contaminated land and eventual restoration and reclamation of the land. There are a limited number of techniques available for treating contaminated land, including the following (Beckett and Cairney, 1993):

- Removal of the contaminating substances from the site for subsequent disposal elsewhere under appropriate containment conditions.
- On-site retention and isolation of the material, e.g. by encapsulation systems or the use of appropriate barriers, etc.
- Dilution of the contaminating substances with clean material.
- The elimination or immobilisation of contaminants through biological, chemical and/or physical treatments.

Among the newest technologies being applied to contaminated land treatment are bioremediation techniques. These utilise the ability of micro-organisms, often in consortia, to degrade a range of organic contaminants and remove heavy metals. This often, though not always, involves enhancing degradation by and activity of the *in situ* microbial community through the manipulation of site conditions, e.g. through the application of nitrogen and phosphate fertilisers (Schepart, 1995). Oil from the grounded *Exxon Valdez* oil tanker which contaminated large areas of beaches and rocky shores in the vicinity of Prince William Sound, Alaska (March 1989) was in part treated through bioremediation (Prince, 1992; Lessard *et al.*, 1995).

One of the problems inherent in using bioremediation technologies to eliminate or immobilise contaminants is the great variability in soil and sediment structure and composition. This can affect the rate and efficiency of bioremediation, e.g. through an impact on the availability of the substance for degradation (see Chapter 8). In addition, there is often a mixed cocktail of contaminants present on a site which may vary in their distribution and concentration across a site. Remediation technologies, therefore, require site specific investigations and are usually selected and specifically designed for the particular site, even a particular area of a site. (See Sayler *et al.*, 1991, for consideration of a range of issues with regard to bioremediation.)

Following remediation of the contaminated land further treatment involves land reclamation or habitat restoration. Land reclamation is a process by which the land is returned to productive use. The final use of the land may be very different from the original use, e.g. a woodland may have been disrupted due to mineral extraction and subsequently reclaimed for agricultural production. Land restoration involves the return of the original ecosystem, i.e. the ecosystem prior to disturbance, to the land. In practical terms this is unlikely to be an entirely achievable goal. There is a grey area between reclamation and restoration based on the inherent limitations of fully restoring a habitat and our limited ability to measure and define ecosystems accurately. Both reclamation and restoration imply the development of a fully functioning and self-sustaining ecosystem with nutrient recycling within and energy flow through the system (see chapter 1). Land reclaimed for productive use will require a degree of subsequent management depending on the end use. (A description of restoration and reclamation techniques and difficulties falls outside the scope of this book; see Beauchamp, 1993, for discussion of this topic.) There are soil and groundwater quality standards set as guidance on the assessment and redevelopment of contaminated land, e.g. ICRCL 59/83: Guidance on the assessment and redevelopment of contaminated land; ICRCL 70/90: Notes on the restoration and aftercare of metalliferous mining sites for pastures and grazing. These often offer guidance on acceptable levels of contamination by named substances linked to final end use.

There are limited funds available for the clean-up of contaminated land. Derelict land grants are available under the Derelict Land Act 1982. Waste Regulation Authorities are given a duty under s. 61(1) of the EPA to inspect from time to time the derelict land in their area. This may include not only landfill sites but broadly interpreted may apply to many other areas where controlled waste is dumped.

There are other possibilities. Part III of the EPA provides local authorities with powers to take action on contaminated land on the basis of a statutory nuisance. There are also powers under the licensing arrangements to take action to encourage the clean-up of contaminated and derelict land.

Special waste

Special waste is defined under the 1980 Regulations (see: the Control of Pollution (Special Waste) Regulations 1980, SI 1980 No. 1709) as any controlled waste which contains one or more of listed substances the presence of which makes the waste dangerous to life. There is a specific list of chemicals (Schedule 1 to the regulations) which are dangerous to life or have a low 'flash point' or are a medicinal product available only on prescription. It is estimated that special waste covers about 2 per cent of UK controlled waste. The largest proportion is from industry but also included are ordinary household products such as battery acids, pesticides and household cleaners.

The statutory controls for special waste are more stringent than for other controlled wastes. The Department of the Environment has noted the following controls on special waste (see: *Sustainable Waste Management: A Waste Strategy for England and Wales*. Consultation Draft, DoE, 1995 p. 93):

● Closer supervision of movements (pre-notification to the WRA).
● Recording of location of deposits within a landfill.
● Fewer waste management licensing exemptions than for other waste.
● Higher licensing charges than for other controlled waste.
● Mandatory Environmental Impact Assessment for the development of facilities (SI 1988 no.1199) (see Chapter 6).

It is likely that the 1991 Directive on Hazardous Waste (EEC Directive 91/156) may be extended to include many more types of wastes within its powers. The potential for harm arising out of special waste requires its segregation from other wastes. This is an expensive operation which requires the waste stream at point of collection to have effective separation of the various types of waste.

Radioactive waste

Radioactive waste arises from a number of different sources including nuclear power stations, reprocessing of spent fuel rods, hospitals and research laboratories (see: 6th report of the Royal Commission on Environmental Pollution, *Nuclear Power and the Environment*, Cmnd 6618 (HMSO, September 1976). Radioactive waste can be gaseous, liquid or solid and must be stored or disposed of safely. A number of hazards arise from radioactive waste depending on characteristics of the radio-nuclides present. For example, waste produced during the reprocessing of fuel rods is highly radioactive, radiotoxic and physically hot. It contains radionuclides which are exceptionally long-lived, i.e. have long half-lives. High-level radioactive waste is defined as containing >37 000 TBq tritium, 37 TBq of beta- and gamma-emitters, 3.7 TBq of strontium-90 and caesium-137 or 0.037 TBq of alpha-emitters with half-lives over 50 years (Clark, 1989). (The becquerel (Bq) is a unit of radioactivity defined as being one disintegration per second.) In contrast low-level waste normally contains short-lived radionuclides (30 years or less) in low concentrations; the bulk of this waste is often organic, e.g. packaging, etc. Techniques for the safe disposal of solid and liquid radioactive wastes are currently being developed by many countries, including the United Kingdom.

The safe disposal of radioactive waste requires that the health of the general population and industrial workers is not put at risk through exposure to radiation. The International Commission on Radiological Protection (ICRP, 1991) estimates that a radiation dose of 0. 05 Sv^{-1} may induce cancer. Exposure levels are kept well below this dose. (The sievert (Sv) is the unit used to express radiation dose to humans. Average background radiation is 2.4 mSv $year^{-1}$.) The impact of any accidental or deliberate discharge of radionuclides to the environment is difficult to predict. The mobility and fate of radionuclides in the environment is, of course, affected by radionuclide chemistry and environmental conditions and will vary with the particular radionuclide. Different radionuclides are also bioaccumulated to different extents by different micro-organisms, plants and animals, e.g. scallops (*Pecten maximus*) readily accumulate manganese and oysters (*Ostrea*) accumulate zinc (Clark, 1989; McEldowney *et al.* 1993). Thus the environmental impact of released radionuclides must be considered on the basis of individual radionuclides. However, radionuclides decay to other elements which may themselves be radioactive. Each radionuclide has a characteristic decay sequence, with a number of different radionuclides formed in series until a stable element is formed. Each radionuclide in this series is chemically distinct, they are after all different elements and each has a different radioactivity and different half-life. Predicting the impact of a sole radionuclide is therefore insufficient: even if there is only one contaminating radionuclide to begin with, the mobility and ultimate fate of all the daughter radionuclides in the decay series should be considered.

The basis for controlling exposure to radioactive waste is through the system of dose limitation recognised by the Radiological Protection Board and recommended by the International Commission on Radiological Protection in 1977 (see: *Radioactive Waste Management* 1982, Cmnd 8607). The Radioactive Substances Act 1993 provides a comprehensive system of controlling the handling of radioactive substances and materials. The 1993 Act is a consolidation of an earlier statute – the Radioactive Substances Act 1960 – which was heavily amended by the Environmental Protection Act 1990 (also see: the Control of Pollution (Radioactive Waste) Regulations 1989, SI 1989 No. 1158). The 1993 Act regulates all aspects of the use and storage of radioactive material and the disposal and accumulation of radioactive waste. There is a system of registration of premises supervised by HM Inspector of Pollution in England and Wales, now the new Environment Agency under the Environment Act 1995. Central controls under the 1993 Act are exercised by the Secretary of State for the Environment and various licences granted under the Nuclear Installations Act 1965. There are various inspectors with enforcement powers and a rigorous system of record keeping and inspection. Transport of radioactive materials is regulated by the Radioactive Material (Road Transport) Act 1991. Current policy on radioactive waste management is under review (see: *Review of Radioactive Waste Policy,* Cm 2919 (HMSO, 1995)).

▶ Genetically modified organisms

A genetically modified organism (GMO) is defined under Part VI (para. 4) of the Environmental Protection Act 1990 as follows:

. . . an organism is 'genetically modified' if any of the genes or other genetic material in the organism–

(a) have been modified by means of artificial techniques prescribed in regulations by the Secretary of State; or

(b) are inherited or otherwise derived, through any number of replications, from genes or other genetic material (from any source) which were so modified.

Inclusion of GMOs in a chapter on waste is for historical reasons.

GMOs or transgenic organisms have new combinations of genetic material in their genome introduced by 'artificial techniques'. These gene combinations cannot be achieved by traditional breeding techniques or other natural methods. For example, there is considerable interest in modifying certain crop plants by the insertion of genes from nitrogen-fixing bacteria, e.g. *Rhizobium,* allowing the plant to fix atmospheric nitrogen and lower the requirement for fertiliser application. Clearly, this GMO could not occur through natural processes.

The 'artificial techniques' applied to micro-organisms, plants or animals include the use of recombinant DNA technology and artificial cell fusion or hybridisation, including protoplast fusion which is primarily restricted to plants (for a full description of these techniques see Old and Primrose, 1989; Glick and Pasternak, 1994). The genetic modification will most commonly involve the insertion of one extra gene in the genome which will sometimes originate from the same species; however, the gene will sometimes arise from a very different species (see above). In the former case it is possible to view the GMO as a variant or strain of the original species; in the latter case the GMO is likely to have very different characteristics from the original species. Some GMOs will essentially be equivalent to a new species, particularly those arising from cell fusion or hybridisation. It should be remembered that GMOs may arise not from the insertion of a gene, but rather from a deletion. For example Ice-minus *Pseudomonas syringae* have the gene deleted that codes for the production of an ice-nucleating protein (Lindow and Connell, 1984). When considering the risks associated with GMO release in the environment (see below) it is important to consider the phenotype of the organism (i. e. its characteristics) rather than the way it was constructed.

The potential commercial applications for GMOs are immense. These applications divide between contained industrial processes, often fermentation processes, and those applications that require the deliberate release of the organism to the environment (Table 9. 4).

Table 9.4 Examples of potential and actual commercial applications of genetically modified organisms

(a) *Applications involving industrial contained processes*

Process or product type	Examples of product or application
Protein pharmaceuticals	Human interferons human growth hormone
Small biological molecules	L-ascorbic acid amino acids
Antibiotics	Improving production of novel antibiotics
Biopolymers	Xanthan gum Plant biopolymers
Immunotherapeutic agents	HIV therapeutic agents
Starch and sugar utilisation	Fructose or alcohol production

(b) *Applications requiring deliberate release (including agricultural systems)*

Process or product type	Example of product or application
Plant growth-promoting bacteria	Nitrogen-fixing bacteria
Bacterial insecticides	Baculoviruses
Developing insect-resistant plants	
Developing virus-resistant plants	
Developing herbicide-resistant plants	
Developing stress- and senescence-tolerant plants	
Modifying properties of plant products	Taste, shelf-life
Developing animals resistant to diseases	
Production of pharmaceutical proteins	Sheep, goat, pig, cattle mammary gland secretions

GMOs raise important issues about the protection of human health and the environment (see: *The Release of Genetically Engineered Organisms into the Environment*, Cm 720 (1989)). The government's approach is to provide research and education but also legal controls. There are various controls under the Health and Safety at Work, etc., Act 1974 and a European Community Directive 90/219/EEC. These have been considerably strengthened by the EPA which provides a detailed statutory framework aimed at minimising the damage to the environment which may arise from the escape or release of any GMOs. This forms an important and comprehensive code for GMOs that seeks to provide a flexible legal framework in a rapidly developing area of science. General controls may be found in ss. 106–108 of the EPA. A risk assessment must be undertaken so that reasonable steps are taken to ensure that organisms imported, acquired or kept are no risk to human health or the environment. The onus lies on those keeping the organisms under their control to provide safe working practices to prevent environmental damage. The principle of BATNEEC applies, namely that the organisms must be kept using the best available techniques not entailing excessive cost. The release of any GMO must also take account of the risks involved.

The deliberate and accidental release of GMOs to the environment poses two types of potential problems:

1. The GMO behaves as an invasive species.
2. The inserted gene or genes spread to other species by horizontal transfer potentially leading to the creation of novel GMOs with new properties.

An invasion is simply the introduction or release of an organism into a region where it was not formerly native. There have been a large number of such invasions by organisms introduced accidentally, e.g. Dutch elm disease, or deliberately, e.g. biological control agents and ornamental plants such as *Rhododendron ponticum*. Many invasions fail and the invading species does not become an ecological problem. However, a number will establish themselves and become a pest species, which may cause a number of ecological effects (Mooney and Bernadi, 1990):

- Damage to plants or habitat
- Competition with native micro-organism, flora or fauna for limited resources
- Imbalance in prey–predator interactions, either through reducing prey numbers or becoming an additional source of prey to native species
- Spread of diseases or parasites
- Breeding with native species producing new hybrids.

The likelihood and mode of transfer of genes from GMOs to other organisms in the environment is different for micro-organisms, plants and animals and will vary with habitat and environmental conditions (Mooney and Bernadi, 1990). The minimisation and assessment of the risk associated with the deliberate release of GMOs to the environment involves consideration of the following factors:

- Specificity (the target of the GMO alone should be affected)
- Predictability (the ultimate fate and mobility of the GMO and its genes should be predictable)
- Reversibility (ideally the released GMO should not survive indefinitely or should be removable, depending on its use)
- Reproduction and dispersibility (depending on the application of the GMO these should be minimal or absent)
- Scale of use (this will affect the number of releases, i.e. the number of potential invasions).

In general we have little appreciation of why one invasion results in the establishment of a pest and another does not. The information necessary for a realistic appraisal of the risks arising from a GMO's release either with regard to invasion or the likelihood of transfer of genetic information may not be complete. Certainly determining and predicting the above characteristics for any GMO is inherently difficult, perhaps most particularly for genetically engineered micro-organisms (GEMs). Our understanding of microbial community dynamics and the rate and extent of gene transfer between micro-organisms in the environment is deficient in many areas (Stewart-Tull and Sussman, 1992). In general, therefore, assessment of the risks associated with releases will be made on a case-by-case basis. Eventually, after a substantial body of evidence has accumulated with regard to safe release, certain categories of GMOs may be given generic permissions. (For a brief and readable introduction to GMO release see Shorrocks and Coates, 1993.)

The Secretary of State for the Environment has various enforcement powers to ensure compliance with the regulations. A prohibition notice may be served on those who are proposing to import, acquire, release or market GMOs or where he believes that such activities involve a risk to the environment. The Secretary of State has wide powers to give consents and impose conditions where it is deemed to be necessary for the keeping, releasing or marketing of GMOs. There is also a system of public registers which contain information, directions, prohibition notices, consent applications and details of the persons who have GMOs under their control.

The above outline of the main legal controls over GMOs is continually under review. Risk assessment of GMOs is subject to differing approaches within different government departments. It is intended to provide a uniform approach by the adoption of common standards of risk assessment in the near future. New regulations have implemented EC Directives on the contained use and deliberate release and marketing of GMOs. The Advisory Committee on Releases to the Environment, part of the Toxic Substances Division of the Department of the Environment, has thus been created a statutory body. Its aims are to provide speedy and reliable procedures to monitor and assess GMOs in line with common practices throughout the European Community (see: Genetically Modified Organisms (Deliberate Release) Regulations 1992, SI 1992 No. 3280, EC Directive 90/220 and *This Common Inheritance: The Third Year Report*, Cm 2549 (HMSO, 1994), pp. 118–19).

This is a fast developing area of science. The legal framework is under review in an effort to keep up to date with recent developments (see: Royal Commission on Pollution 13th Report, Cm 720 and 14th report Cm 1557). Currently the European Commission is reviewing the Directive (EC Directive 90/220) on GMOs (see: ENDS Report 244, May 1995, p. 42, and OJ L297 Vol. 37, 18 November 1994). One possible scenario is that there will be some deregulation of the existing Directive and a focus on risk assessment including the 'likelihood of harm to human health or the environment'.

▶ Mineral extraction

Mineral extraction is an important commercial activity. Mineral extraction is subject to ordinary planning controls (see Chapter 7) with a supervisory function exercised by the Department of Trade and Industry, the Department of the Environment and the Ministry of Agriculture, Fisheries and Food. New and comprehensive powers for the review of old mineral planning permissions and for a periodic review of existing mineral planning permissions are contained in s. 96, Schs. 13 and 14 of the Environment Act 1995. Schedule 13 provides procedures for the future periodic review of all mineral planning permissions which will be phased in over a six year period. Schedule 14 is intended to ensure the future periodic review of all mineral permissions every 15 years. It is envisaged that future guidance will be issued for the preparation and consideration of new schemes and conditions for mines.

In addition to the question of the commercial exploitation of minerals there is a question of mining and quarrying waste. This amounts to approximately 110 million tonnes annually. The activities of mineral extraction, mining and quarrying and the production of waste from these activities have severe environmental consequences (Table 9.5).

Table 9.5 Some environmental impacts from selected mining and quarrying operations

Impact	Coal mine waste	Metal mine waste	Quarry stone pits and waste
Substratum instability	++	+	−
Spontaneous combustion of waste	++	−	−
Steep slopes on tips and excavations	++	+	++
Periodic flooding and water stress	+	−	+
High levels of toxic elements	++	++	−
Compaction of substratum	+	+	++
Extremes of surface temperature	++	+	+
Low nutrient status	++	++	+
Low abundance of soil micro-organisms and soil fauna	++	++	+

++ very pronounced effect.
+ effect present.
− effect negligible or absent.

In addition, acid mine drainage is produced from some mine wastes or during heap leaching. This is highly acidic and contaminated by heavy metals. The environmental consequences of acid mine drainage discharging into surrounding terrestrial and aquatic environments are considerable. Most mining and quarrying waste does not fall within the EPA but other types of wastes generated in the mine or quarry are not exempt. Most of the wastes are inert materials. Wastes may include colliery spoil or china clay wastes. The Town and Country Planning legislation applies to the control of location, size and restoration requirements of the waste tips. In the case of spoil heaps there is legislation contained in the Mines and Quarries (Tips) Act 1969 and regulations in 1971 provide a comprehensive set of requirements concerning the safety and stability of spoil heaps. Landscaping and good practice are included in the regulatory structure.

Colliery spoil is the subject of specific obligations contained in the Coal Industry Act 1994. This is an attempt to ensure that all future tipping obtains the requisite planning permission (see Chapter 7). Research and funding are available from the Department of the Environment as to guidance on good practice.

There is considerable concern about areas of past, present or future mining. In recent years house conveyancers may make a British Coal search (see: Con 29M) which allows the potential buyer of property to ascertain the exact whereabouts of mining works or proposed mining works. Usually this search is accompanied by a map. The Coal Mining Subsidence Act 1991 provides in a single statutory basis remedies for damage attributable to coal mining subsidence. The 1991 Act repeals earlier legislation such as the Coal Mining (Subsidence) Act 1957. A primary duty of care is placed on British Coal for the repair of subsidence damage to housing in mining areas. On the sell-off of British Coal these responsibilities are inherited by the new owners.

Sections 58–60 of the Environment Act 1995 considerably tighten up the regulation of discharges from mines by removing the statutory protections from the owners and operators of mines to be abandoned after 1999. Mine operators must give six months' notice so that pollution prevention measures are taken before the mine can be closed.

The waste hierarchy: waste reduction, reuse and recovery

Waste minimisation is increasingly seen as an important part of a more enlightened understanding of the environment (see: *Centre for the Exploitation of Science and Technology*, 1995) It is therefore essential to see waste disposal as the least attractive option since no benefit comes from the disposal of materials and considerable cost may be involved in ensuring that disposal is environmentally sound. It is also clear that different approaches may be adopted in addressing waste management issues. For example, new provisions have been introduced to regulate litter and abandoned shopping and luggage trolleys (see Part IV of the EPA) through the creation of criminal offences. There is also a duty to keep land and highways clear of litter including a Code of Practice issued by the Secretary of State (see: EPA 1990: Code of Practice on Litter and Refuse. DoE, 1991). There are litter control zones which may include car parks, private roads, industrial estates and beaches. Members of the public may seek redress in the magistrates' court where there is a grievance arising out of a breach of a duty to keep land and highways clear of litter (see s. 89 of the EPA). It remains to be seen if such comprehensive regulations will have any impact on the litter on roads and streets in Britain.

In the waste hierarchy, waste reduction, reuse and recovery are pre-eminent.

Waste reduction

This is a policy intended to reduce waste to the minimum. The government has set various targets:

- To stabilise the production of household waste at its existing 1995 level.
- To reduce the proportion of controlled waste going to landfill sites by 10 per cent over the next 10 years, followed by similar reductions thereafter.

Various strategies have been invoked: better housekeeping in industry; better product design; waste reduction through changing consumer consumption patterns; and the use of Integrated Pollution Control to minimise pollution. A core element in this strategy is information about ways to reduce waste (see incineration and composting above).

Reuse and recovery

Reuse is generally defined as putting materials back into use. Recovery may involve recycling, for example the reuse of glass from bottles. It is also possible to see increased use of composting of organic waste to produce soil or growing medium. Energy may be obtained through the recovery of waste through burning or collecting methane from the decomposition of waste in landfill sites (see above).

In the case of recycling s. 49 of the EPA requires each Waste Collection Authority to prepare a recycling plan. This includes consideration of the use of equipment, and the costs and savings expected from implementation of the plan. There are additional powers for publicising plans and a method of compensation in respect of waste retained by the WCA for recycling (see ss. 49(2), 52, 55 of the EPA). The government's strategies for recycling include various targets.

- To recycle 25 per cent of household waste by the year 2000.
- To commission research on the feasibility of waste exchange networks and promote waste exchange within industry.
- To support the EC Directive on Packaging and Packaging Waste. Recovery of between 50 and 65 per cent of all packaging waste, of which between 25 and 45 per cent is recycled.

Many advantages have been claimed for reuse. Energy savings may be made and new markets encouraged through the sale of waste by-products and an associated reduction in disposal costs.

Obtaining energy from waste represents an important dimension. Energy recovery may come through incineration linked for example to combined heat and power systems. There is a new generation of municipal solid waste plants involving incineration. Other techniques for generation of energy from waste are being developed, e.g. biogas plants (see above).

▶ Conclusions

Sustainable development strategies attempt to reconcile what may appear to be two conflicting ideals: economic development that secures higher standards of living; and the protection and enhancement of the environment. It remains to be seen how sustainable development may be achieved in practice. Undoubtedly waste management will require careful setting of targets. Monitoring the strategy of waste management will require careful assessment of these targets. Evaluating the waste hierarchy of reduction, reuse, recycling, incineration and waste deposit in landfill sites requires a careful cost–benefit analysis. Increasingly the economic evaluation of waste management will have a central role in the success of the strategy for sustainable development.

▶ References and further reading

Beauchamp, G.S. (1993) 'Establishing new landscapes. Reclamation options'. In T. Cairney (ed.), *Contaminated Land. Problems and Solutions.* Blackie Academic and Professional, London. pp. 191–210.

Beckett, M.J. and Cairney, T. (1993) 'Reclamation options'. In T. Cairney (ed.), *Contaminated Land. Problems and Solutions.* Blackie Academic and Professional, London. pp. 68–83.

Clark, R.B. (1989) *Marine Pollution.* Clarendon, Oxford.

Colleran, E. (1993) 'Anaerobic digestion of agricultural and food-processing effluents'. In J.C. Fry, G.M. Gadd, R.A. Herbert, C.W. Jones, and I.A. Watson-Craik. (eds) *Microbial Control of Pollution.* Cambridge University Press, Cambridge, pp. 199–226.

Finstein, M.S. (1993) 'Composting in the context of municipal solid waste management'. In R. Mitchell (ed.), *Environmental Microbiology.* Wiley-Liss, New York, pp. 355-74.

Gascoigne, J.L. and Ogilvie, S. M. (1995) 'Recycling waste materials – opportunities and barriers'. In R.E. Hester and R.M. Harrison (eds), *Waste Treatment and Disposal.* The Royal Society of Chemistry, Cambridge, pp. 91–115.

Gerrard, S. (1995) 'Environmental risk management'. In T. O'Riordan (ed.), *Environmental Science for Environmental Management.* Longman, Essex, pp. 296–317.

Glick, B.R. and Paternak, J.J. (1994) *Molecular Biotechnology. Principles & Applications of Recombinant DNA.* ASM Press, Washington.

Harris, J.C. and Birch, P. (1992) 'Land reclamation and restoration'. In J.C. Fry, G.M. Gadd, R.A. Herbert, C.W. Jones, and I.A. Watson-Craik (eds), *Microbial Control of Pollution.* Cambridge University Press, Cambridge. pp. 169–291.

Hester, R.E. and Harrison, R.M. (eds) (1995) *Waste Treatment and*

Disposal. The Royal Society of Chemistry, Cambridge.

International Commission on Radiological Protection (1991) *1990 Recommendations of the International Commission on Radiological Protection.* ICRP Publication 60, *Annals of the ICRP*, **21**, 1–3.

Lessard, R.R., Wilkinson, J.B., Prince, R.C., Bragg, J.R., Clark, J.R. and Atlas, R.M. (1995) 'Bioremediation application in the cleanup of the 1989 Alaska oil spill'. In B.S. Schepart (ed.), *Bioremediation of Pollutants in Soil and Water.* American Society for Testing and Materials, Philadelphia, pp. 207–26.

Lindow, S.E. and Connell, J.H. (1984) 'Reduction of frost injury to almond by control of ice nucleation-active bacteria'. *Journal of the American Horticultural Society*, **109**, 48–53.

McEldowney, S., Hardman, D. and Waite, S. (1993) *Pollution: Ecology and Biotreatment.* Longman, Essex.

Mooney, H.A. and Bernadi, G. (eds) (1990) *Introduction of Genetically Modified Organisms in the Environment.* John Wiley, Chichester.

National Rivers Authority (1992) *Policy and Practice for the Protection of Groundwater.* National Rivers Authority.

Old, R.W. and Primrose, S.B. (1989) *Principles of Gene Manipulation*, 4th edn. Blackwell Scientific Publications, Oxford.

Porteus, A. (1985) 'Hazardous wastes in the UK – an overview'. In A. Porteus (ed.), *Hazardous Waste Management Handbook.* Butterworth, London, pp. 1–15.

Prince, R.C. (1992) 'Bioremediation of oil spills, with particular reference to the spill from the *Exxon Valdez*'. In J.C. Fry, G.M. Gadd, R.A. Herbert, C.W. Jones and I.A. Watson-Craik (eds), *Microbial Control of Pollution.* Cambridge University Press, Cambridge, pp. 19–34.

Purdue, M. (1990) 'Defining waste'. *Journal of Environmental Law*, **259**.

Sayler, G.S., Fox, R. and Blackburn, J.W. (eds) (1991) *Environmental Biotechnology for Waste Treatment.* Plenum Press, New York.

Schepart, B.S. (ed.) (1995) *Bioremediation of Pollutants in Soil and Water.* American Society for Testing and Materials, Philadelphia.

Shorrocks, B. and Coates, D. (eds) (1993) *The Release of Genetically-engineered Organisms.* British Ecological Society, Field Studies Council, Shrewsbury.

Stewart-Tull, D.E.S. and Sussman, M. (1992) *The Release of Genetically Modified Microorganisms – REGEM 2.* Plenum Press, New York.

Tolba *et al.* (1992) *The World Environment 1972–1992.* UNEP, Chapman & Hall, London.

Watson-Craik, I.A., Sinclair, K.J. and Senior, E. (1993) 'Landfill co-disposal of wastewaters and sludges'. In J.C. Fry, G.M. Gadd, R.A. Herbert, C.W. Jones and I.A. Watson-Craik (eds), *Microbial Control of Pollution.* Cambridge University Press, Cambridge, pp. 129–98.

Westlake, K. (1995) 'Landfill'. In R. E. Hester and R. M. Harrison (eds), *Waste Treatment and Disposal.* The Royal Society of Chemistry, pp. 43–67.

▶ Reports

Department of the Environment: *Contaminated Land,* Cm 1161 (HMSO, 1990).

Department of the Environment: *Recycling Waste Management.* Paper No. 28 (HMSO, 1991).

Department of the Environment: *Sustainable Waste Management: A Waste Strategy for England and Wales.* Consultation Draft January 1995 (DoE 1995).

This Common Inheritance The Third Year Report, Cm 2549 (HMSO, 1994).

UK Annual Report *This Common Inheritance,* Cm 2822 (HMSO, 1995).

Royal Commission on Environmental Pollution (1993) *Incineration of Waste: Seventh Report.* HMSO, London.

PART III
Water

Part III of the book comprises two chapters. In Chapter 10 there is a discussion of the law relating to water and pollution control. In Chapter 11 there is an outline of the law relating to the protection of the coastal and marine environment. Both chapters involve an understanding of the management of the water industry and this is provided in outline in Chapter 10. The Environment Act 1995, establishing the new Environment Agency for England and Wales and the Scottish Environment Protection Agency, is considered in both chapters. The Environment Agency replaces the National Rivers Authority and will have responsibility for the regulation and enhancement of water. The Scottish Environment Agency will take over the functions and property rights and liabilities of the river purification authorities.

Water is an essential to life. Its varied uses at home, in industry and agriculture make it vital to the sustainable development of mankind. Water is essential for a variety of commercial uses including waste disposal, commercial fishing, agriculture and food manufacture, various industrial processes, as a means of transport, and for many recreational activities. Water pollution control is the subject of much recent legislation. The current law is found in six major pieces of legislation: the Water Resources Act 1991, the Water Industry Act 1991, the Statutory Water Companies Act 1991, the Land Drainage Act 1991 and the Water Consolidation (Consequential Provisions) Act 1991. The sixth is the Environment Act 1995. The most recent major legislative change is the new Environment Agency established under the Environment Act 1995, which received the Royal Assent in July 1995, and which will take over the tasks of the National Rivers Authority, set up under the Water Resources Act 1991 and abolished by the 1995 Act. This is a time of great change for the water industry and for the management of water resources, partly as a result of privatisation of the water industry and also because of standard setting by the European Community. Capital investment in the water industry during 1992/93 was £3 billion (see: *This Common Inheritance*, Cm 2549 (HMSO, 1994), p. 98). Anticipated investment between 1989 and 2000 is expected to be £30 billion. More recently, the government has published its policy on water resources that takes account of recent drought conditions and considers improvements in conservation measures and a reduction in water loss from leakage by setting leakage targets for the water industry. (see: *Water Conservation: Government Action*, DoE, 1995).

The Royal Commission on Environmental Pollution published its 16th Report (see: *Freshwater Quality*, Cm 1966 (HMSO, June 1992)) followed by a government response in February 1995. Many of the Royal Commission's proposals are already enacted into law. Tougher controls and monitoring on drinking water standards have led to the first major prosecution of a water company for supplying water unfit for human consumption under the Water Industry Act 1991, after a water pollution incident in Worcester in April 1994 (see: ENDS Report 240, January

1995, p. 9). At the same time it is reported that drinking water standards are improving. The most recent report of the Drinking Water Inspectorate (DWI) claims that 99.3 per cent of tests show compliance with the standards compared to 98.9 per cent in 1993 (DWI, *Drinking Water 1994* (HMSO, 1995)). In this chapter there is an outline of the main legislation and an analysis of the new Environment Act 1995.

Introduction

The focus of this chapter is to consider the arrangements for the management of water and the monitoring, prevention and detection of pollution of inland waters, rivers, canals and groundwater. The setting of standards for water quality and the regulation of drinking water are discussed. The 1990 census on water quality noted that 64 per cent of the rivers in England and Wales could be used for drinking water extraction, and support aquatic life, without major treatment works; in Scotland this was as high as 97 per cent. The same survey found that 11 per cent of rivers were polluted and 25 per cent of rivers might supply drinking water after special treatment in England (see Chapter 12; also see *This Common Inheritance*, Cm 1200 (HMSO, 1990), p. 162).

The different uses and demands made on water require an integrated approach to water management. This means the management of the resource must take account of the variety of uses of water. This includes uses such as water extraction, fisheries, hydro-power generation, navigation, leisure and recreation, and flood defences. The preservation of aquatic ecosystems requires the highest priority.

The water quality found in rivers and groundwater affects the quality of water available for public or private water supply. Pollution of rivers through discharges affects the quality of water and substantially adds to the cost of making water wholesome for drinking or other purposes. The Environment Act 1995 contains powers for the creation of flood defence committees. This is an indication of the potential impact of meteorological fluctuations and potential sea-level rises caused by climate change (see Chapter 12) on the management of water resources.

The pollution of groundwater and surface waters is a serious problem which has a considerable impact on the use of water by man and on aquatic ecosystems. Pollutants in aquatic environments include a variety of organic, inorganic and microbial agents discharged, leached or precipitated from the atmosphere, either singly or as a cocktail, into freshwater systems. Their fate in aquatic environments is controlled by a variety of abiotic and biological factors (Fig. 10.1). In addition physical agents such as heat can pollute water.

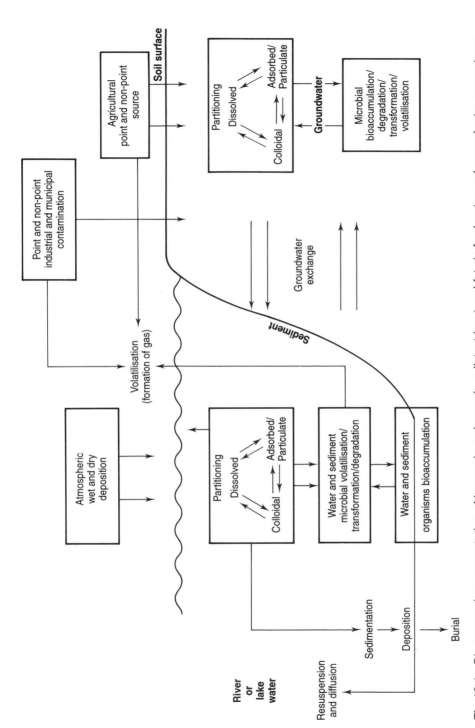

Fig.10.1 Diagrammatic representation of inorganic and organic pollutant input and fate in freshwater and groundwater ecosystems. (Note abiotic factors and the chemistry of the contaminant will affect all of these processes.)

Most electricity generating plants require water to cool and condense steam arising from the turbines. The condenser at a power plant, therefore, requires large amounts of cooling water which is abstracted either from groundwater or from rivers. Most of this is reused in the plant, but a proportion is returned to the environment at a higher temperature. This thermal pollution has a variety of impacts on the ecosystem. There are a number of physical effects including a lowering of water density and viscosity, an increase in the solubility of compounds and of ionisation, and a lowering of the solubility of gases (oxygen deficiency is possible in extreme cases). Plants, animals and micro-organisms are affected in a variety of ways depending on species and their normal temperature range. For example the growth of organisms may be affected and the spawning of fish may be altered depending on species. The density and diversity of micro-organisms may also be affected. There is growing evidence, however, that except in extreme cases of thermal pollution the impact of waste heat on aquatic ecosystems is not as damaging as was originally feared. It appears to be the case that the homoeostatic mechanisms within communities contain any damage (see Mason, 1995, Ch. 7; Langford, 1983).

Pollution of freshwater and groundwater ecosystems is exceptionally diverse in character involving a wide range of agents, for example suspended solids and particulates, organic nutrients, pH, and a wide range of chemicals. In fact some 1500 compounds have been listed as freshwater pollutants. These pollutants arise from a variety of sources, both point sources and non-point or diffuse sources (Table 10. 1) (see below for discussion of point and non-point sources). Any one source of pollution may contain more than one type of pollutant. The specific impact of the pollutants on aquatic ecosystems is difficult to predict but some generalisations can be made (Table 10. 2).

The effects of a toxic chemical on an organism or community depend primarily on the distribution and concentration of the chemical, the length of time that organisms are exposed to it, environmental trans-formations of the compound, e.g. oxidation and reduction reactions and biodegradation, and the bioavailability of the chemical (see Chapter 8). Many of these factors are interrelated and are affected by the physicochemistry of the receiving water and by the nature and lifestyles of the organisms present. For example, exposure time can vary with a number of factors including the environmental longevity of the compound, which is influenced by a number of physicochemical factors, e.g. water pH, and biological factors, e.g. microbial activity (see Chapter 8 for a discussion of factors that affect degradation of organic compounds); the distribution and concentration (partly related to longevity and flow of the water, etc.) of the chemical in the ecosystem; and the lifestyle and life cycle of any given organism. Consider briefly a metal, radionuclide or organic pollutant which after discharge to a river

Table 10.1 Sources and associated types of freshwater and groundwater pollutants

Sources	Key contaminants
(a) Point source (continuous)	
Sewage treatment works ⎱ Septic tanks ⎰	Suspended solids, BOD,* nutrients, ammonia, chloride, micro-organisms
Fish farms	As sewage treatment and in addition biocides
Coalmine drainage	Suspended and dissolved solids, iron, low pH (i.e. acid), chloride
Metal mine drainage	Suspended solids, low pH, sulphates, dissolved and particulate metals
Industrial effluents:	
Chemicals – acids	Low pH
– detergents	BOD
– biocides	TOC†, low pH, toxic compounds
– synthetic resins	BOD
Organic toxic wastes	e.g. formaldehydes, phenols, steroids hydrocarbons, cyanides, nitro and nitroso compounds
Engineering works	Suspended solids, heavy metals, hydrocarbons, variable BOD and pH
Food and drink manufacture	BOD, suspended solids, odours, colloidal and dissolved organics
Petroleum industry	BOD, chloride, sulphur compounds phenols
Power station cooling water	Heat
Metal manufacture	Toxic metals, low pH
Textile industry	Suspended solids, BOD, high pH, i.e. alkaline
Tanneries	BOD, total solids, chlorides, sulphides, chromium, hardness
(b) Point source (intermittent)	
Urban stormwater discharges	Suspended solids, hydrocarbons (from cars etc.), chlorides and urea (from de-icing), metals, micro-organisms, compounds from spillages.
Opencast mining	See coal mining
Farmyard discharges	
Livestock	Suspended solids, BOD, nitrogen. micro-organisms
Silage	Suspended solids, BOD, phenol, carbohydrate

Table 10.1 *continued*

Sources	Key contaminants
Household waste and landfill leachate	Sulphates, chlorides, ammonia, BOD, TOC, suspended solids, micro-organisms, degradation products, e.g. volatile fatty acids, humics, carbohydrates, metals
(c) *Non-point (diffuse) sources*	
Urban run-off	All stormwater discharges
Agricultural run-off	
Fertilisers	Phosphate, nitrate, ammonia, sulphate, chloride, micro-organisms (from sludge and manure spreading)
Biocides	Organochlorine and organophosphorous compounds, etc.
Livestock	See farmyard discharges
Acid rain	Low pH

*BOD, Biological oxygen demand (a measure of oxygen requirement by micro-organisms during the breakdown of organic matter.
†TOC, Total organic carbon requirement

becomes associated predominantly with the sediment. Organisms that remain primarily in the water column will be exposed to the pollutant very little, while sediment-dwelling organisms are likely to be exposed for long periods depending on the longevity of the particular compound. The lifestyle of an organism may vary during its life cycle so the eggs or juvenile stages may be exposed to different extents than adults. It should also be remembered that it is possible for particle-bound pollutants to be unavailable for uptake and, therefore, possibly not induce a toxic effect.

It can be seen that predicting and modelling the impact of pollutants on individual target organisms in aquatic systems is difficult; attempting to predict the impact at community level is even more complex. It is also the case that some aquatic ecosystems are substantially more vulnerable to the adverse effects of pollutants than others. For example, streams that have high levels of nutrients, organics and solutes, e.g. lower clay streams, are well buffered and tend to be reasonably stable when a number of low-toxicity compounds are added. Fragile streams easily disrupted by effluent discharges are generally nutrient and solute deficient but may contain humic compounds, e.g. acid sand streams in the New Forest.

The impact of individual pollutants on any individual organism may

Table 10.2 Environmental impact of pollutants in freshwater ecosystems

Pollutant	Environmental impact	Consequences
High BOD*	Deoxygenation, i.e. reduction in dissolved oxygen content	Change of community structure – sensitive species eliminated and increase in tolerant species
Partial organic degradation	Increased concentrations of ammonia, nitrite and nitrate	Intolerant species eliminated and senstive species reduced
High suspended solids or particles in suspension	Raised turbidity, reduction in light penetration, increased abrasion	Reduced photosynthesis of aquatic plants and algae, abrasion of fish gills, impairment of filter feeding. The fitness of organisms affected
Toxic compounds (organics, metals etc.)	Lowering water quality	Water and/or sediment toxic to some species resulting in changes in community structure and potentially function, nutrient cycling, prey–predator relationships affected, etc. Sub-lethal effects on some species resulting in changed fitness
Sedimentation of organic sludges or inert materials	Anaerobic degradation of sludge resulting in methane and hydrogen sulphide production. Sediment altered by layer of sludge or inert particles blanketing the substratum	Elimination of bottom-dwelling organisms, sediment community changed, reduction in diversity, increase in species exploiting raised nutrient supply of sludge
Nutrient run-off, e.g. nitrate and phosphate fertilisers	Cultural eutrophication, i.e. increased nutrient content	Algal blooms, decline in community diversity[†]
Acid rain[‡]	pH decline, higher concentration of aluminium and other toxic metals	Decrease in community diversity and density. Intolerant species eliminated and may be increase in tolerant species[‡]

* BOD (see Table 10.1 footnote)
[†] See Chapter 8 for discussion of eutrophication.
[‡] See Chapter 12 for discussion of acid rain.

be acute or chronic. Acute effects are rapid, obvious, often fatal and normally non-reversible. Lethal concentrations (LC) of chemicals to selected organisms are often expressed as LC_{50} or LC_{70}, which indicates the percentage of organisms killed at a given concentration of chemical. Since exposure time is important this is normally linked to a specific exposure time, e.g. 48 h-LC_{50} (see Chapter 8 for a full discussion). The Camelford accident on 6 July 1988 is a good example of the potentially acute effects of pollution incidents. Aluminium sulphate (used to floc-culate suspended matter from water at treatment plants) was mistakenly pumped into a water main serving Camelford. This severely affected tap water quality with many people complaining of adverse effects, including a range of symptoms from sore throats to nausea and muscle cramps and joint pains. In order to alleviate the drinking water problem, the water authority flushed out the water distribution pipes into the Rivers Camel and Allen. River water pH dropped to 4.5 and aluminium concentration reached 100 mg l^{-1}. Large fish kills resulted (between 43 000 and 61 000 salmon and brown trout alone were lost) although invertebrates were apparently not affected (Mason, 1995).

Chronic toxic effects occur after long term exposure to low con-centrations or doses of pollutants. These effects are often sub-lethal although on occasion may ultimately cause death. Sub-lethal effects are reflected in a lowering of the growth or reproduction of an organism, i.e. physiological impact, or perhaps impairment of behavioural responses. Chronic pollution may be cumulative with the effect increased by a series of doses. It is possible, however, for a contaminated river to recover from chronic pollution if appropriate remedial and control measures are taken. The effect of chronic exposure of aquatic flora, fauna and micro-organisms to pollutants varies with organism, often with the stage in development, and with specific pollutant. The ultimate impact on community structure and function, the cycling of nutrients, and energy production and transfer through the ecosystem is influenced by the individual organism and population level changes induced by the pollutants. The changes in community structure, density and diversity induced by pollutants can be large (see Haslam, 1990). One example of the impact of low-level chronic pollution is found in the contamination of freshwater, originating either from agricultural run-off or from industrial discharges, by organochlorine pesticides, e.g. polychlorinated biphenyls (PCBs). Organochlorines are recalcitrant (see Chapter 8), hydrophobic and lipophilic, i.e. lipid soluble, so they are readily bioaccumulated and they are biomagnified (see Chapter 8). Predators at the top of food chains including otters have been severely affected by chronic exposure to PCBs in their prey and in water (see Mason, 1995).

Pollutants are often not present singly but mixtures of chemicals contaminate freshwater ecosystems. The chemicals may exert individual influences or they may interact, adding to the difficulty in predicting impacts of pollutants. On occasions the combined effect of the pollutants may be:

1. *additive* where the effect of the pollutants is simply the sum of the effects of the pollutants on their own, e.g. zinc and copper;
2. *synergistic* where the deleterious or toxic effects are significantly increased by interactions between the pollutants, e.g. nickel and chromium;
3. *antagonistic* where the toxicity is reduced due to interactions between compounds, e.g. calcium reduces the impact of aluminium.

Basic ecotoxicology techniques (often using LC values) are currently employed to predict the impact of a given chemical on specified fresh-water organisms in an attempt to quantify the toxicity of the chemical (see Chapter 8). These are largely inappropriate to the prediction of ecosystem-level impacts, or even to predict the response of other organisms to a pollutant. Considerable scientific work should be under-taken to identify ecosystem effects of various pollutants and their impacts on a range of different taxa. An understanding of the mechanisms involved in pollutant damage and the development of monitoring to establish the extent and nature of any ecosystem damage is essential. It should be remembered that the impact of pollutants on the physiological responses of organisms occurs often within minutes or hours; community- and ecosystem-level effects may take months or even years to become evident. The Environment Act 1995 requires con-sideration of the environment and conservation (see below). This sets a considerable challenge to scientists to define impacts on ecosystems and design management strategies to avoid, control and remediate deleterious effects.

River pollution, of course, is important for the quality of drinking water (see above). Equally important is the contamination of ground-water which has considerable impact on achieving drinking water quality standards (see the *Cambridge Water* case below). This is especially the case in South East England where there is a heavy dependence on aquifers for public water supply. Contamination arises from the same range of point and non-point sources and includes the same range of pollutants as surface water (Table 10.1). Particular concerns in the United Kingdom at present relate to pollutants arising from landfill leachate (see Chapter 9); pesticides and nitrates deriving from agricultural land (see Chapter 8) and acid mine drainage; and non-aqueous phase liquids from industry, especially solvents (see Grey *et al.*, 1995, for a discussion of issues and needs relevant to UK groundwater). Contamination of groundwater supplies varies with meteorological conditions. For example flooding may lead to high levels of contamination. The link between groundwater and surface water should not be neglected (Fig. 10.1). Groundwater recharges surface water from springs and seepages into rivers and maintains wetland ecosystems. Any decline in the quantity or quality of groundwater has a subsequent impact on surface water ecosystems and the achievement of river water quality. Remediation of groundwater is often technically complex and expensive to achieve: ideally this precious water resource should be adequately protected from contamination.

An overview of the statutory and regulatory framework

As there have been considerable changes in the statutory framework that applies to water it is useful to give an outline of the major statutes. The Water Resources Act 1991 provides for the management, regulation and operations of water resources. In particular the Act provides for the establishment and the grant of powers and regulatory functions to the National Rivers Authority (NRA) including water management, licensing and extraction, drainage, water pollution control, fisheries management, conservation. These powers have now been transferred to the Environment Agency under the Environment Act 1995.

The Water Industry Act 1991 provides for privatised water companies to carry out the functions of providing water and sewerage services. There are 31 companies serving 10 geographical regions in England and Wales. There is a regulatory body, the Office of Water Services (OFWAT), headed by a director general to regulate the activities of the privatised companies (see: The Water Industry Act 1991). Arrangements in Scotland and Northern Ireland are different. The 1991 Act establishes a Drinking Water Inspectorate (DWI) for the regulation of drinking water supplied for domestic or food production purposes. Such drinking water must be wholesome at the time of supply. Companies are thereby not liable for the supply of water which may deteriorate within a consumer's premises. The only exceptions are copper, lead and zinc. The water companies, within certain exceptions, are required to introduce or modify water treatment systems to reduce the extent that the consumer may be exposed to the harmful effects of these metals.

The Statutory Water Companies Act 1991 applies to the 28 statutory water companies who supply water to customers under various private Acts of Parliament. There are specific powers that apply to these companies distinct from the water and sewerage companies. The Land Drainage Act 1991 applies to the land drainage aspects of water management carried out by internal drainage boards. Many of the powers in the 1991 Act have been consolidated from the now repealed Land Drainage Act 1976. The Water Consolidation (Consequential Provisions) Act 1991 incorporates a consolidation of the various past Water Acts and fills in the gaps in the incorporation of the law undertaken by legislation.

The legislation outlined above envisages several organisations with regulatory functions over water quality. There is also a limited role for local authorities (see below). The main organisations and their key functions in water regulation are as follows:

- Her Majesty's Inspectorate for Pollution (HMIP) oversees discharge consents and supervises the system of integrated pollution control (IPC) under Part 1 of the Environmental Protection Act 1990 and under s. 138(2) of the Water Industry Act 1991 (outlined in Chapter 6). It is intended that from April 1996 the work of the HMIP will be subsumed into the new Environment Agency set up under the Environment Act 1995.
- The quality of drinking water is regulated by the Drinking Water Inspectorate of the Ministry of Agriculture, Fisheries and Food (MAFF). Marine pollution is the specific responsibility of the Ministry of Agriculture, Fisheries and Food (see Chapter 11).
- Under the Water Resources Act 1991, originally the National Rivers Authority (NRA) and now the Environment Agency under the Environment Act 1995, enforce the provisions for the discharge consents under IPC. The discharge of prescribed substances falls under the application of the best available techniques not entailing excessive costs principle (BATNEEC). Waste disposal that falls under Part 2 of the Environment Protection Act 1990 imposes a duty of care to take all reasonable steps to ensure that the disposal is not harmful to others. The NRA works in close co-operation with HMIP, now subsumed into the new Environment Agency. The monitoring of effluent discharges into watercourses and the general quality of rivers fall within its remit. The setting of standards for discharges is an important responsibility. This is carried out through:
  - monitoring of facilities and equipment for sampling and the maintenance of quality assurance;
  - the maintenance of the means to record discharges;
  - maintaining permanent records of discharges and the conditions relating to discharge consents.

As noted above the newly created Environment Agency established under the Environment Act 1995 has been given objectives to protect and enhance the environment taken as a whole and to contribute to sustainable development subject to legislation and taking into account any likely costs.

▶ Water management and pollution

Historical developments and the Environment Act 1995

Part 2 of the Control of Pollution Act 1974 concerns water quality and effluent discharges. After privatisation of the water industry the Water Act 1989 repealed much of the 1974 Act. Reorganisation of the legislation on the water industry took place in 1991 following the Law Commission Report No. 198 *Report on the Consolidation of the Legislation Relating to Water* (Cmnd. 1483) and resulted in the Water Industry Act 1991, with the setting up of the National Rivers Authority (NRA) for England and Wales (in Scotland the Rivers Purification Boards). Since then the Environment Act 1995 has set up a new Environment Agency possessing the powers of the NRA for England and Wales. In Scotland there is a Scottish Environmental Protection Agency with general duties as to pollution control and water. The new Agency for England and Wales has statutory duties under the 1995 Act to promote:

● The conservation and enhancement of the natural beauty and amenity of inland and coastal waters
● The conservation of flora and fauna which are dependent on an aquatic environment
● The use of waters and land for recreational purposes.

The new Agency for Scotland has statutory duties under the 1995 Act to promote:

● The cleanliness of rivers and other inland waters and groundwater in Scotland
● The cleanliness of tidal waters in Scotland
● The conservation as far as practicable of the water resources of Scotland
● The conservation and enhancement of the natural beauty and amenity of inland and coastal waters
● The conservation of flora and fauna which are dependent on an aquatic environment.

Comprehensive powers are provided under the Water Resources Act 1991 for the proper management of water resources. There are general duties on the NRA (now the Environment Agency) to conserve, redistribute, augment and secure the proper use of water resources in England and Wales. This includes powers under s. 20 to make water resource management schemes with water undertakers and under s. 21 to provide the Secretary of State with draft schemes for the minimum flow of inland waters. Part II of the 1991 Act contains powers for the licensing of the abstraction of water (see: ss. 24–37 of the Water

Resources Act 1991). There are detailed regulatory controls over the issuing and modification and revocation of licences under Chapter II of Part II of the 1991 Act.

Section 93 of the Water Industry Act 1991 has a new Part IIIA and s. 93(a) inserted by Sch. 22, art. 102 of the Environment Act 1995. This imposes a duty on every water undertaker to promote the efficient use of water by its customers. Additional powers are contained in new ss. 93 B–D inserted into the Water Industry Act 1991. These powers supplement the powers granted to the Office of Water Services (OFWAT) for the economic regulation of the water companies. Sections 93 B–D allow the Director of OFWAT the powers to determine and publish standards of performance related to the new duties to promote the efficient use of water. In this context it is useful to note that recently published government policy favours the use of water meters (see: *Water Conservation: Government Action*, DoE, 1995).

There are additional powers under Chapter III of Part II of the 1991 Act for dealing with drought. Section 73(1) provides the Secretary of State with powers to make an ordinary drought order where because of 'an exceptional shortage of rain' a serious deficiency of water supplies in an area exists or is threatened. The meaning of the term 'exceptional shortage of rain' is not clear, and the period of time over which this is determined is not stipulated. For example, should average rainfall over a year be used, or is a shorter period, such as four months, appropriate even if rainfall was normal prior to this period? A drought order may provide prohibitions on the use of water and may specify modifications or restrictions to the licensing of the abstraction of water. There are powers to make an 'emergency drought order' where there is a serious deficiency of supply because of shortage of rain and the economic or social well-being of persons in the affected area is likely to be affected as a consequence. An emergency drought order may provide for the same restrictions as set out above for an ordinary drought order. In addition, an emergency drought order may authorise the use of standpipes and water tanks.

The request to make a drought order may be made by the NRA (now the Environment Agency) or the water undertaker. It is an offence to breach a drought order under s. 80 of the 1991 Act. Drought orders are made in the form of statutory instruments and there are procedural rules about public consultation including the holding of a public inquiry under the Drought Order (Inquiries Procedures) Rules 1984 (see: SI 1984 No. 999 and Sch. 8 of the 1991 Act). While there is provision for compensation payable (Sch. 9) where existing rights are affected and loss or damage caused, these provisions are aimed primarily at the entry to or occupation of land or restricting the taking of water or its discharge. There is no provision for any reduction in water bills because of a failure of supplies during a period of drought.

In fact a drought order may be an effective indemnity against any claim for a reduction of water charges. Section 79(3) specifically excludes from compensation payments the inter- ruption of supply by preserving the rights of water or sewerage under- takers to recover their charges. The use of drought orders is likely to prove controversial.

The new Environment Agency has new powers under Sch. 22 of the Environment Act 1995 which inserts into the Water Resources Act 1991 a new s. 79A allowing the grant of a drought permit to a water undertaker. A drought permit may specify the source of water and the period for which water extraction may be granted. This enables water undertakers to have access to a wider variety of water resources than would otherwise be possible. There is a similar system of enforcement for drought permits to that which applies for drought orders under s. 80 of the Water Resources Act 1991.

Water pollution control: the statutory controls

The water pollution control system under Part II of the Water Resources Act 1991 applies to coastal waters and territorial waters extending 3 miles from shore. It also has application to inland freshwaters including lakes, ponds, specified reservoirs, rivers and watercourses. Finally, the definition of controlled water under the 1991 Act extends to ground-water. It may be noticed that the breadth of the definition of controlled water is sufficient to cover almost all water sources, including artificial constructions such as canals.

Pollution control rests on a distinction between 'point' source pollution and 'non-point' pollution explained by Mumma (1995, p. 25):

> Water pollution arises from two kinds of source: 'point sources' and 'non-point' or diffuse sources. As the names indicate, point sources are clearly identifiable sources of discharges into water courses, typified by a drain or a pipe deliberately constructed to conduct effluent from a particular point into a watercourse. Non-point sources are diffuse and not so easily identifiable. Often the discharge is the incidental and unintended consequence of other activity (for instance, the dressing of land with pesticides or nitrate fertilisers or leachate from a landfill). There are, however, areas of overlap; accidents, for instance can cause both point source and diffuse pollution.

Point source contamination of aquatic ecosystems arises from industry, agriculture and fisheries, and the urban environment (Table 10.1). Such contamination may be intermittent or continuous. Inter-mittent pollution events, e.g. urban stormwater discharges exacerbated by heavy rainfall, can be as damaging to an ecosystem as continuous discharges. The concentration of pollutants originating from point sources often tends to decline rapidly with distance from their point of origin. Common diffuse or non-point source discharges arise from sources such as agricultural run-off or acid deposition and may have severe ecological implications (see Chapters 8 and 12). In the case of toxic chemicals, e.g. biocides, diffuse sources of pollution tend to result in low environmental concentrations of the pollutants, their presence and impact often only becoming apparent after accumulation in organisms, e.g. PCBs and otters (above).

Adopting the distinction, in the case of 'point sources' pollution is controlled principally through a regulatory authority giving in advance consent for effluent to be discharged into a watercourse subject to specified conditions and controls. In the case of 'non-point' sources the pollution is primarily intended to be prevented through tight controls precluding discharges from taking place. Where discharges do take place there are legal controls in an attempt to minimise the effects of the discharges. However, both 'point sources' and 'non-point' systems of control are subject to accidental or unintended events. In the case of 'point source' pollution an attempt is made to build into the system of pollution control strategic plans where for example there is unexpected flooding.

The lawful discharge of polluting effluent through the granting of consents must be confined to certain limits in order to prevent pollution becoming too burdensome for the watercourses. Setting limits on lawful discharges is therefore an important part of the system of water pollution control. In the United Kingdom there is a 'water quality objective' (WQO) aimed at ensuring discharges do not exceed certain parameters. WQOs are fixed on the basis of the uses to which the surface water is to be put. It is important to remember that any surface water may have several uses, for example abstraction for drinking water, fish farming, and fishing and other amenity uses, and must be managed appropriately. Once the use of the watercourse is determined then appropriate standards are placed on individual discharges to ensure that the water resource remains within the designated WQO. The standards may vary with discharge and indeed location. If the ability of the water to assimilate and dissipate the impact of discharges is high then relatively low standards are likely to be placed on the discharge. The WQO approach is criticised for two reasons. First, individual quality standards are difficult to enforce and, secondly, minimum values tend to be set to meet the WQO, often meaning that the contaminants are treated little prior to discharge. A further problem relates to insufficient environmental data being available on many substances to set well informed consent levels, even though ecotoxicology tests may have been performed (see Chapters 1, 8 and above). A number of European countries adopt a different philosophy, which is that pollutant discharge should not occur and that recycling or recovery of the pollutant should be encouraged. On the basis of this philosophy uniform emission standards (UESs) are set. UESs limit all discharges to surface water to a uniform standard irrespective of the water use, existing water quality or potential for dilution (see Mason, 1995, Chapter 12 for a discussion of the management of water resources).

Part of the standards for WQOs has come from European Community Directives where dangerous substances form a 'Black List' (see Appendix). In the United Kingdom a similar list is known as the 'Red List' (Table 10.3). There are a variety of Community Directives that contain reference to such substances, such as the Dangerous Substances in Water Directive 76/464/EEC, which sets out a prescribed list of substances and chemicals that are banned or any discharge which must be reduced to safe levels (also see: the Trade Effluents (Prescribed Processes and Substances) Regulations 1989, SI 1989 No. 1156 as amended by SI 1990 No. 1629 and SI 1992 No. 339). The Surface Waters (Dangerous Substances) (Classification) Regulations 1989, SI 1989 No. 2286 provide a list of dangerous substances according to various EC Directives which include mercury (82/176/EEC and 84/156/EEC), cadmium (83/513/EEC), hexachlorocylohexane (84/491/EEC), carbon

Table 10.3   Initial UK Red List

Aldrin
Atrazine
Azinphos-methyl
Cadmium and its compounds
1,2-Dichloroethane
DDT
Dichlorvos
Dieldrin
Endosulfan
Endrin
Fenitrothion
Gamma-hexachlorocylohexane
Hexachlorobenzene
Hexachlorobutadiene
Malathion
Mercury and its compounds
Pentachlorophenol
Polychlorinated biphenyls
Simazine
Tributyltin compounds
Trichlorobenzene
Trifluralin
Triphenyltin compounds

tetrachloride, PCP and DDT (86/280/EEC), and aldrin, dieldrin, isodrin, hexachlorobenzene, hexachlorobutadiene and chloroform (88/347/EEC). There is provision for further Directives to be made as 'daughter Directives' to the main Directive. Also included in the United Kingdom are the Surface Waters (Classification) Regulations 1989, SI 1989 No. 1148.

The Secretary of State is empowered under s. 82 of the Water Resources Act 1991 to set water quality objectives. This involves, in the past the NRA and now the Environment Agency, exercising their water pollution powers to ensure that such objectives are met.

Setting up a statutory formulation for water quality objectives has proved a time-consuming and difficult task (UK Groundwater Forum, 1995). Six categories are to be adopted mirroring the requirements of EC Directives. These are:

1. Fisheries ecosystem (see: EC Directive 75/440 EEC and the Surface Waters (River Ecosystem) (Classification) Regulations 1994, SI 1994 No. 1057 and the Surface Waters (Classification) Regulations 1989, SI 1989 No. 1148)
2. Abstraction for drinking water supply (see: EC Directive 75/440 EEC and the Surface Waters (Classification) Regulations 1989, SI 1989 No. 1148)
3. Agricultural abstractions (see: EC Directive 75/440 EEC and the Surface Waters (Classification) Regulations 1989, SI 1989 No. 1148)
4. Industrial abstraction
5. Special ecosystem
6. Watersports.

The Groundwater Directive 80/68/EEC provides two lists of dangerous substances. List I includes organohalogens, mercury, cadmium, cyanides and substances with carcinogenic properties. Discharges containing any of the substances on List I are prohibited. List II contains many of the substances contained in the Community 'Black List' of dangerous substances and may only be discharged if there is appropriate authorisation (see Appendix for a full description of List I and List II).

Account has also to be taken in the law in the United Kingdom of Directive 91/271/EEC on urban wastewater treatment. This Directive stipulates minimum requirements for the treatment of urban wastewater and disposal sludge. Its aim is to encourage reuse of water and the development of improved wastewater management. Originally in the United Kingdom sewage treatment was designed to avoid disease and odour and to protect potable water sources. Now approximately 30 per cent of all UK potable water supplies are connected with reuse of effluent after abstraction downstream from its discharge point and further treatment. The treatment and disposal of sludge is exceptionally important and accounts for as much as 40 per cent of the operating costs of a wastewater treatment plant. In the United Kingdom approximately 40 million tonnes (wet weight) of sludge are produced annually. There has been considerable debate about the best means of disposing of this waste. The sludge is treated, e.g. by anaerobic digestion and volume reduction processes, not only to minimise nuisance and adverse environmental impacts, but also to make for easy and cheap transport and disposal (see Mason, 1995; Horan, 1990; or Harrison, 1990 for a description of processes). Approximately 67 per cent of sludge is disposed of to land. The largest portion of this is used in agriculture and horticulture while the remainder goes to land reclamation or landfill. Only 4 per cent of sludge is incinerated (see Chapter 9), while 29 per cent is disposed of at sea. Sea disposal will shortly no longer be an option (see Chapter 11) and it is likely that co-disposal of this waste in landfill will become increasingly important (see Chapter 9) since an increase in agricultural use is unlikely.

There is also considerable importance attached to Directive 91/676/ EEC on the protection of waters against pollution caused by nitrate from agricultural sources. This Directive places restrictions on fertiliser use and sets maximum permissible nitrate levels in drinking water. Geographical areas are zoned according to their vulnerability to nitrate pollution (see Chapter 8 for a full discussion of the impact of nitrates on aquatic systems, i.e. cultural eutrophication, and in drinking water).

There are also Directives on fish life. Directive 78/659/EEC is on the quality of freshwaters that require protection or improvement to support fish life. The Directive divides water into salmonid and cyprinid according to fish species to be found in the water. In the United Kingdom the majority of water (88 per cent) is salmonid, the remainder cyprinid. The designation sets water quality standards that must be met within a five year period. There is a Directive on shell fish (Directive 79/923/EEC) which is intended to ensure that Member States will meet designated standards within six years.

Preventative measures

The Environment Act 1995 provides the Environment Agency with new powers to serve a notice on potential polluters requiring them to carry out works to prevent pollution or to clean up water pollution. Schedule 22 of the Environment Act 1995 contains new ss. 161A–C inserted into the Water Resources Act 1991 which make it an offence not to comply with such a notice. There are procedures contained in the new sections for serving notice and, in the event of non-compliance, taking action. If the person on whom the notice is served fails to comply with the notice then powers under s. 161 of the 1991 Act may be used which allow the Environment Agency powers to carry out work and recover costs.

Discharges

The requirement of a discharge 'consent' is authorised under the Water Resources Act 1991 through a consent document that may set the limits on effluent discharged into watercourses or rivers. The 'consent' is analogous to a licence which contains the authorisation for the discharge together with details of procedures and conditions. A consent provides the legality for discharges of effluent. Schedule 10 of the Water Resources Act 1991 prescribes procedures for the obtaining of consents for the discharge of effluent (see: Department of the Environment Circular 17/84). There is a periodic review of consents undertaken by the NRA, now the Environment Agency. There are powers to revoke or modify a consent as a result of the review. However, each consent must specify a period or periods where there cannot be a modification or revocation. A modification or revocation must also contain a specified period, not less than four years, during which a subsequent notice may not be served (see: new ss. 90 A–B inserted into the Water Resources Act 1991 by Sch. 22 of the Environment Act 1995). In a situation where it is deemed necessary to issue a revocation or modification within the protected period, then compensation is payable to the discharger of effluent should there be a modification or revocation. These procedures are intended to give some security to the discharger. A limited amount of deregulation to these procedures has been introduced by amendments contained in Sch. 22 of the Environment Act 1995. This includes the removal of the provision for objectors to be able to call in a consent application and the suspension of modifications or amendments until appeals are heard. The only exception is in a matter where the Environment Agency considers there has to be immediate effect on public health grounds or to minimise pollution.

Consents may take two forms, numeric and non-numeric. Numeric consents specify quantitative limits for discharges, usually expressed in terms of the concentration or load of the determinants. Limits may be expressed as a percentage of the whole or in absolute limits. The former is a standard that the discharge must not exceed at any time. For example, many different discharge consents relate to permitted effluent biological oxygen demand (BOD) (Table 10.1). BOD is a measure of the biologically oxidisable, i.e. biodegradable, material present in an effluent. This is significant because too high a BOD and water is likely to become deoxygenated and, therefore, unable to sustain many aquatic organisms, e.g. fish (Table 10.2). There can be instantaneous spot sampling in order to discover if there is compliance with the standard. The latter is measured over a period of time and compliance is based on a standard that need not be complied with all the time. Non-numeric consents deal with discharges where it is not possible to set quantitative limits. The consent may require technical conditions, which are requirements that apply to the process of discharge to ensure that there is a satisfactory standard.

Discharge consents are issued by the NRA, now the Environment Agency, under Sch. 10 of the Water Resources Act 1991. There are four procedural steps that must be followed after receipt of an application:

1. In two successive weeks notice of the discharge must be published in a local newspaper in the vicinity of where the discharge is intended to take place.
2. A copy of the notice must also be published in the *London Gazette*.
3. The relevant local authority or water undertaker in whose area the discharge is proposed should be informed with a notice setting out the details of the intended discharges.
4. In cases where the discharges are into coastal waters or within or outside the relevant territorial waters then a notice should be served on the Minister for Agriculture, Fisheries and Food and the Secretary of State for the Environment.

If it is considered that the discharge will not have an 'appreciable effect' on the water then the first three steps do not have to be taken and a discharge consent may be granted. Determining what is an appreciable effect falls under the guidance contained in DoE Circular 17/84. Broadly this covers matters relevant to the amenity of the area or of environmental significance, or where the discharge might result in a major change in the flow of the receiving waters or result in changes in water quality that may damage or affect future use of the water. It can, of course, be argued that there are inherent scientific difficulties in accurately predicting the environmental significance of a discharge (see above).

The procedures outlined above also include the receipt of written representations and call-in powers granted to the Secretary of State which may result in the holding of a local inquiry into the application. It is possible for the NRA, now the Environment Agency, to consider the past history of the discharge operator and if necessary conditions may be attached to the discharge. Such conditions as the NRA 'may think fit' include matters such as the place at which the discharge may be made, the nature, volume, origin, composition and rate of discharge, the steps that are taken to provide discharge treatment and the minimisation of the discharge. In addition, conditions may stipulate the facilities for taking samples and the keeping of records and the making of returns.

The regulation of discharges is carefully monitored. Periodic regular reviews are undertaken which may result in notice being served on the discharger revoking consent or setting conditions. Some degree of certainty for the operators of discharges is provided. There is a restriction that conditions when imposed must settle a time period, not less than two years, during which no revocation or variation in the discharge conditions may be made. If a modification or revocation is made within the two year period then compensation is payable. The compensation is not payable in circumstances that are not reasonably foreseen.

There are similar powers of revocation and modification granted to the Secretary of State. These powers are expressed in the form of allowing the Secretary of State to make a direction to the NRA, now the Environment Agency. Such a direction may be made in three situations:

1. To enable the government to comply with any Community Directive
2. To make provision for the protection of public health or of aquatic flora and fauna
3. As a result of advice or representations received by the Secretary of State.

It is noteworthy that the two year rule whereby no modification or revocation may be made does not apply in the case of the first two grounds.

Disposal of waste through sewers

Approximately 6.8×10^6 m^3 (1.5×10^9 gal) of industrial and other waste-water are discharged directly to sewers daily in addition to the 8×10^6 m^3 (1.8×10^9 gal) from domestic sources. The majority of this wastewater is treated by conventional treatment processes at approximately 5000 sewage treatment works. Sewage treatment involves several stages (Fig. 10.2) including: (i) preliminary treatment during which large objects and grit are removed and storm flows are separated; (ii) primary sedimentation during which suspended solids are removed, forming sludge; and (iii) secondary or biological treatment during which dissolved colloidal organics are removed by microbial oxidation, usually in trickling filters or activated sludge tanks. Occasionally a tertiary treatment is undertaken involving further processes to remove bacteria, biological oxygen demand (BOD), suspended solids, toxic compounds or phosphates and nitrates, which results in a high-quality effluent (Mason, 1995; Harrison, 1990, for a description of the treatment process; Horan, 1990, gives a detailed analysis of the processes). Effluent which has undergone tertiary treatment can be abstracted downstream from a discharge as potable water. The extent of treatment provided for wastewater at sewage treatment works depends to some extent on the WQOs for the receiving water. It is important that any industrial or trade effluent entering sewage works should be carefully controlled (see below). This is particularly so since elevated concentrations of toxic compounds entering a plant can severely affect the efficiency and kinetics of secondary treatment, a biological process. In extreme cases the process will break down entirely and the final effluent entering

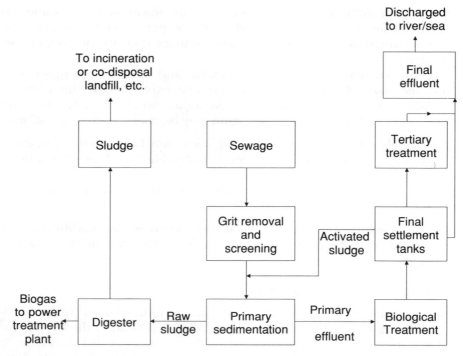

Fig. 10.2 Simplified flow diagram of a sewage treatment process.

water systems will have had virtually no secondary treatment.

The disposal of waste through sewers forms a distinct part of the system of discharge controls. Historically the provision of water and the discharge of sewage has been treated as forming a coherent whole. Since water privatisation, private water and sewerage undertakers provide the public water supply and operate sewage treatment works. This is a lucrative activity operating as a commercial enterprise. There are important environmental controls that are required to be operated by the sewerage undertakers under Chapter III of Part IV of the Water Industry Act 1991. The sewerage undertaker is under a statutory duty to provide a sewerage system under s. 94 of the 1991 Act. This duty, to allow for discharge and disposal of waste, applies to *both* domestic and trade or industrial effluent. Schedule 22 of the Environment Act 1995 introduces into the Water Industry Act 1991 a new s. 101A which provides a duty on sewerage undertakers to provide a public sewer under certain conditions, with the costs being borne by the customer.

Account must also be taken of future trends and the future needs of the industry when making provision for the disposal of trade effluent. The crucial requirement for trade effluent is a trade effluent consent. It is a criminal offence to discharge trade waste without such a consent.

The definition of trade effluent is under s. 141(1) of the Water Industry Act 1991 and is widely drafted to include any liquid wholly or partly produced in the course of any trade or industry carried on in trade premises. Thus the definition is sufficiently broad to include liquid discharges from industry, shops, agriculture, research institutions and launderettes (see: *Thames Water Authority* v. *Blue and White Launderettes Ltd* [1980] 1 WLR 700). The main exception is from domestic premises. The sewerage operator receives an application for consent from the person wishing to make the discharge at least two months prior to the commencement of the discharge. The costs of undertaking the discharge are a central feature of the discussion between the undertaker and the discharger. The emphasis is placed on the discharger to minimise costs by using processes that make discharges less harmful. There is a statutory framework contained in ss. 121(4)(a) and 142 of the 1991 Act.

There are a number of detailed procedural arrangements regarding applications for a trade effluent consent. The application must state the nature and composition of the effluent, the maximum quantity of effluent that is proposed to be discharged in any one day, and the maximum rate of discharge. There is wide provision for agreements to be reached between the discharger and the sewerage undertaker.

The regulatory system for trade effluent discharges rests on a number of enforcement procedures (see: Water Authorities Association, *Trade Effluent Discharges to the Sewer* (September 1986)). A strict liability offence is committed by the occupier who discharges from the relevant trade premises without consent. The enforcement of this requirement may involve the commercial sewerage operator. It is assumed that consent conditions may operate to control effluent discharges. This involves a degree of self-regulation. It is expected that the sewerage operator will control discharges in the light of the most economical costs and available techniques. While it may appear that the undertaker has the crucial decision whether to grant a consent or not, there is an appeal open to the discharger to the Director of Water Services on the basis that any reasonable application for consent cannot be refused by the sewerage undertaker.

There is also some flexibility in the way the system operates. Consent conditions may be varied, revoked or added to by notice issued by the sewerage undertaker under s. 124 of the Water Industry Act 1991. Similar provisions to those discussed above, concerning discharge consents, apply for a two year period. There is a right of appeal to the Director General of Water Services against a variation.

Criminal offences and other remedies for water pollution

The use of the criminal law is a recurring theme in the legislation regulating the water and sewerage industries. The Water Resources Act 1991 contains enforcement through consent procedures where the criminal law applies for failure to obtain the relevant consent. Section 85(1) creates a number of offences to cause or knowingly permit any poisonous, noxious or polluting matter or solid waste to enter any controlled waters. If a defendant is charged with the 'cause' part of the offence it is unnecessary to show that the defendant acted intentionally or negligently (see: *Alphacell* v. *Woodward* [1972] AC 824 discussed below).

Section 90(1) makes it an offence to remove any part of the bed of inland waters so as to cause it to be carried away in suspension. Subsection (2) makes it an offence to cause or permit vegetation to be cut or uprooted so as to fall into inland waters and fail to take reasonable steps to remove the vegetation. Many of these offences employ the term 'causing or knowingly permitting'. The interpretation of this term was considered in the House of Lords case of *Alphacell* v. *Woodward* [1972] AC 824. Polluted water from the appellants' paper factory entered two settling tanks adjoining a river. There was an overflow system which became activated when the water reached a certain level. Owing to a blockage in the inlet to the pumps the polluted water overflowed and entered the river. The defendants failed to prevent the overflow. The defendants were found guilty contrary to s. 2(1)(a) of the Rivers (Prevention of Pollution) Act 1951. Although there was no evidence that the defendants knew that pollution was taking place or that they had been negligent, the House of Lords upheld the conviction on the grounds that, as Lord Salmon explained, although the defendants 'did not intend to cause the pollution they intended to do the acts which caused it'. There is no hard and fast rule that the courts will always adopt a strict interpretation of the statute, thereby finding guilt without proof that the defendant either ought to have seen the pollution or was negligent (see: *Southern Water Authority* v. *Pegrum* [1989] Crim LR 442). The fact of pollution taking place appears sufficient to find criminal liability even if full intention is not proved on the part of the defendant. The interpretation of the statute will largely depend on the facts of each case. The degree of knowledge on the part of the defendant required by the court to uphold a prosecution will be assessed in all the circumstances of the case (see: *Price* v. *Cromack* [1975] 2 All ER 113 and *Wychavon DC* v. *NRA* [1993] 2 All ER 440).

It is also possible to interpret quite widely various statutory defences. One example of judicial approaches to interpretation is the recent decision of the House of Lords in *National Rivers Authority* v. *Yorkshire Water* (*The Times* 21 November 1994 [1994]4 All ER 274, [1995]1 All ER

225). The material facts of the case were that one night when no one was on duty at the sewerage works, an unknown person unlawfully discharged iso-octanol into the sewer. Yorkshire Water Services operated this sewer with a discharge consent for sewage into the River Spen. The iso-octanol was an unauthorised discharge. The first issue raised by the case was whether an offence had been committed. On a strict interpretation of s. 107(1)(a) of the Water Act 1989 Yorkshire Water was in breach of its consent to discharge effluent when a third party caused the discharge to be poisonous and exceed the prescribed limits of the consent. The result of the unlawful addition of iso-octonal was that the discharge by Yorkshire Water was contrary to s. 107. The second issue was whether any statutory defence was available. This involved difficulty over interpretation. The magistrates convicted Yorkshire Water, which appealed. The Crown Court quashed the conviction ruling that the water authority in law had not caused the chemical to enter the controlled water. However, an important point of law was raised and this was accepted on a case stated by the Divisional Court, and the case was considered by the House of Lords. The House of Lords held that the water company had caused poisonous, noxious and polluting matter to enter controlled waters. This finding was decided even though Yorkshire Water was not responsible for the presence of the iso-octanol. There was strict liability in the interpretation of the offence and the magistrates had correctly interpreted the law on this point. However, the House of Lords found that the company had a defence under s. 108(7) and allowed the appeal against conviction. In the interpretation of the special defence contained in s. 108(7), namely that the sewerage undertaker could not reasonably have been expected to prevent the discharge into the sewer or works, the House of Lords took a flexible approach. The case is a good illustration of the approach the courts may be likely to take in the future.

There are other examples of criminal offences in the area of water pollution. There are criminal offences specifically intended to protect fish from the effects of pollution (see above for some discussion). Section 4(1) of the Salmon and Freshwater Fisheries Act 1975 makes it an offence to pollute water containing fish so as to cause the waters to be poisonous or injurious to fish, their food or spawning grounds. There are specific regulations concerning the use of lead weights (see: Control of Pollution (Anglers' Lead Weights) Regulations 1986, SI 1986 No. 1992 and Amendment Regulations 1993, SI 1993 No. 49) and an assortment of regulations concerning the use of certain tri-organotin paints and chemicals (see: Control of Pollution (Anti Fouling Paints and Treatments) Regulations 1987, SI 1987 No. 783). Organotin compounds have a number of applications including use as biocides. Particularly important as a pollutant in aquatic environments is tributyltin (TBT) used as anti-fouling material. Its use has now largely been curtailed, but only after it became evident in the 1980s that commercial oysters (*Crassostrea gigas*) were severely affected by this chemical leaching from ship hulls, etc. It subsequently became evident that other aquatic organisms were adversely affected. TBT and similar compounds, e.g. triphenyltin, tend to accumulate in sediment so that bottom-dwelling organisms may receive particularly high exposure (see Harrison, 1990, for a more detailed discussion).

There is also the potential to take a private prosecution in respect of a breach of the law relating to pollution.

Common law pollution controls

Water pollution is also subject to liability under the common law. Liability for the pollution of groundwater may give rise to an action for negligence, nuisance or under *Rylands* v. *Fletcher* (1868) LR 3 HL 330 (see: Chapter 2):

- Negligence arises from a failure to exercise the care demanded in the circumstances. A plaintiff must show that he is owed a duty of care, that the duty has been breached and that any harm suffered is due to the breach of the duty that the plaintiff is owed. Damages may be awarded upon proof that the harm caused was foreseeable by the defendant.
- Nuisance is an interference with an occupier's use or enjoyment of land where there has been substantial injury to property or personal discomfort.
- The rule in *Rylands* v. *Fletcher* is where a landowner is strictly liable for the consequences of escapes from his property and where the landowner is engaged in a 'non-natural' use of his land. The term 'non-natural' use has never been clearly defined.

Discussion of how the three grounds apply in cases involving water pollution may be found in a recent landmark decision of the House of Lords in *Cambridge Water Company* v. *Eastern Counties Leather* [1994] 2 WLR 53. This case is likely to have a significant influence in the future development of this area of law for some considerable time. The House of Lords has placed restrictions on the availability of liability for past or historic pollution.

The facts of the case are that Eastern Counties Leather plc has manufactured leather at its works at Sawston, Cambridgeshire, since 1879. The processes used organochlorine chemicals (see Chapter 8). Up until the mid-1960s trichloroethene was used and thereafter perchlorethene. In the 1970s scientific evidence emerged that both chemicals were a possible threat to health. In the 1980s the European Community and the World Health Organisation set drinking water standards that permitted only very low quantities of these compounds (see: 80/778/EEC and DoE Circular 20/82; also: Water Supply (Water Quality) Regulations 1989, SI 1989, No. 1147). The EC Drinking Water Directive expects that wholesome water should contain no more than 1 µg l^{-1} organochlorines; in the specific case of tetrachlorethene and perchlorethene the maximum admissible concentration was to be 10 µg l^{-1}. The impact of these standards on the Cambridge Water Company was considerable. The water company had been extracting groundwater from the area of Sawston through boreholes, and by the mid-1980s perchlorethene concentrations in the groundwater were found to be between 70 and 170 µg l^{-1}. As a result of the new standards the water company found it impossible to continue using the extracted ground-water as a source of drinking water. As a consequence the water company moved its boreholes to an unpolluted zone and built a new plant at the cost of nearly £1 million. The Cambridge Water Company sought an injunction and damages from Eastern Leather, which they alleged had caused the pollution. Perclorethene was used by this company to degrease pelts and had been stored on site in drums. It was assumed that the drums had either leaked or that there had been accidental spillage allowing organochlorine to leach into groundwater. The legal basis of the claim alleged is negligence, nuisance and the rule in *Rylands* v. *Fletcher* (*Rylands* v. *Fletcher* (1868) LR 3 HL 330).

The case raises an important question concerning historic pollution. Should there be liability for acts done in the past on the basis of present-day knowledge and standards? The standards that apply to drinking water today and the scientific evidence about the harmful effects of the chemicals were not available at the time the pollution began. It can be seen that liability for historic pollution is an important principle with potentially great financial significance to commercial and industrial activities.

It is valuable to consider historic pollution in its scientific context. There is very often a delay in scientific understanding of the impact of chemicals on health and the environment. More often than not health issues become clear first. The effect of compounds in the environment often remains unclear for prolonged periods. This is particularly the case at ecosystem level where changes can take years to become apparent (see above). The impact may only develop after a threshold concentration is reached in the environment or after accumulation by the biota. The assessment of 'safe' environmental concentrations of chemicals is still largely based on predictions from ecotoxicology studies on single selected species (see Chapter 8). These may subsequently prove to give an inaccurate prediction of the potential impact on other species, communities and ecosystems. Thus even though the prescribed techniques at present have been applied to determining safe environmental loads, they may subsequently prove invalid. Should industrial concerns be held responsible where they have followed current best practice and any future problems remain unknown?

The High Court dismissed the action against Eastern Leather on the grounds that Eastern Leather could not reasonably have foreseen that the chemicals used in its processes could cause harm. Cambridge Water appealed to the Court of Appeal relying on the rule in *Rylands* v. *Fletcher*. There was no appeal made against the High Court's ruling on nuisance and negligence. However, the Court of Appeal upheld Cambridge Water's case against Eastern Leather. The Court of Appeal followed the case of *Ballard* v. *Tomlinson* (1885) 29 Ch D 115, where a brewery successfully sued for contamination of its groundwater taken from its own well. The groundwater had been contaminated by a neighbour's discharge of sewage. The Court of Appeal accepted that Eastern Leather had interfered with a natural right (the water company's ownership of the boreholes and various riparian rights that accrue) and that liability was therefore strict. The water company had shown that the pollution was caused by Eastern Leather and this was sufficient grounds for damages.

On appeal to the House of Lords the nature of liability was considered in relation to the claims made in respect of both nuisance and the rule in *Rylands* v. *Fletcher*. Lord Goff, delivering the speech of the whole House, held that there was no rule of law imposing liability for unforeseeable damage simply because the right affected was a natural right. The House of Lords held that some degree of foresight of risk is required to be proven, even in circumstances where there might be strict liability and in cases where past activities are the subject of present-day litigation. Eastern Leather's appeal was granted on the reasoning that at the time use was made of the chemicals the company could not have foreseen the harm caused by them. As a result Eastern Leather could not be liable in damages (see: *The Wagon Mound (No. 2)* [1967] 1 AC 617 upheld by Lord Goff in the Cambridge Water case).

The decision is of major significance. The House of Lords appears to have limited the effects of imposing strict liability through *Rylands* v. *Fletcher*. This is particularly important in contaminated land cases. Foreseeability of harm is now regarded as a prerequisite for the recovery of damages in nuisance and in *Rylands* v. *Fletcher*. The House of Lords' decision brought some relief to the concerns of commercial enterprises that arose from the Court of Appeal decision because of the threat of the imposition of strict liability for historic pollution. A number of conclusions may be drawn from the *Cambridge Water* case as follows:

1. Historic pollution or retrospective liability, that is liability for past acts, is now made more difficult to prove because foreseeability is a requirement of both *Rylands* v. *Fletcher* and nuisance liability.
   Foreseeability of damage of the relevant type if there was an escape

from the land of things likely to do mischief is a prerequisite of liability.

2. The House of Lords has accepted that liability in nuisance and in *Rylands* v. *Fletcher* is based on strict liability (where fault need not be proven). *Rylands* v. *Fletcher* did not create liability any more strict than liability for nuisance. Strict liability renders the defendant liable where there was an escape occurring in the course of the non-natural use of the land notwithstanding he had exercised all due care to prevent the escape from occurring.

3. The definition of 'non-natural' used in *Rylands* v. *Fletcher* is sufficient to cover the storage of substantial quantities of chemicals on industrial premises. In *Cambridge Water* the House of Lords held that Eastern Leather's use of the land through the storage of chemicals was almost a classic case of 'non-natural' use. No further definition of what 'non-natural' included was attempted but it was accepted that the creation of an industrial estate and employment was not a natural use of the land. Lord Goff explained: 'I myself, however, do not feel able to accept that the creation of employment as such even in a small industrial complex is sufficient of itself to establish a particular use as constituting a natural or ordinary use of the land' (see: [1994] 1 All ER 53 at p. 79e).

4. The House of Lords has sought to remove the differences between nuisance and *Rylands* v. *Fletcher*. Nuisance is moved closer to the law of negligence which reflects a continuing trend in liability during this century (see: Wilkinson [1994] 57 MLR 799) (see Chapter 2).

The House of Lords appears to be adopting principles from the law of negligence and applying them in the law of nuisance and the rule in *Rylands* v. *Fletcher*. If this assumption proves to be valid then it is set to question some fundamental issues. Why should strict liability be retained at all under the rule in *Rylands* v. *Fletcher*? *Cambridge Water* may be the start of a remarkable shift in civil liability whereby negligence becomes the main heading of liability for harm. Foreseeability becomes the crucial issue in determining damages.

The common law has traditionally offered a number of remedies in pollution cases. These comprise declaration or injunction and damages (see Chapter 2). A declaration merely declares the legal rights of the parties. An injunction is a court order which may prohibit, restrain or command a party to do or refrain from doing something that is injurious. It is a discretionary remedy available for serious injury. Damages is compensation payable to someone who has suffered injury. In the *Pride of Derby Angling Association* v. *British Celanese Ltd* [1952] Ch 149 an injunction and damages were granted against British Celanese Ltd for discharging industrial effluent and Derby Corporation for discharging untreated sewage. The impact of a large input of organics into a river from a source such as sewage, through raising BOD (see above), can be exceptionally large. The sewage acts as a nutrient source for microbial (particularly bacterial) growth, enhancing growth and activity. During this growth surge the micro-organisms utilise oxygen, effectively deoxygenating the water. This is reflected in fish kills and other impacts on the biota (Table 10.2). Untreated sewage often contains relatively large quantities of viral and bacterial enteric pathogens. Water contaminated with sewage is a health risk. Industrial effluent can have a variety of impacts depending on its composition (Tables 10.1 and 10.2). Damages may reflect clean-up costs and restocking the river with aquatic life. The House of Lords has held recently that actions in damages and injunctions may be made against public authorities in four situations (*X (minors)* v. *Bedfordshire CC* [1995] 3 All ER 353):

1. A breach of a statutory duty.
2. The careless performance of a statutory duty in the absence of any other common law right of action.
3. Actions based on a common law duty of care arising either from the imposition of the statutory duty or from the performance of it.
4. Misfeasance in public office either with the intention to injure the plaintiff or in the knowledge that the conduct was unlawful.

Finally, the common law has upheld the rights of riparian owners. Owners of land adjoining a watercourse, including estuaries, normally own the river bed but not the water itself. They have the right, however, to receive water subject to the natural usage of the water by other owners upstream (*Young and Company* v. *Bankier Distillery Co.* [1893] AC 698). Thus there is a right to take action as a riparian owner where the natural quality or quantity of the water is unreasonably interfered with. There is a similar riparian right of access to the reasonable enjoyment of the water, now subject to the Water Resources Act 1991. There is also a riparian right to abstract water for ordinary domestic use.

▶ **Water supplies**

Defining the role of the water companies

Water quality is used to describe water that has some use that is provided through reservoirs, groundwater, rivers and the marine environment. Public water supplies comes from a company licensed to supply water under the Water Act 1989. There are 10 water and sewerage companies which provide the vast bulk of water supplies, approximately 2×10^{10} l^{-1} day. The 10 companies also provide sewerage services and are described in some statutes as 'water and sewerage undertakers'. The term public water supplies is in contrast to private water supplies, which refers to water taken from private sources or supplied by unlicensed suppliers (discussed below). There are 28 such smaller private statutory water companies. Many were set up in the nineteenth century and have a long history of supplying water. All suppliers of water must be licensed and the licensing arrangements are undertaken by the Secretary of State for Environment and the Director General of Water Services under s. 6 of the Water Industry Act 1991.

Setting standards for water quality

Public water supplies

Section 68 and Chapter III of Part III of the Water Industry Act 1991 provide that water suppliers or undertakers are under a duty to supply wholesome water and to ensure, as far as it is reasonably practicable, that the sources of the undertaker's supply do not deteriorate in quality. The Act makes it a criminal offence for a water undertaker to supply water that is unfit for human consumption. Part IV of the Water Supply (Water Quality) Regulations 1989 prescribes the steps to be taken by the water undertaker where there is a danger of contamination from copper, lead or zinc present in the consumer's pipes.

Under s. 70(2) there is a defence for the undertaker to show that there were no reasonable grounds for suspecting that the water would be used for human consumption or that the company exercised 'all reasonable steps and exercised all due diligence for securing the water was fit for human consumption on leaving its pipes or was not used for human consumption'. The test of what is wholesome is prescribed under s. 67 of the Water Industry Act 1991 and set out in the Water Supply (Water Quality) Regulations 1989, SI 1989 No. 1147 which have been amended by the Water Supply (Water Quality) (Amendment) Regulations 1989 and 1991. These regulations take account of EC Drinking Water Directive (80/778/EEC). Water supplied for domestic purposes of drinking, washing and cooking or for the purpose of food production will be regarded as wholesome provided it meets three criteria, commonly described as Regulation 3 of the Water Quality Regulations:

1. That the water meets the standards prescribed in the regulations for the particular properties, elements, organisms or substances.
2. That the hardness or alkalinity of water which has been softened or desalinated is not below prescribed standards.
3. That the water does not contain any element, organism or substance whether alone or in combination at a concentration or value which would be detrimental to public health.

The monitoring of water is undertaken on the basis of a discrete water supply zone. This is defined as an area designated by the water company by reference to source and where not more than 50 000 people reside. It is possible that the designation of a zone may have an effect on the monitoring of water quality. In Scotland, for example, the number of small supply zones was high. Gradual improvements have been made to water quality by reducing the number of zones from 682 in 1992 to 663 in 1993 (see: ENDS Report 240, January 1995, p. 10, *Drinking Water Quality in Scotland 1993* (Scottish Office, 1995)).

The regulations contain 11 national standards that are interpreted over either three-monthly or twelve-monthly periods. There are specific parameters (66 in total) and descriptive standards for the testing of water quality. These are categorised into six groups:

1. Organoleptic (4 parameters), e.g. colour, odour
2. Physicochemical (15 parameters), e.g. temperature, pH, conductivity
3. Substances undesirable in excessive amounts (24 parameters), e.g. nitrates, oxidisability, zinc
4. Toxic substances (13 parameters), e.g. arsenic, cadmium, pesticides
5. Microbiological (6 parameters), e.g. faecal coliforms, sulphite-reducing clostridia
6. Minimum concentration of softened water (4 parameters), e.g. total hardness, alkalinity.

Consumers' taps within the supply zone are used to monitor supply. The exact number of samples depends on the population served, the parameter and the water source. The Secretary of State has powers to authorise sampling from strategic points other than consumers' taps. There are guidelines for the method of taking samples as a result of a recent ruling from the Court of Appeal (see: *Attorney General's Reference* (No. 2 of 1994) [1995] 2 All ER 1000). (See Gray, 1994, for a full analysis of drinking water quality.)

It is clear from the above outline that there is a degree of self-regulation in the application of water quality standards. In the first instance the monitoring of water quality is undertaken by the water companies subject to checks by local authorities and the Drinking Water Inspectorate. Local authorities receive regular amounts of information from water companies on the quality of drinking water in their area. The local authority may also take its own samples. If it is dissatisfied with the results of its findings it is under a duty to inform the water company. If it fails to receive adequate satisfaction then a report may be made to the Secretary of State for enforcement action. Monitoring consists of taking a minimum number of samples over a specified time scale. There is a Public Register of results of monitoring that must be made available on demand. Annual reports are made by local authorities in a prescribed manner and water companies, in their annual reports, must include a commentary on the supply of water.

There are considerable enforcement powers available under s. 18 of the Water Industry Act 1991 where there is reasonable cause to believe that a public water supplier is in contravention of any enforceable statutory duty. This includes contravention of regulations or lapses in the system of monitoring supplies. Section 19 provides some exception from prosecution in cases where the breach is trivial and does not warrant prosecution or where there is an undertaking to stop current practices and introduce changes. Prosecution proceedings may be instituted in respect of s. 70 of the 1991 Act for the offence of supplying water unfit for human consumption.

The procedures for enforcement are straightforward. A 'notice of intention to enforce' is first issued giving the undertaker time to respond. This response may include a programme of work or the introduction of new measures to facilitate or to comply with the required standards for drinking water quality. The Secretary of State may take into consideration the parameters covered by the Drinking Water Directive and may make provisional or final orders to ensure compliance.

The Drinking Water Inspectorate is responsible for initiating enforcement action on behalf of the Secretary of State in the following circumstances:

● When water quality is breached and the breach is not trivial or where it is likely to recur.
● When there is a breach of one of the enforceable regulations, for example Regulation 3 of the Water Quality Regulations (see above), such as sampling analysis or providing information on water treatment.
● When existing undertakings or time-limited relaxations authorised by Regulation 4 expire before the necessary improvements have been made.

Normally no action will be taken in circumstances where the company takes remedial action and demonstrates that there is compliance with the regulations.

It was envisaged that the standards of water quality set by the Drinking Water Directive would be fully implemented by 1985. In practice this has not proved possible. As a consequence, and under intense criticism, the Secretary of State has intervened to relieve water companies of the onerous duties of achieving the standards by receiving from water companies undertakings to carry out works to achieve the required standards in the future. Consistent with this approach the Department of the Environment has invited local planning authorities to view sympathetically planning applications by water companies to construct treatment works (see: DoE Circular Guidance on Planning 1991).

Private water supplies

The definition of a private water supply is any supplies of water provided otherwise than by a statutorily appointed water undertaker (s. 93 of the Water industry Act 1991). In recent years private water suppliers have become more numerous, especially, for example, in answering the increasing demand for bottled water. There is no legal prohibition against water suppliers or undertakers who wish to supply water in their private capacity. Private water suppliers have much the same requirements placed on them as public suppliers. There are similar requirements for wholesome water in regulations consolidated in the Private Water Supplies Regulations 1991, SI 1991 No. 2790. The 1991 Regulations set out a two-fold classification system and require local authorities to monitor private suppliers on the basis of the classification. Category 1 water is used for domestic purposes; category 2 water is used for food production or in premises used as staff canteens, educational, hospital and other residential use or camp sites or in other places providing short-term accommodation on a commercial basis. The regulations cover most matters relevant to the setting of water quality standards. The regulations provide that local authorities may serve a notice specifying the steps that are necessary to bring the water supply up to the standard of 'wholesome water' and a period of at least 28 days when objections may be made to the notice. The regulations specify:

- How local authorities are required to classify private suppliers in their areas.
- The parameters for which local authorities are required to monitor private supplies, including the frequency of monitoring and the taking of samples.
- The right of local authorities, with certain exceptions, to enter into arrangements for the taking of samples and their analysis.
- The maximum charges local authorities are permitted to make for sampling and analysis.

The 1991 Act maintains the long-standing obligation on local authorities to be kept informed about the wholesomeness and sufficiency of water supplies in their respective areas. Local authorities are given powers to secure the improvement of private water supplies or connection to a mains supply. This includes powers to serve a notice on the occupier of land where the source is situated and specify the improvement steps to be taken and the time scale for the improvements to be implemented. Such a notice must also be submitted to the relevant Secretary of State for confirmation. In certain circumstances there may be a public local inquiry or hearing at the discretion of the Secretary of State.

The Drinking Water Inspectorate also has a role in respect of private water supplies. It is responsible for the provision of scientific advice and for monitoring the arrangements made by local authorities. It also oversees the responsibility of local authorities to comply with the relevant regulations noted above (see: DoE, and Welsh Office (1994), *Private Water Supplies – A Guide to the Laws Controlling Private Water Supplies*).

The increasing popularity of bottled water is a commercial development that is relatively lightly regulated. The Drinking Water in Containers Regulations 1994, SI 1994 No. 743, sets some standards for bottled water, broadly in line with the requirements of EC Directive 80/778/EEC. Local authorities have a duty to enforce these standards. The sale of bottled water also comes under the provisions of the Food Safety Act 1990 and the Act gives local authorities powers as food authorities.

There is little regulation over the contents of bottled water. The regulation of the use of various labels to describe bottled water is surprisingly lax. Mineral waters that are described as 'natural mineral waters' fall under the Natural Mineral Waters Regulations 1985, SI 1985 No. 71, which implements EC Directive 80/777/EEC on the marketing and exploitation of mineral waters. Official recognition of a 'natural mineral water' requires the applicant to apply in writing to the local authority giving details of the source of supply, the physical, chemical and microbiological properties of the water and evidence that the source and the supply are not polluted. Details are published in official journals and, if recognition is to be accepted in the EC, in the *Official Journal of the EC*.

▶ Pricing and the regulation of water companies

In common with other utilities such as gas, electricity and tele-communications, water has a regulator (OFWAT) responsible for the economic regulation of the water companies (Water Industry Act 1991). Water is a natural monopoly and is essential for life. Privatised companies, despite operating in the commercial sector, recognise the importance of the public service element in their activities. At the time of privatisation a balance was required in the regulation of pricing. One objective was to allow companies sufficient funds to finance investment and improve services and the infrastructure of the water supply system. A competing objective was to protect consumers from unjustified price increases due to the virtual monopoly power of the water companies. The balance that is required from the regulator is set out in s. 2 of the Water Industry Act 1991. Water and sewerage companies may fix charges for their services in accordance with a charges scheme which is under the overall control of the Director of OFWAT. The formula for pricing is based on a simple mechanism expressed as RPI + K (i.e. the Retail Price Index + some factor 'K' determined by OFWAT). In applying the pricing mechanism a number of factors have to be taken into account. Some parts of the country have greater physical costs to take account of in the supply of water and in the treatment of sewage. The size and revenue of companies vary throughout the country. Comparison between water companies is difficult in terms of performance and profitability. Some offshore discharge outlets in southern England require capital investment to bring them up to the required standards and such differences make for unevenness in the costs of the different water companies. Finally there are unknown factors in predicting future developments. Tighter regulatory Directives from the Community may add to the costs. Demand and supply are in flux, depending on variables such as weather conditions and economic performance of different sectors of the economy. There is no national water grid equivalent to the electricity grid and the absence of a national grid adds to problems of supply.

Setting the 'K' factor in the pricing mechanism requires careful judgement. The 'K' factor is assessed taking into account two components: first, various mandatory quality improvements; second, increased efficiency in the industry. Clearly each water company must be assessed and a calculation made for each company on the basis of both components. Initially it was intended that the 'K' factors would be set for 10 years. This was intended to give the industry some degree of certainty. In the interests of consumers and shareholders this degree of predictability in the early stages of privatisation was regarded as an important consideration. A review of the 'K' formula could be triggered by either the water regulator (OFWAT) or the water companies. After five years the first review, initiated by OFWAT, was completed in July 1994. The review took account of the planned capital investments and additional quality improvements. Various modifications to the 'K' factor resulted from the 1994 review and these were disputed by two water companies, who referred matters to the Monopolies and Mergers Commission. Currently water companies have become the subject of intense public interest since the announcement by Northwest Water in March 1995 that £180 million was to be repaid to shareholders (Baldwin, 1995, p. 65). Allegations of excess profits and controversy over the use of disconnection powers have influenced public opinion about the operation of the industry. The next five years will provide opportunities to resolve some important questions that involve key decisions about the industry. Questions to be resolved about the future of the water industry include: (i) the possible impact of the new Environment Agency; (ii) the impact of future European Directives including ecological water quality (a scientifically demanding problem); (iii) the impact of the financial performance of the industry on pricing;

and (iv) public perceptions about the management of the water industry.

▶ Community policy and Directives on water

The extensive involvement of the Community in the environment is a classic example of how the European Union has been able to expand its role. Water policy was one of the first subsectors of EC environmental policy and it has now developed into a comprehensive area of Community activity (Haigh, 1994). Many of the changes, including the large-scale investment in improving standards and in the introduction of new legislation, noted above, have come about because of the Community's role in developing water policy. For example, the Drinking Water Directive 80/778/EEC provides an important set of standards for water quality. In the future it is intended that there will be two sets of Directives: one dealing with water quality through a reformed drinking water Directive and the other set providing discharges to waters. Such changes require considerable time, given the deliberations that are often required before agreement is reached. In the case of drinking water it is envisaged that there will be a number of new developments. A new drinking water Directive will replace Directive 80/778/EEC and some parts of 75/440/EEC. A new Directive on the ecological quality of surface waters is to revise Directive 80/778/EEC. A revised groundwater Directive will replace 80/68/EEC. Further proposals are being considered by the Commission in the area of bathing water (see Chapter 11).

▶ Conclusions

The water industry is undergoing a period of change and expansion. As a scarce resource used for a variety of purposes it is essential that there is effective water management, not only to conserve the resource but also to maintain its quality. Water management and pollution controls are at the centre of the future development of environmental law. The law is heavily influenced by scientific and technical expertise. It is undoubtedly the case that scientists are faced by a number of challenges in the development of water environmental law. For example, what techniques should be employed to monitor and predict the impact of discharges on aquatic ecosystems? Are discharge consents based on WQOs appropriate for pollution control or are UESs a more realistic basis for water protection? What are the best techniques for setting environmental standards and how is a balance to be struck between cost to industry and environmental protection? Since the philosophy underpinning the government's environmental policy is towards sustainable development, it seems appropriate to minimise and if possible avoid discharges. If this is the case the challenge for scientists is the rapid development of clean technologies.

There is continued pressure from public opinion and the work of pressure groups maintains water pollution at the centre of media attention. Privatisation of the water industry has affected public understanding and perceptions about the water industry. Differing perceptions about water emerge from the different agencies involved. There is a change in the perception of water as a natural resource and in abundant supply, to understanding water as a commodity with value added in the maintenance of water quality and its supply. This change of thinking involves volatile political issues, and the consequences of political and economic considerations combine to set challenges for the future regulation and management of the industry.

▶ References and further reading

Baldwin, R. (1995) *Regulation in Question: The Growing Agenda.* London School of Economics, London.

Churchill, R., Warren, L. and Gibson, J. (1991) *Law, Policy and the Environment.* Basil Blackwell, Oxford.

Department of the Environment (1995) *Freshwater Quality: Government Response.* DoE, London.

Drinking Water Inspectorate (1995) *Drinking Water 1994.* HMSO, London.

Gray, N.F. (1994) *Drinking Water Quality: Problems and Solutions.* John Wiley, Chichester.

Grey, D.R.C., Kinniburgh, D.G., Barker, J. A. and Bloomfield, J.P. (1995) *Groundwater in the UK. A Strategic Study. Issues and Research Needs.* Groundwater Forum Report FR/GF 1.

Haigh, N. (1994) *Manual of Environment Policy: The EC and Britain.* Longman, Essex.

Harrison, R.M. (ed) (1990) *Pollution. Causes, Effects and Control.* The Royal Society of Chemistry, Cambridge.

Haslam, S.M. (1990) *River Pollution an Ecological Perspective.* John Wiley, Chichester.

Horan, N.J. (1990) *Biological Wastewater Treatment Systems. Theory and Operation.* John Wiley, Chichester.

Howarth, W. (1990) *The Law of the National Rivers Authority.* National Rivers Authority, London.

Langford, T.E. (1983) *Electricity Generation and the Ecology of Natural Waters.* Liverpool University Press, Liverpool.

Macrory, R. (1989) *The Water Act 1989.* Sweet and Maxwell, London.

Mason, C.F. (1995) *Biology of Freshwater Pollution*, 3rd edn. Longman, Essex.

Mumma, A. (1995) *Environmental Law.* McGraw-Hill, London.

National Water Council (1978) *River Quality.* National Water Council.

NRA (1992) *Policy and Practice for the Protection of Groundwater.* National Rivers Authority, London.

NRA (1993) *Low Flows and Water Resources.* National Rivers Authority, London.

OFWAT (1991) *Paying For Water: A Time for Decisions.* OFWAT.

OFWAT (1993) *Paying for Quality: The Political Perspective.* OFWAT.

OFWAT (1994) *Future Charges for Water and Sewerage Services: The Outcome of the Periodic Review.* OFWAT.

Royal Commission on Environmental Pollution 16th Report (1992) *Freshwater Quality.* June 1992 (Cm 1966).

Richardson, G. (1995) 'EU Water Policy: Uncertain Agendas, Shifting networks and Complex Coalitions'. Unpublished paper, the University of Warwick.

Richardson, G., Ogus, A. and Barrows, P. (1983) *Policing Pollution.* Oxford University Press, Oxford.

Richardson, G., Maloney, W. and Rudig, W. (1992) 'The dynamics of policy change: lobbying and water privatisation'. *Public Administration,* **70** (2), pp. 157–75.

Stewart, M. (1994) 'Modelling water costs'. Office of Water Services Research Paper No. 2 and Warwick Economic Working Paper No. 9416.

Stewart, M. (1994) 'Modelling water costs'. Office of Water Services Research Paper No. 3, January.

Stewart, M. 'Modelling sewage treatment costs'. Office of Water Services Research Paper No. 4, January.

UK Groundwater Forum (1995) *Groundwater in the UK: a Strategic Study.* UK Groundwater Resources, June.

Additional information

The main environmental law journals all provide very good coverage of water management and pollution issues. There is a dedicated journal devoted to water: *Water Law* (Publishers: Wiley Chancery). Also see: ENDS.

Protection of the coastal and marine environment

Water resources include coastal and marine habitats. It is estimated that at least 70 per cent of the earth's surface is covered by seas. Oceans and seas serve as a primary source for life. In modern times, in common with the exploitation of many natural resources, the oceans are seen as a resource for food, for minerals and metals, for energy generation, for transport and for many forms of recreational use. Increasingly the oceans are used as dumping grounds for waste disposal and sewage discharges. The self-renewing properties of the seas are seriously under threat from pollution. Pollution from rivers, estuaries and coastal areas affects the marine environment. Pollution from ships and waste disposal at sea have a significant impact on the coast and marine life. The transportation of oil in bulk carriers and mishaps causing oil pollution have an impact on the self-generating qualities of the seas. Over-fishing and a failure to conserve fish stocks has also had an impact on the sea as a food resource.

▶ Introduction

The coastal and marine environment provides a distinctive challenge for environmental law. The dedication of a specific chapter to the coastal and marine environment is recognition of the need to isolate the specific problems confronting the marine ecosystem and identify the relevant laws that apply. A wide variety of sources and different forms of law are relevant to the protection of the marine environment. Legal responses to the diverse challenges arising from the protection and conservation of marine ecosystems involve laws at the level of the Member State, involving both community law and international law. As Kiss and Shelton (1993, p. 277) explain:

> Deterioration of the marine environment demands legal responses with some universal aspects and others that are individualized, according to the different regional and local problems. In numerous cases regional or even global cooperation is required, even where the

issue appears to be a local question like the cleanliness of several kilometres of coastland.

The marine environment is a rich source of food. Fish stocks taken from the sea in the waters of the North-East Atlantic have supported large fishing communities for generations. It is estimated that:

Total fish catches in the North Sea rose from an annual average of 1.7 million tonnes in the late 1940s to a peak of 3.2 million tonnes at the beginning of the 1970s and have now stabilised at around 2.4 million tonnes. (see: *This Common Inheritance*, Cm 1200 (1990), para. 12.40, p. 172)

These fish stocks are at risk from over-fishing. Excessive catches and catches of juvenile fish have a major impact on the reproductive capacity of a fish population and the ability of the population to regenerate. In addition, there is increasing evidence that pollution of the marine environment is having an adverse effect on fish. This in part is being manifested as morphological abnormalities in the fish; other impacts are not yet clear.

Marine pollution is due to a diverse number of causes and effects (Table 11.1; Fig. 11.1; Clark, 1989; GESAMP, 1990). These pollutants may arise from both point and diffuse sources (see Chapter 10). They may be continuous or intermittent and may originate from man's activities on land or on the sea (Table 11. 1). Indeed, pollution from land may be the most significant, particularly in coastal regions. Diffuse sources of marine pollutants include run-off of fertilisers and pesticides from agricultural land. Point sources include sewage outfalls, industrial effluents, mining wastes, etc., and contribute a wide variety of different pollutants to marine habitats (Table 11.1). Pollutants are also discharged to the marine environment through rivers carrying their pollutant load to the sea. Gaseous and particulate atmospheric emissions, primarily from land-based sources, may also contribute to the marine pollutant load through wet or dry deposition (see Chapter 12).

The significance of pollutants in marine ecosystems became apparent to the public in the late 1980s. In 1988 there was an epidemic of phocine distemper virus in the common seal populations which spread from the Danish to the UK coast. Approximately 16 000 dead seals were washed up on beaches. The cause of this massive epidemic was thought to have been through the action of polychlorinated biphenyls (PCBs) and other pollutant chemicals impairing the seals' immune systems. Also in 1988, there was a large toxic algal bloom of *Chrysochromulina polylepsis* in the spring and early summer. The coasts of Norway and Sweden were severely affected, with large numbers of marine invertebrates dying. Trout and salmon died at fish farms although most wild fish were able to avoid the contaminated area. The algal bloom was attributed to

Table 11.1 Sources and types of marine pollutants

Pollutant type	Source
Chemical pollutants	
Heavy metals	Sewage and sewage sludge, power stations, industrial waste, anti-fouling paints, metal processing, tanneries
Radioactivity and radionuclides	Nuclear power plants and nuclear reprocessing plants
Halogenated hydrocarbons and other toxic organics	Agricultural run-off of biocides, plastics, industrial plants, fish farming.
Acid and alkalis	Industrial effluent, textile industry, engineering works, metal mine drainage, etc.
Sulphur, chloride, phenols, etc.	Range of industries, e.g. petroleum industry
Organic or high BOD wastes	Sewage and sewage sludge, oil refining and extraction industry, shipping, e.g. bilge water, food and drink manufacture effluents, paper and chemical industry
Nutrients	Sewage and sewage sludge, fish farms, phosphate and nitrate run-off from agricultural land or river run-off.
Thermal pollution	Power plants
Particulates and suspended solids	Mining wastes, pulp mills, power stations (pulverised fuel ash), dredging spoils, plastics, engineering works, textile industry, sewage and sewage sludge, food and drink manufacture, tanneries

(*Source* : Adapted from Hughes and Goodall, 1992)

cultural eutrophication of the coastal waters arising primarily from fertiliser run-off from land (see Chapter 8).

The impact of pollutants is dependent on a variety of factors including the local physical conditions, for example tides, currents, water depth, the nature of the sediment. These will influence the concentration and duration of exposure of an organism, population or community to a pollutant. The littoral zone is particularly prone to fluctuations in conditions such as temperature, wave action, etc. This zone also tends to be relatively high in nutrients (many originating from land run-off) and has a highly diverse flora, fauna and microbial community which is dense and active. The deep sea, in comparison, is

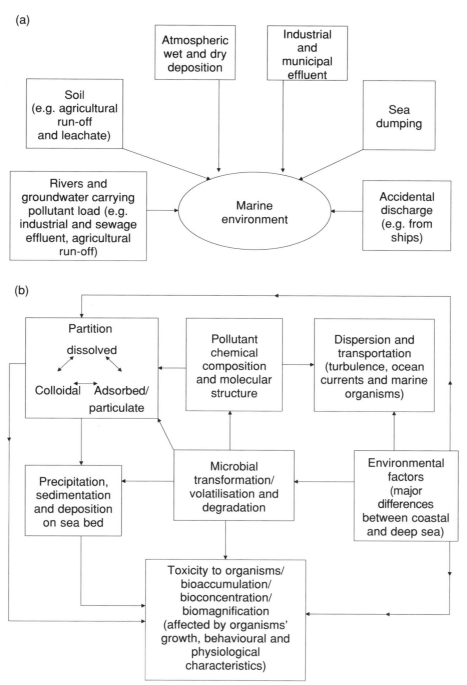

Fig. 11.1 (a) Sources of marine pollutants. (b) Factors affecting the fate and impact of pollutants in marine environments.

in general relatively stable, low in nutrients and with less biological activity. The biological characteristics of the ecosystem are also important in determining the impact of pollutants. At the individual or population level the sensitivity of the organism to the compound and its tendency to bioaccumulate the compound are important (see Chapters 8 and 10). The life cycle of the organism and its lifestyle will also affect an organism's exposure to pollutants. Some marine organisms are pelagic, that is they either float (planktonic) or swim (nectonic) in the water. Other organisms are bottom dwelling, that is benthic. Some organisms have diurnal patterns of behaviour. Their way of life will affect their exposure to a chemical, e.g. if it remains pre-dominantly in the water phase or associates with the sediment. The characteristics of the particular pollutant are important: its longevity, its chemistry and distribution, etc., in the marine environment affect the impact on organisms (see Chapters 8 and 10 for further discussion of these points, and Hughes and Goodall, 1992, for additional discussion). The impact of pollutants at community level is complex, but it is possible that the density and diversity of communities will be adversely affected and that energy flow-through and nutrient cycling within an ecosystem may be disrupted. As with terrestrial ecosystems (see Chapter 8), in marine ecosystems it is possible for pollutants to be biomagnified through a food chain with predators, e.g. birds, aquatic mammals, predator fish, at the top of the food chain accumulating most pollutant and being greatly affected. The impact of pollutants in marine ecosystems is difficult to predict and often difficult to monitor and study. It should be remembered that there can be major population shifts with season, for example phytoplankton community composition and density fluctuate with season, and some fish are migratory, adding to the difficulty of assessing and predicting pollutant impact.

Marine pollution can also originate from man's sea-based activities. The dumping of waste at sea offers an apparently cheaper alternative based on the economic argument that land-based disposal is too expensive. This is to justify short-term decision making. When measured over the longer term the pollution of the marine environment is costly. Oil pollution can be caused by the spillage of oil from vessels and from oil exploration. These pollution incidents often have major acute effects including large bird and other animal kills. They may also result in chronic pollution with shorelines and sediment remaining con-taminated for many years (see below). The *Torrey Canyon* disaster in 1967 illustrated the inherent dangers of the transportation of oil in bulk carriers when large quantities of spilt oil caused hazards to fisheries, coastal resorts, marine wild life and humans. Other disasters such as *Amoco Cadiz* and the *Exxon Valdez*, and more recently in January 1993 the Shetland tanker accident, have shown the scale and potential severity of pollution from bulk oil carriers. It should not be forgotten that ships may discharge oil pollutants during their normal passage and that deep sea oil installations contribute to the hydrocarbon pollutant load.

There are a number of government departments in the United Kingdom with responsibilities that cover marine pollution. The Department of Transport is concerned with the control of oil and chemical pollution at sea and since 1979 there has been a Marine Pollution Control Unit (MPC) responsible for counter-pollution measures in the North Sea. The Secretary of State for Transport is under a duty to make an annual report to Parliament under s. 26 of the Prevention of Oil Pollution Act 1971. Dumping of waste at sea is controlled through a system of licences operated by the Ministry of Agriculture, Fisheries and Food. In the case of pollution from offshore installations the responsibility lies with the Department of Trade and Industry (DTI) to deal with pollution. The DTI works with the MPC and, in cases of oil pollution involving naval vessels, with the Ministry of Defence. Finally the Secretary of State for the Environment has responsibilities for the protection of wildlife in England.

This chapter provides an outline of the main legal powers found in international law, in Community law and in the national law of the United Kingdom for the control of pollution and the management of the marine environment.

Sources of law

The main sources of law that apply to the marine environment are international law, Community law and the national law of the United Kingdom. The law covers matters as diverse as marine pollution and ownership of the seas. Marine pollution does not recognise national boundaries but legal frontiers are helpful in defining responsibility and regulation of the marine environment. Primarily international law in this area rests on the assumptions that there can be co-operation between states and that through international regulation the protection of the marine environment may best be achieved. This is a fast developing and specialised area of law with particular emphasis on transfrontier pollution (see: *Trail Smelter Arbitration* (1938) and (1941) 3 U.N.R.I.A.A).

International law

There are a number of international organisations that are relevant to marine pollution and a number of international conferences that provide a forum for discussion of particular areas of marine pollution. There is an International Maritime Organisation (IMO) which is part of the United Nations, with a membership of about 125 states and headquarters in London. It acts as a facility to extend co-operation between governments on shipping matters. The Marine Environment Protection Division of the IMO draws up conventions on shipping and marine pollution. There is a United Nations Convention on the Law of the Sea which has been ratified by over 60 states since it was agreed in 1982. The United Nations Environment Programme followed from the Stockholm Conference in 1972, where 113 states participated and a Declaration on Human Environment was agreed. The programme was established with its headquarters in Nairobi, Kenya. Protection of the marine environment is part of the United Nations Environment Programme. There is an International Convention for the Prevention of Pollution from Ships (MARPOL), signed in 1973 and later amended by Protocol in 1978. The Convention, which came into force in October 1983, is intended to eliminate international pollution of the marine environment.

There are a number of regional conventions and in 1984 the North Sea states met together to discuss prevention of pollution of the North Sea. There have been conferences held in 1987, 1990 and 1995 with the result of a number of declarations elaborating agreed general principles.

International law is important in designating ocean waters into zones. In 1982 the diffuse number of treaties and conventions was codified by a global convention signed by the majority of states of the world. The United Nations Convention on the Law of the Sea (UNCLOS) 1982 provides five distinct categories of marine space:

1. The sovereignty of the coastal state is defined to include internal waters consisting of ports, harbours and bays whose openings do not exceed 40 km.
2. A coastal state may exercise its territorial sea as a sovereign zone up to 20 km. Foreign shipping may have rights of passage but the sovereign state may legislate to protect its marine environment.
3. A coastal state is defined as consisting of the sea and seabed to the outer limit of the continental plateau, that is to the beginning of the deep seabed.
4. An exclusive economic zone consists of the maritime area that extends between the territorial sea and a line situated 360 km from the coast. This designation has existed from the 1970s and gives the coastal state rights to exploit the resources of marine life in the zone. The coastal state is under a duty to ensure that there is environmental protection of the area.
5. Waters outside the designated zones outlined above are described as the high seas. These are open to exploitation by international shipping.

International law also consists of a number of treaties and conventions with certain environmental protection afforded to the various oceans of the world. As noted above, the United Nations

Environment Programme attempts to set out a programme for regional seas which was initiated in 1974. The programme covers 10 areas where regional plans are under development or are operative. In addition there are a number of treaties which apply to the North Sea and the North-East Atlantic. There is a 1983 Treaty dealing with oil-based pollution. The 1972 Oslo Dumping Convention, amended by subsequent protocols, applies to the North Sea, the North-East Atlantic and the adjacent Arctic seas. In 1974 the Helsinki Convention for the Protection of the Marine Environment of the Baltic Area adopted a comprehensive approach to pollution control. There is a United Nations Environment Programme for regional seas. The Barcelona Convention came into force in 1978 and applies to the Mediterranean. It is hoped to extend the principles of combating pollution to other seas through a series of framework conventions. These include the Persian Gulf, the Red Sea and the Gulf of Aden, parts of the Indian Ocean, the South Pacific, the Caribbean and parts of the South Atlantic. There is a Standing Conference on Stradling Stocks and Highly Migratory Species which attempts to persuade states to conserve fish stocks. The United Kingdom ratified the Agreement on the Conservation of Small Cetaceans [small marine mammals] of the Baltic and North Seas in July 1993 to protect dolphins and porpoises in the North Sea and to fund research into preventing them from being caught in fishing nets.

European Community law

Community law is also an important source of law for setting standards to protect marine habitats. Community law is increasingly part of the law of the United Kingdom. Article 130R. (3) requires that the Community should take account of available scientific and technical data when considering its environmental policy. Section 156 of the Environmental Protection Act 1990 permits the Secretary of State to make regulations to give effect to Community law concerning atmospheric pollution or waste on land, and to control injurious substances or radioactive wastes.

Community Directives relating to the sea include Directive 76/464/EEC which applies to the pollution caused by certain dangerous substances discharged into the aquatic environment of the Community. There are a number of Directives on the quality of shell fish, and Directive 76/160 on the quality of bathing waters, discussed in more detail below. There are Directives prohibiting the discharge of specific chemicals into an aquatic environment.

United Kingdom law

National laws are important in tackling marine pollution. For example there are a variety of laws in the United Kingdom preventing tankers from discharging oil or waste while at sea (see: the Merchant Shipping Act 1979 and the Merchant Shipping (Prevention of Oil Pollution) Regulations 1983, SI 1983 No. 1398). Many of these laws implement international agreements or set out in United Kingdom law obligations introduced by the European Community. For example, the Merchant Shipping (Salvage and Pollution) Act 1994 implements the International Convention on Salvage 1989 (Cm 1526) and various international conventions and protocols for oil pollution damage. In the United Kingdom s. 1 (1) of the Territorial Seas Act 1987 sets the territorial seas to be 12 nautical miles. Included within the definition of 'relevant territorial waters' under the 1987 Act are a number of straits used for international navigation. Under the Fishery Limits Act 1976 the United Kingdom set up an Exclusive Fishing Zone of 200 nautical miles. Since 1978 the United Kingdom Crown Court has jurisdiction over indictable offences committed on board or by means of a foreign ship in UK territorial waters. British ships are registered under the Merchant Shipping Act 1988.

▶ Conservation of the sea

In 1983, after protracted negotiations, a legally enforceable Common Fisheries Policy (CFP) was agreed by the Member States of the Community. Past attempts to arrive at a common policy had been unsuccessful and current attempts to find a workable fishing policy among all Member States remain controversial. The competence of the Community to make laws for the conservation of the biological resources of the sea has been approved by the Court of Justice of the European Communities (see: Cases 3, 4 and 6/76 *Kramer et al.* [1976] ECR 1279). The agreement in 1983 has four elements. First, all community fishermen are entitled to fish within the Community's 200 nautical mile limit of their own shores. The 200 nautical mile limit came into operation in January 1977 and represented a considerable expansion in the territorial scope of Community law. Within this framework Member States are free to reserve fishing to their own fishermen and those fishermen with traditional fishing rights. Fishing the Atlantic and North Sea fish stocks is subject to additional controls. There are allowable catches that are divided into national quotas. The Total Allowable Catch (TAC) is fixed annually on the basis of Regulation 4194/88 (OJ 1987 L 375/1). Fishing from vessels flying the flag of a particular country may be stopped for a specific period.

Secondly, the Community operates a price system and market organisation for fish that come within the price system. There is also an external trade policy. Regulation 379/81 (OJ 1981 L 379/1 amended by Regulation 3468/88 OJ 1988 L 305/1) sets the guide prices, classification, market standards, packaging and labelling of fish products. Thirdly, there are international negotiations conducted by Community representatives on behalf of all the Member States that concern access to waters and conservation of fish stocks. Finally, there are structural provisions for market development and modernisation of the industry that include redeployment of resources. The Common Structural Policy falls under Regulation 101/76 (OJ 1976 L 20/19).

Community fishing policy, the subject of quotas and the use of exclusion of certain types of ships in conservation zones have all been highly controversial areas of Community policy and often the subject of litigation before the courts (see: Case 63/83 *R.* v. *Kirk* [1984] ECR 2689, and the *Factortame* litigation [1991] 1 AC 603). Concerns remain that diminishing fish stocks in the North Sea and Atlantic require a tougher policy if the replenishment of an important food source is not to be severely impaired. The Sea Fisheries Regulation Act 1966 has been amended by s. 102 of the Environment Act 1995. The Environment Agency, sea fisheries committees and ministers have been granted powers to regulate fisheries for environmental as distinct from fish management purposes. Membership of the sea fisheries committees may now include experts in environmental matters. The Sea Fish (Conservation) Act 1967 contains powers to restrict fishing for sea fish. The 1967 Act has been strengthened by s. 103 of the Environment Act 1995. A new s. 5A provides powers to make an order for the purposes of conserving the marine environment. This includes conserving the natural beauty or amenity of marine or coastal areas. In effect these are important conservation powers to restrict fishing or to prohibit the carriage of specified types of net for marine environmental purposes. It is likely that it will become increasingly necessary to make use of conservation powers of this kind.

Section 104 of the Environment Act 1995 also contains powers for the new Environment Agency to operate a fixed penalty system for dealing with offences under legislation protecting salmon and freshwater fish under amendments made to s. 37 of the Salmon and Freshwater Fisheries Act 1975. A new s. 37A sets out detailed procedures and fixed penalties. There are additional miscellaneous powers for setting standards for fish farm intakes and outfalls to be screened to protect wild fish stocks.

The Environment Act 1995 also attempts to provide the Environment Agency with unified grant-in-aid powers derived from the Ministry of Agriculture, Fisheries and Food. The 1995 Act also unifies the administration of the grant and approval of fish passes.

The above description of the specific laws that apply to the marine environment must also be placed in the general context of conservation in the United Kingdom. In s. 11 of the Countryside Act 1968 there is a general duty on ministers and government departments to have regard to the conservation of the natural beauty and amenity of the countryside. In previous chapters it has been noted that this duty is balanced by various duties found in the National Parks and Access to the Countryside Act 1949, the Countryside Act 1968 and the Wildlife and Countryside Act 1981. Broadly these Acts provide that due regard should be given to the needs of agriculture and forestry and to the economic and social interest of rural areas. The Environment Act 1995 provides the Environment Agency with the aims and objectives of protecting or enhancing the environment in order to achieve sustainable development. The future of marine conservation will be to achieve the exacting requirement of balancing the competing needs and uses of the sea with its proper management and conservation.

▶ Coastal management

Marine Nature Reserves (MNRs) occupy tidal and coastal waters. Land or water can be designated from the high tide mark to a line three miles from the baseline under the Territorial Sea Act 1987 and s. 36 of the Wildlife and Countryside Act 1981 on a similar basis as National Nature Reserves. There is a procedure whereby designation may be made by the Secretary of State for Environment which allows representation from interested parties and if necessary a public inquiry. The Nature Conservancy Council manages MNRs and is given powers to make by-laws. The scope of by-laws is set out in s. 37 of the Wildlife and Countryside Act 1981. Restrictions may be made on the killing, taking and disturbance of animals as well as the deposit of litter. There are provisions included under s. 37 for the restriction or prohibition of people and vessels to the MNR. However, this does not apply where there is a right of access to tidal waters or the right of passage. In reality this limitation curtails the usefulness of these powers.

Coastal flood defences are the responsibility of the Ministry of Agriculture, Fisheries and Food through the NRA (now the Environment Agency) (see Chapter 10). The NRA is directed in its work by local flood defence committees composed of local landowners and local authority councillors. The control of coastal erosion falls to the district councils bordering the coast under the Department of Environment. In effect the district councils are responsible for the coastal zone inwards of the sea. They receive some funding for coastal protection schemes from MAFF but most costs are met directly by the councils. The impact of the predicted sea level changes associated with global warming (Chapter 12) may substantially increase the costs of already expensive sea defences (see Clayton and O'Riordan, 1995, for a discussion of coastal processes and management).

▶ Pollution control

Discharge of effluent

The regulation of the discharge of effluent under the Water Resources Act 1991 has been examined in Chapter 10. There are other statutory provisions relevant to the marine environment. The Dangerous Substances in Harbour Areas Regulations 1987, SI 1987 No. 37, provide extensive regulations for the carriage, loading and unloading, and storage of dangerous substances within harbour areas. The regulations require periods of notice to be given to the harbour master where it is intended to berth any dangerous substance. There must be provision by the harbour authorities of an emergency plan and regulations over the entry, access, method of carriage and handling of dangerous goods. The correct forms and procedures, including the labelling of the dangerous substances, are also included within the regulations. Vessels carrying dangerous substances must display flags and conform to the procedures set out in the regulations.

A range of waste is discharged to the sea from land, including untreated or partially treated sewage which may pose a health risk (see below). It may also contribute to cultural eutrophication of coastal water. In some cases where exceptionally high BOD waste is released then estuaries may become deoxygenated, with major impacts on the flora and fauna (see Chapters 8 and 10). A range of other industrial waste may be discharged (Table 11.1), the impact of which will depend on the particular compounds involved and on a variety of other factors (see above). Attempts can be made to determine the toxicity of specific chemicals to selected marine organisms in ecotoxicity tests. The limitations of predicting other species' reactions, community and eco-system-level impacts from such studies have already been discussed (see Chapters 8 and 10). Power production in the United Kingdom also contributes to marine pollution. Thermal pollution can arise in coastal regions and estuaries from the discharge of cooling water from power stations (see Chapter 10).

Radioactive waste management

Nuclear power stations are permitted to discharge radioactive effluent to marine environments. These are site specific and depend on the receiving water (see Chapter 10). Currently, controls are set in terms of the total amount of radioactivity released and the maximum levels of specified radionuclides discharged. Reprocessing plants which reprocess the spent fuel rods from nuclear reactors are similarly controlled in levels of discharges. It is proposed that discharge authorisations will be set at the same low-dose level for all new nuclear installations and, wherever possible, existing ones (see: the government's White Paper, *Review of Radioactive Waste Management Policy* (Cm 2919, July 1995, HMSO). This proposal appears to be adopting the same strategy as that of uniform emission standards (UESs) followed in some European countries (see Chapter 10).

The mobility, distribution and fate of discharged radionuclides in the marine environment vary with the chemistry of the radionuclide and the physicochemical characteristics of the receiving water. These factors influence the biological availability of the radionuclide. The uptake and accumulation of radionuclides varies with organism and with particular radionuclide, as discussed above for pollutants generally. Radionuclides change to other isotopes during radioactive decay; this means that any prediction of the impact of a radionuclide on marine habitats must include consideration of the potential fate and impact of all its decay-daughters (see Chapter 9). A number of discharged radionuclides may have no stable counterparts and essentially not occur naturally in the biosphere – assessing their likely environmental fate and biological interactions may be exceptionally difficult. This of course can also be said for many man-made chemicals which do not occur naturally.

The regulation of radioactive waste under the Radioactive Substances Act 1993 has been amended by the Environment Act 1995. The new Environment Agency and the Scottish Environment Protection Agency will take over the functions of HMIP in England and Wales and Her Majesty's Industrial Pollution Inspectorate in Scotland. The authorisation procedure whereby the Ministry of Agriculture, Fisheries and Food determines applications for the disposal of radioactive waste will be directed by the new Environment Agency. The government's White Paper, *Review of Radioactive Waste Management Policy* (Cm 2919, July 1995, HMSO) contains details of how radioactive waste management policy should share the same principles as apply more generally to environmental policy. Sustainable development requires a number of supporting principles:

● The use of the best possible scientific information.
● Where there is uncertainty and potentially serious risks exist precautionary action may be necessary.
● Ecological impacts must be considered, particularly where resources are non-renewable or effects may be irreversible.
● Cost implications should be brought home directly to the people responsible – the 'polluter pays' principle.

It is intended that the government will maintain and develop a regulatory framework that will take account of the above principles. The framework will assume that the producers and owners of radioactive waste are responsible for bearing the costs and managing and disposing of the waste, including the cost of regulation and research.

Bathing Water Directive

EC Directive 76/160/EEC (OJ No. L31/1) is an innovative Directive that requires the Member States of the Community to provide a quality standard for bathing water. There is much anecdotal evidence about illness developing after swimming and surfing, etc., in coastal water. The illnesses range from gastroenteritis to ear infections, even to more serious disorders including paralysis. It has proved epidemiologically very difficult to verify the link between swimming and such illnesses. This is partly because the reported illnesses are so varied and partly because the population using beaches is often transient. Many people spend holidays at the seaside and only develop symptoms when they return to their homes. The infectious agents causing the illness are likely to be varied, with different incubation periods before symptoms become apparent, adding to the epidemiological complexity. It is thought that viruses may be particularly important in causing bathing water-related illness. Recent studies using volunteer bathers may be helpful in establishing the validity of the link. It appears that the main contribution to the health risk from bathing water originates in the discharge of untreated or only partly treated sewage effluent into coastal waters.

The water quality criteria for the Bathing Water Directive are based on water quality assessed through the presence of bacterial indicators of faecal pollution. A range of bacteria occur as normal flora in the human gastrointestinal tract and these are excreted in faeces. Estimating the numbers of these bacteria, e.g. *Escherichia coli,* faecal streptococci such as *Streptococcus faecalis,* and *Clostridium perfringens,* in water gives an indication of the amount of faecal pollution and therefore the risk of enteric pathogens being present in a water body. Isolating and enumerating pathogens themselves is more time consuming and difficult than determining the presence of indicator organisms. However, one assumption must stand if indicator bacteria for faecal pollution are to be useful in determining the disease risk associated with water. The indicator organisms must survive longer in the water than pathogens. There is evidence that this is not always the case, depending on species of indicator bacterium and species or type of pathogen, particularly in seawater, e.g. *E. coli* does not appear to survive as long in seawater as certain enteric viruses. This raises a question about the safety of the monitoring technique accepted and used internationally.

There are a number of distinctive features about the EC Bathing Water Directive. First, the Directive may be phased in over a period of time: two years for countries to bring their laws into line with the Directive and 10 years to bring the standards of bathing water into conformity with the Directive. Secondly, the requirements of the Directive may be waived where there are exceptional circumstances such as bad weather. For example, heavy rain can overwhelm a treatment works resulting in poorly treated effluent being discharged. The United Kingdom has found it difficult to comply with the Directive. It was found in 1989 that 25 per cent of the designated bathing waters failed to reach even the minimum standards of the Directive. Complaints that the United Kingdom failed to take adequate measures to ensure the quality of bathing waters at various resorts have been upheld in *Commission* v. *UK* (see: ENDS Report 222, July 1993, p. 47, Case C-56/90). The United Kingdom had argued that there was no requirement to authorise all bathing beaches under the Directive. In designating beaches to qualify to come within the standards set by the Directive, the United Kingdom adopted the criteria of counting the number of bathers in the water at any one time. As a result, only 27 beaches were designated in the United Kingdom and many well used beaches were excluded. The court rejected this approach and also the argument that the 10 year period to comply with the Directive could commence on the basis of the time of designation. The outcome is that another 389 beaches were required to be designated and the standards of the Directive applied and had to be in place within the 10 year period (1977–87).

The United Kingdom has about 475 beaches. Since 1990 it has sought to bring the majority within compliance of the Directive. A £2 billion investment programme is under way to meet the standards. It is clear that there have been a number of improvements. The compliance rate for England and Wales in 1994 was 82.5 per cent, Scotland 69.5 per cent, Northern Ireland 93.7 per cent. There is still room for improvement (see ENDS Report 238, November 1994, p. 24). It remains to be seen how far future arrangements to improve bathing beaches will meet the required standards set by the Directive.

There are proposals from the Commission to strengthen the standards by replacing the current Directive with a new Bathing Water Directive to be implemented by the end of December 1995. The proposed Directive will require better publicity about the standards of beaches, and the prohibition of bathing areas where the pollution constitutes a threat to human health. In addition there is a new category of excellent quality for bathing waters. The new Directive will require: (i) an improved standard for faecal streptococci which are thought to mimic the survival of enteric viruses better than other indicator bacteria; and (ii) improved monitoring of water quality to enforce a zero limit for enteroviruses. Techniques to determine the number of enteroviruses in water are difficult and will need improvement if numbers are to be monitored regularly. The Department of the Environment has commissioned studies that have found that the new draft Directive would cost £1.6–4.2 billion and extra operating costs of £70–150 million. There is controversy over the desirability of spending such costs as

PART IV
Atmosphere

The atmosphere provides essential gases for aerobic respiration and photosynthesis and contains a large and important pool of compounds for some biogeochemical cycles, e.g. carbon, nitrogen and oxygen. The balance of gases in the atmosphere supports life as we know it on this planet. Good air quality, whether at work or at home, is essential for human health. A range of medical problems such as asthma and bronchitis are aggravated and possibly induced by poor air quality. Asthma, in particular, is one of the fastest-growing diseases in the United Kingdom. It is estimated that 20 per cent of children may be suffering from this complaint. Poor air quality can also have an effect on animal and plant life. Long-term effects of poor air quality can change the quality of water and soil. Atmospheric pollution may also damage the fabric of buildings, e.g. acid rain. Air pollution contributes to global warming with potential for serious and long-term impacts on the environment, agriculture, climate and sea level that are not easily reversed or predicted. In an influential report from the Royal Commission on Pollution (HMSO, 1994), it is estimated that carbon dioxide emissions from road transport in the United Kingdom will increase significantly over the next 25 years (p. 40). Other global effects resulting from atmospheric pollution include ozone depletion in the stratosphere. The local and regional impacts of atmospheric pollutants also have major health, agricultural and environmental effects which can be either acute or chronic. In the United Kingdom there are memories of the 1950s' smogs in London caused by the combination of domestic coal fires and industrial pollution. Traffic fumes trapped at ground level during December 1991 produced excessively high levels of nitrogen dioxide in London. The accumulation at ground level of photochemical smog is a major problem in urban environments. High ozone concentrations occur in periods of warm weather in cities, and also occur in rural areas over high ground. Recent world events have highlighted the potentially acute effect of industrial releases to the atmosphere. The discharge of 30–40 tonnes of methylisocyanate to the air after a disaster at a chemical plant in Bhopal, India, in December 1984 resulted in 3300 deaths and 200 000 injuries many of them serious, e.g. blindness. The explosion and fire at the Chernobyl nuclear reactor in 1986 released 50–100 million curies of radioactivity into the atmosphere. The plume of radionuclides (287 million curies of radio-isotopes) from the reactor spread over large areas of Eastern and Western Europe 7–10 days after the accident, up to 400 million people were exposed to radiation and agricultural and environmental systems were contaminated. Such an incident highlights the fact that atmos-pheric pollution does not recognise national boundaries. Consequently air pollution requires action, not only in the individual state but also by the European Community and by international law. The law in the United Kingdom has recently been consolidated in the Clean Air Act 1993. This supplements Parts I and III of the Environmental Protection Act 1990. Part IV of the Environment Act 1995 contains additional controls on air quality in line with its proposals contained in *Air Quality: Meeting the Challenge* (DoE, 1995).

▶ The atmosphere

Atmospheric pollution has a variety of impacts on natural ecosystems, agricultural systems, the built environment and human health. It has been defined as:

> . . . the presence in the atmosphere of substances or energy in such quantities and of such duration liable to cause harm to human, plant, or animal life, or to damage human-made materials and structures, or change in the weather or climate, or interference with the comfortable enjoyment of life property or other human activities. (Elsom, 1992)

Air pollutants may be either gaseous or particulate (see below) and can be defined to include energy releases (above). The impact of pollutants in the atmosphere occurs at the local, regional and global scale. These are not mutually exclusive and releases to the atmosphere may have consequences on several scales. For example, the Chernobyl nuclear reactor explosion caused both local and regional contamination by radioisotopes. Substantial local air pollution arises from road traffic emissions. This pollution, however, also has a global impact by contri-buting to the load of greenhouse gases and ozone depletion in the stratosphere through the production of gases such as carbon dioxide and nitrogen oxides.

Substantial environmental problems arise from nitrogen dioxide and sulphur dioxide emissions, originating from a variety of sources. Legislation controlling their release relates to the emission source (see below). Northern European countries have been aware of the local and regional impact of oxides of nitrogen and sulphur dioxide emissions for some years. Sulphur dioxide has a direct effect on plant growth and health through impairing stomata and chloroplast function, and reducing carbon dioxide fixation and thereby photosynthesis (Crawford, 1989). Reduced photosynthesis has a number of knock-on effects such as impaired root function due to less photosynthate being available to the root. The impact of this on plant growth varies with the pollutant concentration but can be considerable (Table 12.1). Commonly recorded concentrations of sulphur dioxide in the United Kingdom are: <1.0 ppm in industrial areas; 0.02–0.05 ppm in urban areas; and 0.001–0.05 ppm in rural areas. Clearly levels of these pollutants are high enough even in rural areas to affect plant growth and yield (Table 12.1). Plants vary in their sensitivity to these pollutants, tree species being among the most susceptible to damage (Roberts, 1984). Sulphur dioxide and the nitrogen oxides may also have a direct effect on human health by exacerbating or possibly inducing respiratory problems and infections.

Sulphur dioxide and oxides of nitrogen gases have further significant impacts. They are converted in the atmosphere to sulphuric acid and nitric acid respectively (see Harrison, 1990, for possible mechanisms; and McEldowney *et al.*, 1993). Wet and dry deposition of these acids to the environment has a number of important consequences. The term acid rain was first coined in 1872 by Robert Angus Smith to describe polluted air around Manchester. He noted that the local air damaged vegetation, bleached fabrics and corroded metals. By the mid-1960s large areas of Europe were experiencing acid precipitation of below pH

Table 12.1 The effect of sulphur dioxide (SO_2) on plant growth

SO_2 concentration (ppm)	Duration of exposure (months)	Effect on plant growth
0.076–0.150	1–3	Significantly reduced yield in most species
0.038–0.076	>2	Reduced yields in some species
<0.038	Prolonged	Beneficial (if S limited soil), no impact, or minor yield reductions in most species
0.067	4.5	51% reduction in yield of *Lolium perenne* (on agricultural grass)

(*Sources*: Bell and Clough, 1973; Roberts, 1984)

4.0–4.5 (Elsom, 1992) and it became apparent that other countries, e.g. the United States, were also experiencing acid rain. The effects of acid precipitation are extensive and aquatic environments undergo general degradation because of increased acidity (McEldowney *et al.*, 1993). The effects include:

1. The diversity of the phytoplankton community declines and is often dominated by dinoflagellates.
2. The abundance and diversity of macrophyte plants decreases. *Sphagnum* (a moss) often dominates.
3. Bacterial activity declines and fungal species dominate the microbial community. The nutrient cycles are impaired and organic matter tends to accumulate.
4. The diversity of invertebrates and zooplankton declines.
5. Waters affected by acidification often contain no or at best only few fish species. This ultimately results in a decline in birds and mammals which rely on fish in their diet.

Terrestrial ecosystems are similarly degraded by acidification, in particular the decline of forests is thought to be influenced to a large extent. There are a variety of possible effects on trees (McEldowney *et al.*, 1993):

1. The direct stress of poor air quality on plant growth.
2. Increased acidity in the soil leaching out essential mineral nutrients, especially Mg^{2+}, resulting in mineral deficiencies in the plant. Soil acidity also increases the concentration of available Al^{3+}, a toxic element to many plants. Acid precipitation can leach nutrients directly out of leaves; again Mg^{2+} is considered particularly important here.
3. High concentrations of nitrogen oxides result in over-availability of nitrogen. This has a variety of impacts including stimulating plant growth and therefore the demand for limiting mineral nutrients, increasing sensitivity to frost damage and inhibiting the development of mycorrhizae.

Trees thus stressed are vulnerable to damage from a variety of factors, such as disease, snow and frost, wind, insects, etc. It should be noted that there is some debate about all the factors influencing defoliation and tree death. It is believed that ground-level ozone, peroxyacetyl nitrate (PAN) (see below) and other atmospheric pollutants may also contribute to the effect. There can be no doubt of the severity and intensity of defoliation and that the effect increased towards and beyond the end of the 1980s. For example, in the United Kingdom trees suffering from slight to severe damage (through to dead trees) increased from 56 per cent in 1987 to 74 per cent in 1990. Similar figures have been reported in Austria, Bulgaria, Finland, Hungary,

Germany, Spain, Sweden and many other countries (Elsom, 1992). In general deciduous trees are affected less than conifers. Birds resident in affected forests have been found to produce fewer and lower-quality eggs. This appears to be due to a lack of calcium in tree foliage resulting in caterpillars consumed by the birds containing little calcium after eating the foliage (Drent and Woldendorp, 1989). This type of domino effect is difficult to predict, and the true extent of the ecological impact of acid rain is still being evaluated. There are clear indications, however, that other vertebrates and invertebrates in terrestrial environments are also adversely affected.

The damage to forest and water systems has often been observed at sites remote from industrial emissions or urban areas, indicating that these atmospheric pollutants may travel large distances before undergoing wet or dry precipitation. Indeed, pollutants originating in the United Kingdom have been suggested to cause acid rain damage in countries such as Sweden. Ironically, large chimney stacks were incorporated in many factories in an attempt to protect the local environment from acid precipitation and dilute and disperse the emissions in the atmosphere. The unfortunate result appears to have been to discharge the emissions into air streams that carried the pollutants to many vulnerable habitats on a regional scale. Clearly all possible implications of pollution control measures must be carefully considered before they are implemented.

The effects of acid rain are not restricted to natural ecosystems. The acidification of soils and watercourses has a potentially significant health impact. Acidification results in the release of toxic heavy metals such as cadmium, nickel, lead, mercury and manganese from soils. These may contaminate drinking water supplies and be bioconcentrated by fish (see Chapters 8 and 10). In some countries the concentration of these elements in drinking water may exceed national drinking water standards. The effects of acid rain are also clearly demonstrated on buildings. Metal is corroded by the acidic precipitation and stonework, in particular limestone, marble and sandstone is eroded. In many European cities there is considerable concern about the best way to protect historic buildings.

Techniques to protect the atmosphere must clearly be adopted at both national and international levels. International recognition of the problems may be found in Article 1(a) of the *Convention on Long Range Transboundary Air Pollution* (UN Economic Commission for Europe, Geneva, 13 November 1979). The European Community has introduced emission controls in an attempt to improve air quality throughout the Community.

Global warming is one of the biggest environmental problems facing the world at present. So-called greenhouse gases in the atmosphere are transparent to short-wave radiation from the sun but adsorb long-wave terrestrial radiation which would otherwise escape to space. The energy trapped within the atmosphere acts to warm it and long-wave radiation is re-radiated to the earth, warming the surface. The main gases that contribute to the greenhouse effect are carbon dioxide, methane, nitrous oxide and various chlorofluorocarbons (CFCs). Low-level ozone and water vapour can also contribute to the effect. This, of course, is a natural process and is essential for maintaining the earths temperature above freezing. Concern arises because the concentrations of greenhouse gases have been increasing in recent years (Table 12.2). This is primarily due to man's activities including the burning of fossil fuels for energy production and deforestation by burning to clear land for agriculture. Forest burning not only adds directly to the carbon dioxide in the atmosphere, but also removes an important sink for CO_2, i.e. the loss of trees reduces CO_2 utilisation in photosynthesis.

Predictions have been made that if the production of greenhouse gases goes unchecked then as soon as the 2030s CO_2 levels will be double those prior to the industrial revolution. This would result in a global temperature rise of between 2 and 5 °C. There are a variety of models predicting the impact of this on the earth's climate. They include predictions of changes in temperature and rainfall with latitude and region. For example, several of the models indicate that important areas of grain production in North America and Russia will become warmer and drier, significantly reducing the yield in these important areas of food production. In contrast some predictions suggest that the United Kingdom will become wetter. Recent models indicate that the

Table 12.2 Concentrations and importance of greenhouse gases in the atmosphere

	Carbon dioxide CO_2	Methane CH_4	CFC11	CFC12	Nitrous oxide N_2O	Low-level ozone O_3
Pre-industrial concentration	280 ppm	0.8 ppm	0	0	288 ppb	11 ppb
1990 concentration	353 ppm	1.72 ppm	280 ppt	484 ppt	310 ppb	21 ppb
Current rate of annual accumulation	1.8 ppm	0.015 ppm	9.5 ppt	17 ppt	0.8 ppb	0.02 ppt
Lifetime in the atmosphere (years)	50–200	10	65	130	150	<1

(*Source* : Adapted from Elsom (1992). Original source UN IPCC (Intergovernmental Panel on Climate Change) 1990 *Scientific Assessment of Climate Change* Report of Working Group I. Nairobi: UNEP)

United Kingdom and northern Europe are likely to become colder due to changes in the Gulf Stream induced by global warming. Regional changes in precipitation, snow melt and evapotranspiration have important implications for river flow. This will affect a variety of activities including agriculture, groundwater levels, drinking water availability, and river management (flooding, erosion and sedimentation) (Elsom, 1992). Not only will there be changes to the pattern of precipitation and temperature across the globe, but the frequency and intensity of storms will be changed, probably increasing.

Global warming will also cause a rise in sea level. This is for two reasons: first, melting ice on land will contribute to sea level rise; and, second, thermal warming of surface water will increase the volume of sea water. The predictions for the increase in sea level vary considerably. For example, values for sea level rise predicted for the year 2100 range from 20 to 165 cm, to 3.5 m. Taking the former prediction this means that sea levels by the year 2030 will be 20 to 100 cm higher than at present. Even this increase in sea levels mean that low-lying land is at risk from flooding. This includes the Caribbean and Pacific coral islands, and major tropical and subtropical river deltas such as the Nile delta of Egypt, the Ganges–Brahmaputra–Meghna delta of Bangladesh and the Mississippi delta of the United States. The Netherlands is vulnerable unless coastal defences are significantly raised and reinforced, as are low-lying areas in the United Kingdom. Many of these areas are densely populated and have high agricultural or industrial productivity. The economic burden of strengthening existing coastal defences or developing new ones will be immense. The sea-level changes will be gradual, but storms will undoubtedly result in periodic inundations of these areas, inevitably leading to loss of life and considerable agricultural and commercial damage. It should not be forgotten that sea-level rises will also have an impact on coastal habitats. There will be changes in the pattern of coastal erosion and ingress by sea water into terrestrial habitats and groundwater. Vulnerable coastal habitats such as marshes and swamps will be damaged with the probability of species loss. Even the productivity, diversity and density of sea water species are likely to be affected by warmer seas (Elsom, 1992).

Increased concentrations of carbon dioxide in the atmosphere have a direct effect on crop productivity. This varies with the biochemical pathway by which plants fix carbon dioxide during photosynthesis. Plants designated C_3 plants, primarily temperate species such as wheat, rye, rice, barley, legumes, most grasses and forest species, increase their photosynthetic efficiency with carbon dioxide concentration (to a maximum of 1000 ppm carbon dioxide) increasing yields by 10–50 per cent. In contrast, C_4 plants, e.g. corn, sugar-cane, maize, millet, sorghum, are unlikely to show any net benefit from higher concentrations of carbon dioxide in the atmosphere. Increased carbon dioxide concentrations in the atmosphere may raise the efficiency of water use in plants through a reduction of transpiration through stomata (inducing partial closure of stomata), thus increasing their resistance to water stress. These effects have not been demonstrated beyond experimental systems. The balance between the effect of climate change on agricultural yields and any improvements in yield that may accrue from raised CO_2 is unknown. The impact of climate change and elevated CO_2 on natural terrestrial ecosystems is also difficult to predict, but is likely to be large (Bolin *et al.*, 1986). We are embarking on a global experiment the outcome of which is difficult to predict. There is no doubt, even if CO_2 emissions are extensively limited over the next few years, that we are committed to global climate changes. This atmospheric pollution is a global issue and is being addressed at an international level through various conventions (see Chapter 3). (For a full discussion of the impact of raised concentrations of atmospheric CO_2 see Bolin *et al.*, 1986.)

There are additional implications to human health in global warming. Tropical diseases such as malaria, yellow fever and dengue fever are likely to extend their geographical range. Indeed, the Intergovernmental Panel on Climate Change (IPCC) has reported evidence that this has already started to occur.

It should not be forgotten that pollutants can interact, affecting the extent of subsequent impacts. One example of atmospheric pollutants interacting draws the acid rain and global warming problems together. Global warming has tended to be masked in parts of the world where fossil fuel burning has resulted in a thin smog of polluting particles, predominantly composed of sulphate particles (see below). Sulphates, however, have a short life in the atmosphere, between 4 and 5 days, and only spread a few hundred kilometres from their emission point. Carbon dioxide has a long atmospheric life (Table 12. 2) and spreads throughout the atmosphere (*New Scientist*, 1 April 1995, p. 5). The development of regulations to protect the natural and man-made environments and human health from the deleterious effects of atmospheric and other pollutants must, in addition, attempt to take account of synergistic pollutant effects.

Air pollution

Historical foundations

The history of attempts to regulate and control air pollution goes back many centuries. Air pollution stands out as one of the most obvious symptoms of environmental deterioration. Consequently attempts have been made over several centuries to control atmospheric pollution.

There is, therefore, a significant historical contribution reflected in current legislation. Smoke and fumes may cause ill-health and in the London of the seventeenth century there were many fatalities due to respiratory diseases caused or exacerbated by air pollution. An attempt to provide a statutory solution to air pollution began with various Alkali Acts. The first was passed in 1863 which was followed by numerous Acts and then consolidated in the Alkali, etc., Works Regulation Act 1906, part of which still remains in force today. The Alkali Inspectorate was established and left to apply at its discretion the regulation of many industrial processes. The alkali legislation required that the inspectorate should require industrial processes under its inspection to use the best practicable means to prevent noxious gases or fumes escaping into the environment. This set a standard for the future development of the law.

During the nineteenth century the courts recognised the problem of air pollution but were slow to provide compensation to the individual for personal injury or discomfort. In the famous case of *St Helens Smelting Co.* v. *Tipping* (1865) 11 HLC 642, the House of Lords considered the case of Tipping, who owned a large estate in St Helens. Tipping claimed that his land was rendered useless for agricultural purposes due to air pollution from a neighbouring copper smelter. The House of Lords found in Tipping's favour. He received damages for the value of his land and an injunction against the continued operation of the copper smelter. However, the courts were unwilling to award damages for personal discomfort. This finding led to a fundamental weakness with the law (see: *The Royal Commission on Noxious Vapours* Parl. Pap. 1878 XLIV 14). Only gradually did the courts move from this position and in 1869 a majority of the judges decided that on a narrow basis personal liability would arise from any injurious harm caused by the nuisance of noise or dirt from a railway (see: *Hammersmith and City Rly.* v. *Brand* (1869) LR 4 HL 171). This is a clear illustration of the question of costs. Railway companies and foundry owners were required to pay for their nuisance or inconvenience, but settling costs and passing these on to the consumer was commonplace. Settling the best practicable means required a balancing act between the cost of statutory controls and the technologies available, and the economic realities of the industry.

Integrated Pollution Control

In Chapter 6 we noted the development of Integrated Pollution Control (IPC) as a technique of environmental law. IPC requires the disposal of solid, liquid or gaseous wastes in the way that will cause the least environmental damage. IPC requires that the best possible environmental option should be adopted. This is intended to ensure that IPC should form a system of pollution control that avoids damaging the environment. Over 5000 processes and activities are covered by IPC including not only air pollution but all forms of pollution. Her Majesty's Inspectorate of Pollution (HMIP, now the Environment Agency under the Environment Act 1995), operates the system of IPC, which has statutory force under Part 1 of the Environmental Protection Act 1990. The 1990 Act also conforms to Community requirements. In addition to providing prior approval of various industrial processes, IPC requires the operator to use the best available 'techniques' not entailing excessive costs (BATNEEC) (see Chapter 6). This procedure is intended to provide suitable management systems over the whole process (see: the Environmental Protection (Prescribed Processes and Substances) Regulations 1991, SI 1991 No. 472, SI 1992 No. 614 and SI 1994 No. 1329). Recognition of the UK's system of IPC may be found in the European Commission's Integrated Pollution Prevention and Control proposals for all Member States (see: COM(93) 423 OJ No. C 311, 17/11/93). Member States are expected to ensure that new installations do not operate without a permit and existing installations must obtain a permit by 30 June 2005.

There is a consultation paper covering amendments to the regulations defining the scope of industrial pollution control under Part 1 of the Environmental Protection Act 1990. It is envisaged that there may be changes in the relaxation of controls on manufacturers of glass- or fibre-reinforced products (see: ENDS Report 245, June 1995, pp. 34–5. *Proposed Further Amendments to the Prescribed Processes and Substances Regulations*, DoE, 1995).

IPC raises an important general question about who has legal jurisdiction and responsibility to monitor and control air pollution. There are two parallel systems of control, which in effect means overlapping jurisdictions for HMIP (now the Environment Agency under the Environment Act 1995) and local authorities for the monitoring of processes that fall within IPC and release prescribed substances into the atmosphere. Primarily the HMIP within the Environment Agency will have responsibility for IPC even though local authority control is also possible. In practice there has to be agreement and collaboration over the remit of the two systems of control. The creation of the new Environment Agency will provide opportunities to formally determine the respective responsibilities between HMIP and local authorities. There are signs that a national air quality strategy is to be implemented. Part IV of the Environment Act 1995, discussed in more detail below, provides for action at both local and national level. It is intended to publish a national air strategy at the end of 1995 setting standards and targets for the main pollutants and offering a time scale for improvements.

Energy and air pollution

Atmospheric pollution is in many instances directly related to energy production, e.g. carbon dioxide and sulphur dioxide gaseous emissions (see above), and this is dependent on energy consumption. *Climate Change – The UK's Programme* (DoE, 1994) outlines aims to reduce carbon dioxide emissions by 10 million tonnes by the year 2000. There are a number of elements to this programme and some have been referred to in previous chapters in this book (see Chapters 5 and 6). It is, therefore, necessary only to summarise the main elements of the 1994 Programme. Achieving the target of emissions reduction involves a wide variety of fiscal and economic devices. In the case of energy consumption in domestic premises, there are building regulations to ensure more energy-efficient buildings. Domestic appliances must conform to energy consumption standards. There is a system of eco-labelling currently under review as part of the EC's SAVE programme. There are two Directives intended to come into force from 1 April 1996 (see OJL 136, Vol. 38, (HMSO, 21 June 1995)). The Directives require appliance manufacturers to provide standard labels and information notices to dealers. The information and labels must be displayed. Energy consumption ratings are included in the published information. There are specific requirements for washing machines and tumble driers. Domestic consumers of energy have to pay an 8 per cent VAT on energy use since April 1994 and this is set to increase. An Energy Saving Trust was established in November 1992 to promote energy conservation.

In the case of non-domestic energy use there are various initiatives. These range from the Department of Trade and Industry's Energy Management Scheme and the initiatives promoted by the Department of Environment's Energy Efficiency Office. Transport policy which may contribute to the control of emissions to the atmosphere includes the addition of a tax on fuel and the possible introduction of toll roads.

The use of renewable energy sources is also an important strategy. The Non-Fossil Fuel Obligation (NFFO) provides that electricity companies must purchase a proportion of their electricity from renewable and nuclear sources. This is intended to guarantee a market for renewables over a set period and on this basis investment may be made in the renewable industry. The Department of Trade and Industry may make an order setting out the sources from which renewable energy is to be purchased and the amount that may be claimed. In practice the nuclear industry receives the largest amount under the order. There have been several NFFO orders (made by statutory instrument), which are beneficial for renewable energy companies. NFFO orders have been made in 1990, 1991 and 1994. It is intended to make the fourth in 1996 and the fifth in 1998. Wind farms have benefited under the various orders, giving rise to concerns about planning such projects (see: *Renewable Energy* (PPG 22), DoE, 1993).

The promotion of Combined Heat and Power (CHP) schemes and energy-saving initiatives is an important contribution to the reduction of air pollution. Schedule 22 of the Environment Act 1995 introduces an amendment to s. 3 of the Electricity Act 1989 to enable CHP operators to compete more efficiently with other forms of non-fossil fuel under the fossil fuel levy arrangements.

The Community has put forward specific proposals to promote the reduction of energy use and carbon dioxide emissions. In the case of energy efficiency there is a Programme on Energy Efficiency (SAVE) introduced by EC Directive 93/76/EEC (OJ No. 1 237/28). Member States must draw up and implement plans for the energy certification of buildings, the assessment of heating, air conditioning and hot water costs, thermal insulation, inspection of boilers and energy audits for buildings with high energy consumption. There is a Directive on the monitoring of greenhouse gas emissions (EC Directive 93/389/EEC OJ No. L 167/31) to establish a monitoring programme for carbon dioxide and other greenhouse gas emissions. In 1993 the Council set up an alternative energy programme (ALTENER) (see: 93/500/EEC OJ No. L 235/41) setting out specific actions for the greater use of renewable energy. This initiative includes proposals for technical studies and measures including grant assistance to develop and exploit renewable sources of energy.

An important initiative is contained in the Home Energy Conservation Act 1995 where provision is made for the drawing up of local energy conservation reports in relation to residential accommodation. Local authorities in Scotland, England and Wales and the Housing Executive in Northern Ireland can be designated energy conservation authorities. Section 2 of the Act provides that it is the duty of every energy conservation authority to prepare a report setting out measures 'that the authority considers practicable, cost-effective and likely to result in significant improvement in the energy efficiency' of residential accommodation in its area. Significantly the report should include an assessment of the cost of energy conservation and an assessment of the extent to which carbon dioxide emissions into the atmosphere would be decreased as a result of the measures. The 1995 Act also provides that the energy conservation report shall contain an assessment of the impact of reduced emissions into the atmosphere of oxides of nitrogen and sulphur dioxide.

Transport

The control of air pollution in the United Kingdom must include consideration of pollution caused by the motor car. In Part V of the Department of Environment's paper, *Air Quality: Meeting the Challenge* (DoE, 1995), it is noted that since 1970 the number of road vehicles in the United Kingdom has increased by 11 million. Nationally it is estimated that road transport is a major source of air pollution:

> ... responsible for 51 per cent of emissions of nitrogen oxides, 47 per cent of black smoke, 90 per cent of carbon monoxide and 37 per cent of volatile organic compounds. In urban areas, road transport is the principal source of pollution, in London responsible for up to 76 per cent of nitrogen oxides, 94 per cent of black smoke, 97 per cent of volatile organic compounds, 99 per cent of carbon monoxide and 22 per cent of sulphur dioxide pollution.

As Grant (1995, p. 2) has noted:

> The central paradox can be stated thus: government transport policies generally have a relatively marginal or incremental impact on the choices faced by consumers. If, however, government attempted to make radical changes in conditions of use (for example allowing cars to be driven on alternate days on the basis of their number plates), it would encounter substantial resistance from the electorate.

The environmental impact of sulphur dioxide and nitrogen oxides in the form of acid rain and direct effects on plant health and human health has already been noted (see above). A key source of carbon monoxide in urban environments is petrol-burning vehicles. The adverse effects of carbon monoxide arise from its ability to bind with haemoglobin, reducing the oxygen-carrying capacity of the blood.

Volatile organic compounds (VOCs) include reactive hydrocarbons which have a range of potential effects. They may have a direct impact on human health, for example some are carcinogens. In addition to this VOCs are significant contributors to the formation of photochemical smog. The reactive hydrocarbons and oxides of nitrogen arising from vehicle exhausts undergo photochemical oxidation in sunlight, in particular at UV wavelengths (<310 nm). A series of complex reactions produces a number of different products (see Harrison, 1992, for a full description of the reactions). The most important of the oxidants produced are ozone and peroxyacetyl nitrate (PAN). The end result is photochemical smogs, which are a major problem in many cities. The oxidants have several impacts. They induce a burning sensation in the eyes and nose, and sore throats. More seriously, individuals suffering from chronic respiratory problems such as asthma may be severely affected. Recently the Committee on the Medical Effects of Air Pollutants has considered recent research on air pollution and recommended further research in this area (see: Report of the Committee on the Medical Effects of Air Pollutants, HMSO, 1994).

Ozone also has a deleterious effect on materials such as fabrics and rubber. Chronic and acute exposure of plants to photochemically produced oxidants such as ozone and PAN has a deleterious effect. Leaves become necrotic, yields are reduced, and the quality of agricultural produce declines. The environmental impact of low-level ozone in the greenhouse effect has already been noted (see above).

Particulates also arise from the exhaust of motor vehicles. Other sources of particulates include the burning of fossil fuels, various industrial processes and natural processes. Solids or liquids can be suspended in the atmosphere in particles of sizes between 0.1 and 25μm in diameter. The majority of particles are below 1 μm and approximately 20 per cent consist of sulphate or sulphuric acid; other common constituents are carbon and hydrocarbons, e.g. polyaromatic hydrocarbons. Smoke includes particles of <10 μm diameter. In the United Kingdom and Europe the amount of particulate matter is measured on the basis of soiling properties. A known volume of air is passed through a filter paper so that particles present in the air are captured leaving a stain on the filter. The concentration of smoke in the atmosphere is then estimated by determining the density of the stain. The blackness of the smoke is an indication of the concentration of particulates. Smoke emission from petrol engines is seven times less than that from diesel engines (see Harrison, 1990, for a full description of measurement and analysis of particulate and other atmospheric pollutants; also see Elsom, 1992, for a discussion of particulate and gaseous air pollutants).

The acute effects of particulates on human health are partly reflected in their sulphurous content but particles themselves appear to have an important influence. Short-term exposure to particulates exacerbates respiratory illness, and when combined with exposure to sulphur dioxide pulmonary effects may result. Chronic, long-term exposure causes an increased prevalence of respiratory problems, including chronic bronchitis. There is evidence to suggest that particulates may be partly responsible for the increase in asthma in children.

Atmospheric particulates also have severe environmental consequences. Excessive quantities of airborne particles may coat the surface of leaves and block leaf stomata. Thus, the amount of light reaching the chloroplasts and the uptake of carbon dioxide are reduced, resulting in lowered rates of photosynthesis and plant growth. Particles containing reactive components, such as toxic hydrocarbons, may have additional adverse effects specific to the chemical.

The impact of atmospheric particles on the soiling of buildings, fabrics, etc., is well known. Not only does this result in substantial economic costs in cleaning, but particles often enhance corrosion. The atmospheric effects of particles are considerable, for example there may be a substantial reduction in visibility. It has even been suggested that particulates may act as nuclei for the condensation or freezing of water in the air, causing an increase in local precipitation. Particle content in the atmosphere is increasing. It is likely that this will have an effect on global warming, but there is some uncertainty and debate about whether warming will be reduced or enhanced (see Elsom, 1992; Harrison, 1992; and O'Riordan (1995) for full discussion of the impacts of particles).

Currently the Community is set to develop a road transport policy but the steps necessary to reduce road transport pollution are also being taken. Directive 91/441/EEC (see SI 1992 No. 2137) limits emissions of carbon monoxide, hydrocarbons and oxides of nitrogen from new passenger and light goods vehicles. This has been extended by Directive 93/59/EEC to new light commercial vehicles and vans (see SI 1993 No. 2201). Directive EC 91/542/EEC limits the emissions of carbon monoxide and oxides of nitrogen from new heavy commercial vehicles (see SI 1992 No. 2137).

There are Directives (EC Directive 75/716/EEC OJ No. L307/22, and EC Directive 87/219/EEC OJ No. L91/9) setting standards for the content of fuels and the lead content of petrol (see: the Motor Fuel (Sulphur Content of Gas Oil) Regulations 1990, SI 1990 No. 1097 and the Motor Fuel (Lead Content of Petrol) Regulations 1981, SI 1990 No. 1523). Alkyl lead compounds such as tetraethyl lead and tetramethyl lead are used as anti-knock additives in petrol. After combustion in the engine over 70 per cent of the lead enters the air; much of this is deposited locally but a significant amount (up to 24 per cent) may travel considerable distances, becoming dispersed. Lead has an atmospheric residence time of up to 2 weeks. In urban areas concentrations of atmospheric lead may be between 10 and 10 000 ng m^{-3} depending on local conditions, compared with lead concentrations between 5 and 500 ng m^{-3} in rural areas. Lead in petrol, particularly in urban areas, is a large contributor to the total lead intake of adults and children, but it should be remembered that there are other sources of human lead exposure, e.g. lead piping for drinking water (see Chapter 10). The link between lead from traffic and increased lead blood levels has not in fact been fully established, though evidence is growing that this is the case. There is as yet no unequivocal evidence that atmospheric lead has significant effects on the central nervous system, with a subsequent impairment of, for example, the mental ability of children. Such a link is tenuous at present but may in future become clearer. It is an interesting point that this type of impact has largely been accepted as real by the public and government policy has been influenced. It should be noted that atmospheric lead will also contaminate soil and water through precipitation. Lead is a toxic metal and will inevitably have ecological impacts, depending on the pattern of deposition and concentration. High exposure to lead results in a decrease of species abundance and diversity (McEldowney *et al.*, 1993). There is an additional reason for the reduction of lead in petrol. Catalytic converters, which remove other gaseous pollutants from exhaust emissions, do not function properly with leaded petrol.

Attempts to make engine construction meet improved environmental standards have been gradual, dating back to the early 1970s. The construction and certification of vehicles is regulated under the United Kingdom Construction and Use Regulations under the Road Traffic Act 1988. Emission standards are set for different categories of vehicle: passenger cars, light commercial vehicles and heavy goods vehicles.

The future policy on road transport is based on a number of different approaches. The influential Report of the Royal Commission on Environmental Pollution (Royal Commission on Environmental Pollution, 18th Report, *Transport and the Environment* (HMSO, 1994)), has caused a substantial re-think of the motorway building programme and reliance on road transport. The report recognised that future expansion in road traffic was not sustainable and that restrictions on future growth are required. Limitations on air pollutants, especially carbon dioxide, are an important requirement for the future. Attempting to meet the World Health Organisation's targets for air quality is another requirement. The government's own paper, *Air Quality: Meeting the Challenge* (DoE, 1995, p. 24), sets out four instruments of road transport policy:

1. Planning policies and setting local transport priorities to reduce the need for travel.
2. Develop environmental responsibilities in partnership with public service and fleet operators.
3. Tighter enforcement of emissions regulations and targeting the vehicles most likely to damage the environment.
4. Set out effective guidance to the public on environmentally friendly motoring.

The introduction of lead-free fuel and the tax differential for unleaded petrol are examples of how policy developments in this area may be implemented with relatively modest success. Road duties are set to rise at least 55 per cent on average to help meet the UK's targets and reduce emissions. The United Kingdom has identified transport as the key sector for improving air quality. It remains to be seen whether the pragmatic approach to road transport will achieve improvements when public sector transport, including rail, is subject to privatisation. Vested interest and government policy are not always compatible.

▶ Control of noxious emissions and dark smoke

United Kingdom legislation

The Clean Air Act 1993 contains the main provisions on air pollution and the control of dark smoke. The 1993 Act replaces and consolidates earlier Clean Air Acts 1956 and 1968 and the Control of Smoke Pollution Act 1989. There are various Circulars from the DoE that provide useful and workable guides (see: for example, Circular 9/93 Exchequer grant-aid in smoke control areas). There are a number of Community Directives on industrial emissions (see below). It is an offence for dark smoke to be emitted from a chimney of any building or of any fixed boiler or industrial plant or from any industrial or trade premises. Dark smoke is defined according to the Riglemann Chart which acts as a type of calibration curve. This chart provides Local Authority Environmental Health Officers with the standard means to measure and monitor dark smoke emissions. The chart is calibrated from 0 to 5 and the standard for dark smoke is set at 2. (See above for discussion of particulates and measurement of atmospheric concentrations of particulates.)

Liability is placed on the occupier of a building or the person who is in possession of a boiler for the use of a chimney. In industrial or trade premises there is strict criminal liability on the occupier of premises or any person who causes or permits the emissions. The offences are mainly summary ones and there is a requirement under s. 51 to notify the occupier of the premises or the person in possession of the boiler or plant, in writing within four days, of the alleged offence. Statutory exceptions to strict liability may be found in s. 1(4) of the 1993 Act. Broadly these exceptions are based on lighting up a furnace or when the failure to prevent smoke emissions was not reasonably foreseen. There is also under s. 2(4) of the 1993 Act a defence for the defendant to show that the alleged emission was inadvertent, and that all practicable steps had been taken to prevent or minimise the emission of dark smoke.

Further exceptions are provided in a number of regulations (see: Dark Smoke (Permitted Periods) Regulations 1958, SI 1958 No. 498 and the Clean Air (Emission of Dark Smoke) Exemption Regulations 1969, SI 1969 No. 1263), which specify exemptions in the lighting of a furnace, or due to some failure of apparatus that could not be foreseen or the use of unsuitable fuel when suitable fuel was unobtainable. In industrial and trade premises it is for the defendant to bear responsibility for showing that no dark smoke was emitted where material is burned on the premises.

Regulation of smoke and emissions of grit and dust is covered by the Clean Air Act 1993. Section 4 requires that new furnaces should be smokeless. There are limits on the rate of emission of grit and dust (see s. 5 of the Clean Air Act 1993 and the Clean Air (Emission of Grit and Dust) from Furnaces Regulations 1971, SI 1971 No. 162). There are regulations for the fitting of grit- and dust-arresting plant and also certain exemptions which may be granted at the discretion of the local authority and subject to appeal to the Secretary of State for

Environment (see: the Clean Air Arrestment Plant (Exemptions) Regulations 1969, SI 1969 No. 1262).

Sections 10 and 11 of the Clean Air Act 1993 provide for the measurement of grit, dust and fumes emitted from furnaces. There are also powers for the control of the height of chimneys under s. 14 of the 1993 Act (see: Clean Air (Height of Chimneys) (Exemption) Regulations 1969, SI 1969 No. 411). The tendency to utilise tall stacks (chimneys) for emissions to the atmosphere while helping to protect local environments has been blamed for enhancing the distance travelled by pollutants. The effect may be to transfer adverse impacts to regions distant from the original source (see acid rain above).

There are proposals to deregulate and repeal certain parts of the Clean Air Act 1993 as part of an overall deregulation strategy (see: Department of the Environment, *A Proposal to Repeal Provisions of the Clean Air Act 1993*, July, 1993).

In addition to the regulation of emissions such as grit and dust there are also smoke control areas that are subject to smoke control orders under s. 18 of the 1993 Act. Procedures for making, enforcing and the prohibition of smoke in such areas are covered by ss. 18 to 22 of the 1993 Act. The powers are vested in the Secretary of State to require the creation of smoke control areas by a local authority. Setting standards is part of the Air Quality Standards Regulations 1989 (SI 1989 No. 317). There are also a number of orders that apply to fireplaces in domestic dwellings (see: s. 11(4) of the Clean Air Act 1956) and regulations for smokeless fuels (see: the Smoke Control Areas (Authorised Fuels) Regulations 1991, SI 1991 No. 1282, and the Smoke Control Areas (Authorised Fuels) (Amendment) Regulations 1992, SI 1992 No. 72). These regulations provide local authorities with powers and obligations in smoke control areas over domestic and industrial premises.

Finally, the problem of stubble burning in agricultural areas, usually in the autumn months, is now regulated by the Crop Residues (Burning) Regulations 1993, SI 1993 No. 1366, made under s. 152 of the Environmental Protection Act 1990. The burning of stubble by farmers produced considerable quantities of particulates and contributed to some extent to increases in atmospheric carbon dioxide. Farmers adopted the policy of stubble burning for several reasons. It requires limited manpower, is low cost and has the advantage of helping to maintain nutrient levels in soils. Undoubtedly, a substantial problem exists for the agricultural industry for the disposal of ligno-cellulosic waste.

Industrial emissions

The European Community has introduced a number of initiatives to improve industrial air emissions. There is a Directive on Air Pollution from Industrial Plants (see: EC Directive 84/360 EEC OJ No. L 188/20). This requires Member States to provide prior authorisation for industrial plant in various industries such as energy, metal processing and production, manufacturing industries in terms of non-metallic mineral products, chemicals, waste disposal and others. The principles employed in deciding on the authorisation include BATNEEC (noted above, and see Chapter 6), and that the plant concerned does not emit significant amounts of pollutants, including: sulphur and nitrogen and their compounds; carbon monoxide; organic compounds excluding methane (e.g. VOCs); chlorine and fluorine and their compounds (these have a range of toxic impacts and contribute to the depletion of ozone in the stratosphere, see below); dust; asbestos; and glass and mineral fibres. The Directive also requires Member States to adapt existing plant to meet higher standards set by the Directive. In addition to the arrangements contained in the Directive it is envisaged that there will be further Directives containing emission limits fixed for large combustion plants, municipal waste incinerators and hazardous waste incinerators. The above arrangements are part of the Integrated Pollution Control strategy for the environment (see: Prescribed Processes and Substances Regulations 1991, SI 1991 No. 472) (see Chapter 6).

The EC Large Combustion Plants Directive 88/609/EEC OJ No. L 336/1, applies limits on the emissions of certain pollutants from combustion plants that are rated at a minimum of 50 MW thermal input. There are exemptions for certain plants. The aim is to reduce sulphur dioxide and oxides of nitrogen by setting national ceilings for Member States (see above for health and environmental impacts). There are three phases, from 1990 to 2003, for implementing the Directive. There is a UK programme for reducing emissions published by the Department of Environment (see: Department of the Environment, 1990, *Programme and National Plan for Reducing SO_2 and NO_x Emissions from Large Combustion Plants*. The quotas that are set in the United Kingdom are subject to revision to ensure that the targets of the Directive are met. Changes such as the use of different fuels may have implications for the target. Her Majesty's Inspectorate of Pollution (now the Environment Agency) has set new targets to take account of the current situation (see: ENDS Report 245, June 1995, p. 29). There are implications for the electricity industry arising out of the Directive. Meeting emissions targets is probably easier through gas rather than coal generation of electricity.

There are a number of Directives on Municipal Waste Incinerators, including EC Directive 89/369/EEC OJ No. L 163/32 on the prevention of air pollution from new (authorised from 1 December 1990) municipal waste incineration plants. There is also an EC Directive 89/429 EEC OJ No. L 203/50 that applies to plant before 1 December

1990 and this includes a timetable for new municipal waste incineration plants. There are proposals for a Directive on the Incineration of Hazardous Waste (OJ No. C 130/1, 21 May 1992). Any proposed incinerator plants first require to be authorised and limits are set on the legally permitted emissions (see Chapter 9 for a discussion of possible problems arising from incineration processes). Finally there is a Directive on Pollution caused by asbestos, EC Directive 87/217/EEC OJ No. L 85/40, that requires Member States to ensure that asbestos releases into air, water and land are reduced at source and prevented. The principles involved in setting standards fall under BATNEEC, discussed above, reinforced by the Trade Effluents (Prescribed Processes and Substances) Regulations 1989, SI 1989 No. 1156.

This area of the law is not static. New developments in terms of scientific understanding lead to new Directives. The EC has introduced Regulation 91/594/EEC OJ No. L 76/1 on substances that may contribute to the depletion of the ozone layer in the stratosphere. This covers various chlorofluorocarbons (CFCs), halons, carbon tetrachloride and 1,1,1-trichloroethane. There are restrictions in the United Kingdom on the importation, supply and storage of non-refillable containers containing CFCs for use in refrigerants or air conditioning machinery. The reactions reducing the ozone concentrations in the stratosphere are varied depending on the compounds involved. It is, however, worth while indicating the types of reactions that occur:

1. Nitrous oxide

$$O_3 + NO \longrightarrow O_2 + NO_2 \tag{12.1}$$

$$O + NO_2 \longrightarrow O_2 + NO \tag{12.2}$$

2. Chlorine

$$O_3 + Cl \longrightarrow O_2 + ClO \tag{12.3}$$

$$O + ClO \longrightarrow O_2 + Cl \tag{12.4}$$

CFCs contribute to the breakdown of ozone after their dissociation in the atmosphere, catalysed by sunlight, i.e. photodissociation, to produce Cl, as shown in the following equations:

$$CF_2Cl_2 \xrightarrow{\text{sunlight}} CF_2Cl + Cl \tag{12.5}$$

$$CFCl_3 \xrightarrow{\text{sunlight}} CFCl_2 + Cl \tag{12.6}$$

(For a full analysis of these reactions see Harrison, 1992.)

The ozone depleting potential (ODP) of chemicals varies. The most potent ODPs are CFC 11 ($CFCl_3$) and CFC 12 (CF_2Cl_2) (Table 12. 3). There are several points worth noting with regard to ozone depletion. Undoubtedly major contributors to ozone depletion are used in

Table 12.3 Percentage* of ozone removed by selected halocarbons

Halocarbon	Per cent removal
CFC 12	40.0
CFC 11	30.4
CFC 13 (CF_3Cl_3)	11.7
Carbon tetrachloride	7.6
Methyl chloroform	5.1
Halon 1301 (CF_3B)	3.7

(*Source* : Elsom, 1992)
* Weighted by ozone depletion potential based on 1985 emissions.

domestic appliances and in various industries. These are now being controlled (above) and will be phased out. Care must be taken that replacement chemicals do not themselves have ODP. Other sources of compounds that deplete stratospheric ozone may be less easy to control. For example, oxides of nitrogen may be released as the result of microbial denitrification of nitrogen-based fertilisers used in the agricultural industry. Estimates about the contribution this will make to ozone loss vary from 1–4 per cent to 20 per cent in the first 25 years of the next century (Elsom, 1992). Clearly, considerably more research is required before a full understanding of the impact of this process is achieved.

The significance of the layer of ozone in the stratosphere is the ability of ozone to adsorb ultraviolet (UV-B or 280–320 nm) radiation from the sun. A depletion of this layer has significant health and environmental effects because the biosphere is exposed to higher levels of UV radiation. In humans the exposure to higher levels of UV radiation is linked to substantial increases in the incidence of skin cancers. A wide variety of plant species, including some important crop species, e.g. soya beans, are sensitive to increased UV exposure. Plant structure and function is impaired and growth reduced. Aquatic plants, including phytoplankton, also appear to be adversely affected. Similarly a wide range of aquatic animals, e.g. crabs, zooplankton, have been shown to be adversely affected at the egg, larval, juvenile and/or adult stage. Terrestrial animals show a tendency to cancers and show an impaired immunological system.

The seriousness of ozone depletion cannot be doubted. The impact has varied slightly between the southern and northern hemispheres. In the region of the Antarctic there has been the formation of a 'hole' in the ozone layer in the spring. The depth and size of this hole varies on a biennial cycle, i.e. is deeper every second year. The position and area covered by the 'hole' also varies, but often reaches as far as Australia. Ozone depletion over the Arctic appears to be more diffuse. There is a drop in ozone content over a fairly large region rather than the formation of a 'hole'. Again the severity of this decline varies with year (Elsom, 1992; Harrison, 1992). At present the global loss of ozone is between 1 and 2 per cent annually. Even if ODPs were stabilised at pre-1990 levels it would be 70 years before ozone loss ceases.

Finally there is a proposed Community Directive on volatile organic compounds (VOCs). These are emitted from sources such as motor cars, landfills, during solvent usage and through various industrial processes such as oil refining and from natural sources. Examples of commonly encountered VOCs in urban areas include toluene, propane, ethane, ethylene, isobutane and benzene. Their longevity in the atmosphere varies with their reactivity. The most reactive degrade within a few hours while the least reactive may remain undegraded for several days. Many are carcinogens and in addition contribute to the formation of photochemical smog (see above). The current law on VOCs falls within the controls under Part 1 of the Environmental Protection Act 1990 and such controls will have to take account of Community Directives. This is likely to be in the form of a Directive on solvents (see ENDS Report 241, pp. 32–3). There is also likely to be a Directive on fuel-produced VOCs. This is in two stages: stage I controls set limits on losses due to petrol storage and stage II concerns loss from vehicles during the process of refuelling. This may require the installation of vapour recovery equipment at petrol stations.

The Department of the Environment has published a paper, *Reducing Emissions of VOCs and Ground Level Ozone: A UK Strategy* (DoE, 1993). It is noted that:

> According to the Department of the Environment (DoE), emissions of VOCs from industrial solvent use amounted to 454 000 tonnes in 1988, 18 per cent of the total and the second largest source after vehicle emissions. The DoE's latest projections, presented to the Committee last November, suggest that controls under the Environmental Protection Act 1990 will reduce the sector's emissions by 44.5 per cent by 1999. (ENDS Report 241, pp. 9932–3)

Concerns about levels of VOCs have been voiced by the House of Commons Environment Committee (see: *House of Commons Environment Committee, First Report Session 1994/5, Volatile Organic Compounds*, Vol. 1, HMSO, 1995). The dilemma confronting Parliament is to balance the burden on industry of the high cost of VOC controls and the requirement of substantial reductions in emissions as part of international agreements and Community objectives. In 1991 the Geneva protocol to the 1979 UN Economic Commission for Europe Convention on Long-range Transboundary Air Pollution stipulates that Member States should take action to control VOC emissions.

The government's response to the Committee report is that new fiscal arrangements are being considered to provide incentives for the sale of less polluting vehicles (ENDS Report 245, pp. 32–3). There are also detailed specific responses to VOCs in the chemical and solvent industries. It is likely that coming to terms with the emission of VOCs will direct government policy to the development of strategies for making less use of motor transport in the United Kingdom.

▶ Community developments

Attempts in the 1980s to develop a European Community policy on air pollution focused on the setting of air standards. One approach taken by the Community is to provide pollutant-specific Directives (Table 12.4).

In 1980 EC Directive 80/779/EEC (OJ No. L 229/30) set limits and guidelines for sulphur dioxide and suspended particulates. Certain limit values were set to be achieved by Member States. Guide values were set containing target standards. These included standards intended to achieve long-term protection for human health and the environment. There are also limits to be achieved within certain zones, specifically designated where it is necessary to limit foreseeable pollution. In 1985 the Nitrogen Dioxide EC Directive 85/203/EEC (OJ No. L 87/1) sets standards to be achieved by 1994 on nitrogen dioxide (see above for environmental impacts). The Directive contains principles for the evaluation of zones worthy of special environmental protection. In the United Kingdom implementation of the Directive is through the Air Quality Standards Regulations, SI 1989 No. 317, which set standards on sulphur dioxide, suspended particulates and nitrogen dioxide emissions.

In 1982 the Directive on lead in the air, EC Directive 82/884/EEC (OJ No. L 378/15), set limits on the value of lead (see above for impacts) which Member States must have achieved by December 1987. It also includes the requirement for plans to be drawn up by December

Table 12.4 EC Directives on specific pollutants

Sulphur dioxide and suspended particulates	Directive 80/779/EEC
Lead	Directive 82/884/EEC
Nitrogen dioxide	Directive 85/203/EEC
Ozone	Directive 92/72/EEC

1989 on future improvements. There is also a Directive on Air Pollution by Ozone, EC Directive 92/72/EEC (OJ No. L 297/1). This Directive sets up a system for the harmonisation of procedures across the Community for monitoring, exchanging information and warning the public about air pollution caused by ozone at ground level and the consequences of such pollution to humans and vegetation. The Directive sets standards for the monitoring of ozone concentrations and addresses the effects of pollution on health and vegetation (see above), supplying information to the population and issuing warnings where there are dangerous levels. These standards are referred to in the Directive as thresholds and there is legislation to provide the Secretary of State with powers to set up monitoring stations and issue warnings (see: Ozone Monitoring and Information Regulations 1994, SI 1994 No. 440). It is intended that Member States will monitor levels of ozone and report to the European Commission within four years (1996) after the implementation of the Directive.

In 1994 the Commission proposed a new framework Directive on ambient air quality assessment and management (COM (94) 109 final, OJ No. C 216/4 6/8/94). It is expected that there will be 13 further Directives on individual pollutants. These will include a revision of the existing Directives on nitrogen, sulphur, lead and hydrocarbon particulates and ground-level ozone. Additional pollutants will be covered by Directives on cadmium, carbon monoxide and benzene. In all, including ozone, there will be 14 air pollutants subject to regulation (see: *Chemistry and Industry*, Vol. 13, 3 July 1995, p. 483).

Grant (1995, p. 177) has noted that the Directives have a number of limitations. There is a time difference as to when the different Directives setting air quality standards were adopted. Different philosophies apply to different Directives. There are variations in the time Member States have taken to implement Directives and differences in monitoring strategies throughout the Community. Long-term policies on air pollution have different priorities among Member States. Taking all these factors into consideration it is argued that Directives that are pollutant specific may give rise to lack of standardisation and variations throughout the community appear inevitable. Grant favours a different approach:

> A more standardized approach would be adopted with common reporting standards; setting pollution limits to be attained within ten to fifteen years; and setting provisional ceilings. (Grant, 1995, p. 178)

The Community has a number of issues to address. The first is how effective its strategy will appear when air pollution problems arise in specific zones in the Community. Second, there appear to be differences between Member States on the strategy to be adopted for the control of air pollution and the improvement of air quality. How will such differences be reconciled, if at all? Clearly, given the potentially regional or global impact of certain air pollutants, decisions made by individual states have an effect beyond their own boundaries.

The UK's approach is a reactive and flexible one geared towards assessing the effects of air pollution. This may be criticised as not providing a sufficiently clear set of standards, such as those envisaged in the Community's Air Quality Framework Directive. Reconciling such differences will confront the United Kingdom in the coming years.

Air quality and sustainable development: setting standards

The government has embarked on a strategy to develop air quality as part of its overall strategy for sustainable development and its conclusions are contained in *Air Quality: Meeting the Challenge* (DoE, 1995). The principal elements in the strategy are as follows:

- Set standards and targets for a new framework of national air quality.
- Introduce a new system for local air quality management based on the creation of standards.
- Set effective controls of emissions, particularly from vehicles.
- Local air quality management improved through the setting of standards.
- Co-ordination of all activities in the management of air quality achieved through new powers and duties on both local and central government.

It is expected that the new Environment Agency will have a role. Part IV of the Environment Act 1995 provides the necessary legislation for a National Air Quality Strategy. The National Strategy will set a framework for air standards and targets for nine major pollutants. Local authorities will be given a new role to conduct reviews of air quality and to designate 'Air Quality Management Areas' where reviews have shown that air standards and quality have not been achieved because they have not met the targets set in the National Strategy.

Part IV and ss. 80–91 of the Environment Act 1995 only provide a framework for a National Air Quality Strategy. Further legislation and detailed arrangements will be contained in regulations and guidance under the 1995 Act. The Secretary of State will publish guidance and a National Strategy setting air quality standards at the end of 1995.

Conclusions

The Government's response to air quality, although a belated one, has come about through public pressure and the influence of the European

Community. It is sometimes the case that by challenging the basic assumptions that underline government policy, a more fundamental analysis of air pollution problems may be produced. For example, the Royal Commission on Environmental Pollution in October 1994 published an important analysis of transport policy and its effects on air pollution (see: Royal Commission on Environmental Pollution, 18th Report, 1994, p.1).

There are a number of scientific challenges associated with establishing a successful regulatory framework to control atmospheric pollution and achieve good air quality. The most obvious is the need for continued investigation of the health and environmental impacts of atmospheric pollutants. For example, it has only recently started to be established that the rise in the number of children suffering from asthma may be linked in part to traffic pollution. It is not yet known which pollutant (or pollutants) in vehicle exhausts is responsible for this effect although some evidence suggests particulates. If this is the case then a policy controlling the use of diesel engines may be appropriate since these produce the most particulate emissions. Little is known about the synergistic or antagonistic impacts, if any, of different atmospheric pollutants, and understanding of the impact of pollutants on natural ecosystems is often limited.

Crucial to determining the impact of air pollutants and ensuring good air quality is the establishment of adequate and efficient monitoring procedures (see: Harrison, 1992, for analytical techniques) – a requirement clearly recognised in the Government Strategy (see above). Apart from the technical ability to measure pollutant concentration there are questions as to the appropriate places to establish monitoring stations. Should they be sited in residential areas, in city centres, near busy roads or at other sites? Individuals' exposure to air pollutants will inevitably vary throughout a day as they move about. To add to the complexity, this movement and therefore exposure levels will vary with the individual. Should monitors be at child's height, adult height or higher? How often should measurements be taken – hourly, daily, less frequently, or should frequency vary with season? Should there be one monitor or several monitors? Certainly the area over which a single monitor operates will vary with a number of factors, including local topography, the atmospheric longevity of the pollutant, and weather conditions. It is important to establish the best possible monitoring system to ensure that measurements are representative of an individual's or a community's exposure to the pollutants. The Expert Panel on Air Quality Standards has recommended various air quality standards, e.g. carbon monoxide 10 ppm measured as a running 8-hour average (see: *Report of the Committee on the Medical Effects of Air Pollutants*, HMSO, 1994).

It is relatively easy to specify the emission rate of a single point source such as a chimney stack at an industrial plant and to develop predictive models for the transport and dispersal of any emissions. In urban areas there may be thousands of different point sources contributing to impairment of air quality. In this case emission inventories are often produced, estimating the overall amount of air pollutants produced in a given area from all sources, both industrial and domestic, e.g. combustion processes (power plants, cars, etc.) (see Harrison, 1992). This is useful for longer-term modelling, e.g. annual, but presents problems for shorter time scales because of seasonal and diurnal variations. Reliable predictive models of air pollutant fate, and ideally the impact of the pollutants, are essential for the control of air pollution and the development of appropriate regulations to protect human health and the natural and built environments.

▶ References and further reading

Bell, J.N.B. and Clough, W.S. (1973) 'Depression of yield in ryegrass exposed to SO$_2$. *Nature, London,* **241**, 47–9.

Bolin, B., Doos, Bo.R., Jager, J. and Warrick, R.A. (1986) *The Greenhouse Effect, Climatic Change, and Ecosystems (Scope 29).* John Wiley, Chichester.

Crawford, R.M.M. (1989) 'Studies in plant survival. Ecological case histories of plant adaptation to adversity'. In *Studies in Ecology,* Vol 11. Blackwell, Oxford.

Drent, P.J. and Woldendorp, J.W. (1989) 'Acid rain and eggshells'. *Nature, London,* **339**, 431.

Elsom, D.E. (1992) *Atmospheric Pollution. A Global Problem,* 2nd edn. Blackwell, Oxford.

ENDS Report (1994) *Integrated Pollution Control – The First Three Years.*

Grant, W. (1995) *Autos, Smog and Pollution Control.* Edward Elgar, Aldershot.

Harrison, R. (ed.) (1990) *Pollution: Causes, Effects and Control,* 2nd edn. Cambridge Society of Chemistry, Cambridge.

Holman, C. (1991) *Air Pollution and Health.* Friends of the Earth, London.

Leeson, J.D. (1995) *Environmental Law.* Pitman, London.

McEldowney, S., Hardman, D., Waite, S. (1993) *Pollution: Ecology and Biotreatment.* Longman, Essex.

Mumma, A. (1995) *Environmental Law Meeting UP and EC Requirements.* McGraw-Hill, Maidenhead.

Roberts, T.M., (1984) 'Effects of air pollution in agriculture and forestry'. *Atmos. Environ.* **18**, 629–52.

Weale, A. (1992) *The New Politics of Pollution.* Manchester University Press, Manchester.

▶ Reports

Department of the Environment, *Climate Change – The UK's Programme* (HMSO, 1994).

Department of the Environment, *Improving Air Quality – A Discussion Paper on Air Quality Standards and Management* (1994).

Department of the Environment, *Ozone in the United Kingdom 1993: Third Report of the United Kingdom Petrochemical Oxidants Review Group Air Quality Division* (London, 1994).

Department of the Environment, *Air Quality: Meeting the Challenge* (1995).

Report on the Consolidation of Certain Enactments Relating to Clean Air (1992) Law Comm. No. 209; Scot. Law Comm. No. 138.

Royal Commission on Environmental Pollution, 18th Report, *Transport and the Environment* (HMSO, 1994).

▶ Useful information

Since 1993 there is available an Enhanced Urban Monitoring Network of the Department of the Environment which provides information on air quality (01800 556677).

13 Noise

Experiencing modern-day living is to recognise how noise may be a pollutant which in excess may damage health. Historically noise was linked to the workplace either in traditional heavy industries such as steel and shipbuilding or in light manufacturing. Noise at work has been governed by strict health and safety legislation but this falls outside the remit of this book. Domestic noise is potentially a more chronic problem and can be regarded as an environmental issue. In everyday life the experience of high-street traffic or living near large urban conurbations brings an awareness of noise as an irritation and annoyance. Prolonged exposure to noise can cause severe ear damage. In this chapter the legal remedies and controls on noise are examined. How is noise measured and what are the measures to be taken to reduce noise and minimise the risk to health? Setting standards for noise also requires effective enforcement measures.

Measuring and defining noise

There is no overriding legal definition of noise. While this is unsatisfactory, the law does have an important role. Instead of providing a workable definition of noise, the law has focused on the means to control noise and has recognised the difficulties of measuring noise. In 1963 the Wilson committee made a useful contribution when it defined noise as 'sound which is undesired by the recipient' (see: *Noise*, Cmnd 2056 (1963)). Noise is measured in decibels (db).

Objective measurements of noise do not equate with the nuisance noise may cause. It is commonly agreed that the polluting nature of noise has both objective and subjective elements. The objective element provides some basic criteria for the measurement of noise. The subjective element (see: *Gaunt* v. *Fynney* (1872) 8 Ch App 8) implied in noise pollution is that the noise is unwanted. This unwanted element makes legal definition difficult. Relevant considerations as to whether noise is unwanted may include questions of excess use or whether the use is reasonable or necessary. A variety of levels of noise are

Table 13.1 Noise Levels

0 db	Threshold of hearing
10 db	Leaves rustling
30 db	Quiet bedroom at night
40 db	Average living room
50 db	Living room with distant traffic noise
60 db	Busy office
70 db	Conversational speech
75 db	Major road with heavy traffic
88 db	Heavy lorry on busy road
90 db+	*Potential loss of hearing from prolonged exposure*
100 db	House near airport
125 db	Jet aircraft taking off
140 db	Threshold of pain

(*Sources*: Adapted from C.S. Kerse, 1995; *This Common Inheritance* Cm 1200;
D. Van Wynsberghe *et al.*, 1995)

experienced in everyday life (Table 13.1). The human ear is surprisingly
sensitive to noise: it can detect approximately a one decibel change in
sound intensity. Prolonged exposure to noise above 90 db may cause
damage to hearing, though the level where harm to human health may
occur may vary according to the duration of exposure and the sensitivity
of the individual.

There are attempts to limit noise levels for various activities through
international agreements and the European Community. Controls on
noise may fall into two broad categories: public law controls that include
the role of local authorities; private law remedies that allow the citizen
to pursue remedies in the courts.

▶ Public law controls

The haphazard development of the law in this area is indicative of the
difficulty of providing a coherent analysis of noise for the purposes of
legal definition and control. Local authority by-laws and local Acts of
Parliament have provided a miscellaneous number of rules and regulations on noise. The first major legislative attempt to bring order to this
confusion was the Noise Abatement Act 1960. The Act codified existing
local authority powers. Part III of the Control of Pollution Act 1974
introduced further changes to the law. This was further consolidated by
the Environmental Protection Act 1990 (hereinafter EPA).

It is also noteworthy that noise may be considered as part of planning
law (see Chapter 7). Some planning authorities have included the

control of noise when drawing up their statutory plans. The use and imposition of planning conditions under s. 106 of the Town and Country Planning Act 1990 may lessen the necessity to impose the stricter noise condition in the EPA. In many large-scale developments the use of development control may require close liaison between environmental health, planning, transport and local authorities (see: ENDS Report 237, October 1994, p. 34). The first wide-ranging guide to planning and noise was issued in October 1994 by the Department of the Environment (see: PPG24 *Planning and Noise*, HMSO, 1994). The aims of the guidance are to provide planners and developers, alongside local communities, with some degree of certainty about the particular types of developments that are acceptable or those in which special measures may be required to mitigate the impact of noise. The guidance provides an important contribution to the debate about noise by setting out certain noise bands to assist local authorities in determining applications within residential areas.

Nuisance

Various statutory nuisances exist. Subsections 79(1) (g) and (6) of the Environmental Protection Act 1990 (the EPA) make it a statutory nuisance to emit noise from premises which is prejudicial to health or is a nuisance. Normally the power to take action to stop the nuisance is given to the local authority, but there are specific procedures to be used when action is taken by an aggrieved citizen. The local authority has powers to serve a notice on the owner or occupier of premises to stop the noise (s. 80 of the EPA). This is subject to an appeal procedure. An aggrieved citizen, due to a complaint about nuisance caused by noise, may make a complaint to the magistrates under s. 82 of the EPA. This procedure may result in an abatement notice if the magistrates are satisfied that the nuisance exists or, though temporarily abated, is likely to recur on the same premises. This procedure is available against the person causing the noise or the occupier or owner of the premises.

One difficulty, often caused by changes in this area of law, is that recent legislation may overturn regulations currently in operation to provide abatement notices or other forms of relief to aggrieved citizens suffering noise pollution. The House of Lords has recently accepted that enforcement notices made under legislation prior to the EPA 1990 would remain valid even though the EPA repealed many of the statutory powers under earlier legislation (see: *Aitken* v. *South Hams DC* [1994] 3 All ER 400).

A further example of a statutory nuisance is provided in s. 2 of the Noise and Statutory Nuisance Act 1993 which amends s. 79 of the EPA to make it a statutory nuisance for noise to be emitted from or caused by a vehicle, machinery or equipment in a street. Statutory nuisances have a legislative history that may be traced back through the Control of Pollution Act 1974 and the Public Health Act 1936 (see: Ormandy and Burridge, *Professional Practice Note*, 1995). There are also powers to allow a local authority officer to enter, open or remove a vehicle or machinery or equipment in a street to abate the nuisance arising from street noise. The 1993 Act also extends the powers of the local authority by empowering them to impose charges on premises for the recovery of expenses incurred in abating nuisance under Part III of the EPA (Environmental Protection Act 1990).

The Environment Act 1995 provides an extension to Scotland of the framework for nuisance control under Part III of the Environmental Protection Act 1990 in England and Wales.

Noise abatement zones

Section 63 of the Control of Pollution Act 1974 provides local authorities with the powers to designate an area or part of an area as a noise abatement zone. There are inspection powers whereby the local authority is under a clear legal duty to inspect an area from time to time (s. 57(b) of the Control of Pollution Act 1974). There are comprehensive powers for procedures to draw up noise abatement zones. This includes serving notice on each owner advertising the noise abatement zone. There are also procedures for taking objections. This includes receiving written objections within six weeks, and proposing the order after considering all the relevant objections. The implications of making a noise abatement order are that the local authority is required to measure noise levels from premises within the area designated in the order (see: the Control of Noise (Measurement and Registers) Regulations 1976, SI 1976 No. 37). Records of measurements must be kept and copies of such records forwarded to the occupier or owner of premises. There is an appeal system (see: The Control of Noise (Appeals) Regulations 1975, SI 1975 No. 2116) to the Secretary of State for the Environment. The main sanction for breach of a noise level that is exceeded within a noise abatement zone is a court order. It is also a criminal offence.

The designation of a noise abatement zone requires the local authority to measure the noise levels and record these details in a Noise Level Register. This register must contain various details for each premises within the zone. Details of the address, particulars of noise and the dates on which each entry is made must be recorded (see: s. 64 of the 1974 Act).

Local authorities have a number of other powers available to them in respect of noise. The local authority may make *noise level determinations for new buildings*. This may involve the use of a noise abatement notice and the recording of acceptable noise must be registered in the Noise Level Register which sets out what is an acceptable noise level for the building. There are procedures for appeal and the serving of notice on the occupier or owner of premises. Local authorities may also make a *noise reduction notice* which may specify the time of day, the particular days required and the duration of noise levels. There are appeal procedures in respect of such a notice.

Miscellaneous noise controls

There are a variety of special provisions introduced to deal with specific problems of noise, e.g. construction site noise (see ss. 60 and 61 of the Control of Pollution Act 1974). This provides for the regulation of construction site noise and the serving of notice subject to the correct procedures.

Traffic noise falls under s. 1 of the Road Traffic Regulation Act 1984. Controls may be placed on traffic flows and for the restriction and regulation of heavy vehicles, e.g. access to town centres or through built-up areas or where there are schools and children playing. Vehicle noise is regulated under the Road Traffic Act 1988 and the Road Vehicles (Construction and Use) Regulations 1986, SI 1986 No. 1078. It is an offence to exceed the limits on noise prescribed by the regulations. Under the Noise and Statutory Nuisance Act 1993 (discussed below), it is a statutory nuisance to emit a noise from machinery, vehicle or equipment in a street.

Aircraft noise is the subject of specific regulation. Section 76 of the Civil Aviation Act 1982 exempts actions for trespass or nuisance in respect of the flight of aircraft over property. This exemption takes account of a number of factors such as the height of the aircraft, weather conditions and the ordinary circumstances of air travel, such as authorised flight paths, and that the aircraft is not flown in a dangerous manner. Also exempt under the Air Navigation Order (see: Air Navigation Order, SI 1989 No. 2004), made under the Civil Aviation Act 1982, are the conditions under which noise and vibration may be caused by aircraft on aerodromes. In the case of aircraft taking off and landing regulations are provided under the Air Navigation (General) Regulations 1981, SI 1981 No 57. The aircraft must satisfy certain safety requirements to come within the exemption from liability.

Outside the exemption there may be liability arising from the operation of aircraft. For example s. 76(2) of the Civil Aviation Act 1982 provides strict liability where items fall from the aircraft during take-off or landing or while in flight. This may also cover damage caused by sonic boom. Aircraft engine noise is regulated by the Air Navigation (Noise Certification) Order 1990, SI 1990 No. 1514. This order takes account of various EC Directives (see Directive 80/51 and 83/206).

Airport noise is regulated by a mixture of regulatory powers. The Secretary of State or the Civil Aviation Authority has various powers under the Civil Aviation Act 1982. These powers are of a miscellaneous variety in terms of the proper management of airports. Section 63 of the Airports Act 1986 provides powers to make by-laws including the control of aircraft operations and limits on the noise and vibration coming from the airport. The licensing functions of the Civil Aviation Authority may also include aerodromes. Licensing air operators is also a means of seeking to achieve standards of performance (see: the Air Navigation (Aeroplane and Aeroplane Engine Emissions of Unburned Hydro-carbons) Order, SI 1988 No. 1994). A general duty exists to minimise the effects on the environment, as far as it may be practicable, of noise, vibration, atmospheric pollution (see Chapter 12) or any other cause attributable to the civil aviation use of aircraft (see s. 68(3) of the Civil Aviation Act 1982).

Noise and neighbours

The Noise and Statutory Nuisance Act 1993, a private member's Bill, came into force on 5 January 1994. The 1993 Act provides local authorities with new powers to investigate and deal with noise nuisances that arise in streets. Noise emitted from a vehicle, machinery or equipment in the street may be a statutory nuisance. One important addition is the intrusive impact of burglar alarms. The 1993 Act reinforces controls contained under ss. 91 and 92 of the Control of Pollution Act 1974 in respect of rights of entry to premises to silence audible alarms. Abatement notices may be more conveniently served by fixing the notice to the vehicle, premises or machinery or equipment. The hours at which loudspeakers may be used in the street are also prescribed under s. 7 of the 1993 Act which amends s. 62 of the Control of Pollution Act 1974.

There is also a licensing system of public entertainment undertaken by local authorities. This is provided for in Sch. 1 of the Local Government (Miscellaneous Provisions) Act 1982. It applies automatically to indoor events with the exception of music associated with religious places or functions.

The Department of Environment working party (see: *Neighbouring Noise Working Party, Review of the Effectiveness of Neighbour Noise Controls* (DoE, 1995) has recommended new powers and a new offence of night-time disturbance, including confiscation powers to deal with the increasing problems of neighbourhood noise.

▶ Private law remedies

The citizen may rely on the powers of the local authority discussed above. It is also possible to take a private action for nuisance. The plaintiff must show on the balance of probabilities the existence of the noise that constitutes the nuisance. The courts may consider a variety of issues such as the nature of the locality, the duration of the noise, the harm suffered by the plaintiff and the social and economic consequences of the defendant's actions, and the state of mind of the defendant and the effects of noise on the plaintiff. Concluding whether there is a nuisance and setting damages or granting an injunction to stop the nuisance requires a careful balance of the issues in dispute. Individual action by a citizen may not be as effective as group action taken on behalf of a group of local residents (see: *Gillingham Borough Council* v. *Medway (Chatham) Dock Company Ltd* [1992] 3 WLR 449).

▶ Conclusions

Noise is fast becoming one of the worst effects of modern-day living. Schemes for proper noise insulation are becoming more common. There are grants available for noise installation in respect of aircraft noise and traffic noise. There are limited compensation schemes available under the Land Compensation Act 1973 in respect of highways or road schemes built after 17 October 1969. Highway authorities may undertake works to mitigate the consequences of traffic improvements or the building or updating of highways. The question of noise pollution is also a matter of public awareness and perception. Cost-effective measures to provide a sensible policy for noise reduction appear more attractive than attempts to control noise pollution. Van Wynsberghe estimates that 'some environmental noises are twice as intense as they were in the 1960s' and this intensity is expected to double every 10 years (Van Wynsberghe *et al.*, 1995, p. 514). The future of strategies for noise reduction lies in greater awareness of the risks to health of noise pollution and greater sensitivity to the needs of others.

▶ References and further reading

Department of the Environment (1995) *Noise Control: The Law and its Enforcement.* Shaw and Sons, Kent.

Kerse, C.S. (1995) *The Law Relating to Noise.* Oyez, London.

Leeson, J.D. (1995) *Environmental Law.* Pitman, London.

Miller, C. and Wood, C. (1983) *Planning and Pollution.* Clarendon Press, Oxford.

Ormondy, D. and Burridge, R. (1995) *Professional Practice Note.*
Penn, C.N. (1979) *Noise Control.* Shaw and Sons, Kent.
Van Wynsberghe, D., Noback, C.R. and Carola, R. (1995) *Human Anatomy and Physiology*, 3rd edn. McGraw-Hill Inc., New York.

▶ Reports

Annual Report of the Institution of Environmental Officers 1992/3.
Neighbouring Noise Working Party, Review of the Effectiveness of Neighbour Noise Controls (Department of Environment, 1995).
PPG24 Planning and Noise (HMSO, 1994).
Report of the Noise Review Working Party (HMSO, 1990).

PART V
Conclusions

14 The environment: future directions?

The future directions of environmental law resist easy prediction. Environmental law has continued to evolve in an organic way. Historically, environmental law grew out of a response to problems of pollution and the demands of public health. This evolutionary process has continued responding to new scientific developments and the development of new processes. Environmental law is becoming less reactive and more proactive. Towards the end of the twentieth century, it is clear that environmental law and regulation is dependent on scientific understanding and the continuous development of new techniques of assessing the quality of human development.

The challenge of environmental law in the 1990s

Environmental law retains many of the characteristics of its historical development. It is composed of many distinct core subjects such as contract, tort, criminal law and public law. Environmental law cases are heard before the ordinary courts, though the development of planning law and public inquiries has been an example of a growing specialism away from ordinary administrative law. It is also clear that environmental law draws on specific and specialist statutory provisions, such as public health legislation and statutes on the control of pollution. Significantly, in recent years environmental law has been subject to considerable change, reflecting changing attitudes among policy makers and politicians to environmental problems. Pressure groups and campaigns have an important impact in shaping and informing public opinion (see: Maloney and Jordan, 1995, pp. 1137–53). Such changes appear to provide environmental law with its own conceptual framework and distinct contribution to the way legal rules may be framed. Legal rules tend to rely on detection after the event of their breach. Courts provide an examination of what has occurred and only rarely evaluate future risks. Environmental law must attempt to predict outcomes and take steps in anticipation of risks. Principles such as 'the polluter pays', techniques such as 'eco-labelling' and the development of environmental impact assessment and integrated pollution control are examples of the distinct contribution environmental law is making to the general development of new concepts in law. Environmental lawyers place reliance on scientific data and methodology in measuring and understanding anthropogenic impacts on the environment and providing monitoring techniques. Science is used to help predict outcomes and deal with the impact, often unpredictable, of man's activities on the environment. Scientists will increasingly need to understand the impact of legal rules on the environment. Evolving legal rules to serve the needs of the scientist presents one of the formidable challenges for the future.

At international, European and national level, environmental policies are being shaped, albeit belatedly, that begin to take account of the challenges to the environment in the final years of the twentieth century and beyond the year 2000. The UN Earth Summit in 1992 drew attention to the need for international action to tackle global problems such as climate change, biodiversity and forest loss. This highlights the fact that man's environmental impacts do not recognise national boundaries and action is required on an international basis. The end of the twentieth century has seen the realisation that environmental protection and conservation rest heavily on the implementation of policies such as clean technology, waste minimisation and sustainable development. In January 1994 the UK government embarked on a national strategy for sustainable development (UK Annual Report: *This Common Inheritance*, Cm 2822 (HMSO, 1995)). The UN Commission on Sustainable Development met for the second time in New York during May 1994 and reviewed progress to date. The European Community's Fifth Action Programme provides a framework for action on sustainable development. The newly created European Environment Agency has in part been developed in recognition of the importance of information on the environment to environmental assessment and monitoring, and to verification of European Community Directives. The creation of the Environment Agency for England and Wales and the Scottish Environment Protection Agency recognises the importance of strategic planning for the future of the environment. Are such changes adequate to the challenges ahead? The lessons for future generations are summarised by Tolba *et al.* (1992):

> Concern for the environment is as old as human civilisation. History abounds with examples of the wide variations in human understanding of the environment and in our ability to maintain it in a healthy condition. Those societies that managed to provide their material, cultural and spiritual needs in a sustainable manner were those that succeeded in reconciling their needs and aspirations with the maintenance of a viable environment. Whenever the outer limits

of the physical environment were exceeded, civilizations declined or even vanished.

Sustainable development

A crucial part of the future strategy for the environment is sustainable development defined by the Brundtland Commission in 1987 as intended to meet 'the needs of the present without compromising the ability of future generations to meet their own needs'. The recent UK Annual Report, *This Common Inheritance* (see: Cm 2822 (HMSO, 1995, p. 12)), has noted that the common theme in the sustainable development strategy adopted by the government for the environment has been 'to establish more specific targets and objectives, together with quantified indicators of progress' for different parts of the environment (UK Strategy, 1994). Concerns about climate change and biodiversity (the United Kingdom ratified the Convention on Biological Diversity on 3 June 1994) are among future priorities.

There are a number of key elements in this strategy (see: Cm 2822 (HMSO, 1995, pp. 9–38)).

- A high priority to the definition of environmental objectives and targets.
- Publication of a set of indicators in areas such as air quality, water quality, land, wildlife and habitats and the impacts on these of social and economic change.
- Education about the environment including the consideration of the government's Panel on Sustainable Development.
- Priority to improve relationships between industry and government.
- Clarify the need for environmental regulation and the use of fiscal instruments including taxation of pollution.
- Set the agenda and priorities for sustainable development.
- To provide advice and recommendations on actions to achieve sustainable development.
- To promote strong economic development in harmony with true stewardship of the environment.

Objectives and strategies: techniques of environmental law

It is clear that setting objectives and adopting strategies for the environment is a multi-disciplinary task. Monitoring how environmental laws are obeyed is the first step. This is an evolutionary process whereby learning how procedures and processes work will help ensure a better understanding of regulation and law. Ensuring adequate enforcement of environmental law at national and European Community level sets immense challenges for the future of environmental law. It is also essential to set priorities that make environmental enforcement an essential value in society (Kramer, 1993, pp. vi–vii). There is a wider concern for the impact of pollutants on the biosphere as a whole.

In the chapters in Part I of the book we examined the variety of techniques and institutions that are involved in an attempt to resolve environmental problems. Concepts such as Best Practicable Means or the Best Practicable Environmental Option have become common in the articulation of principles of environmental law. As the Tenth Report of the Royal Commission (Tackling Pollution – Experience and Prospects, Cmnd 9149 (1984)) explained, the term involves the use of different sectors of the environment to minimise damage overall. In its widest context it involves a consideration of the financial implications in the calculation of the best practicable means to deal with environmental pollution. Section 7 of the Environmental Protection Act 1991 takes this concept further with the Best Available Techniques Not Entailing Excessive Costs (BATNEEC). This formulation considers what is economically possible, what is environmentally practical and what is legally achievable within existing legal powers. BATNEEC is adopted at national, European and international levels.

In environmental law other important techniques available include Integrated Pollution Control (IPC) and Environmental Impact Assessment (EIA) (Chapter 6). These are likely to dominate environmental law and science in the twenty-first century. Alan Gilpin has noted in his study of EIA throughout the world, that in 35 countries EIA systems are established and many are performing well.

> So how will EIA go in the twenty-first century? Certainly, the signs are favourable. All the countries which have adopted EIA systems have invariably made significant advances in economic growth since the 1970s, reflected in improved material well being and the health of entire societies. (Gilpin, 1995, p. 161)

The concept of Best Practical Environmental Option (BPEO) developed by the Royal Commission on Pollution (see: Fifth Report, Cmnd 6371) provides opportunities to set emission standards for specific proscribed processes and substances. This might encourage the development of scientific and technological responses to pollution control within a legal framework. In particular, emphasis might be placed on the following:

● The development of appropriate, perhaps continuous, monitoring procedures on discharges together with regular and effective monitoring of the receiving environment. This must be achieved within a realistic economic framework.

- Improved methods for assessing potential harm arising from a pollutant (or mixture of pollutants) at single species level and on the structure and functioning of ecosystems.
- The development and application of waste minimisation and clean technologies (i.e. the prevention of waste).

The aim is to limit damage to the environment to the greatest extent achievable subject to reasonable cost (Tromans, 1987). Currently the Royal Commission on Environmental Pollution is undertaking a study of the basis on which environmental quality standards are set (see: ENDS Report 243, April 1995, p. 3).

Setting standards is often controversial and may appear haphazard. There are many examples of different forms of standards setting, such as emission controls, or design standards such as eco-labelling and specifi- cations such as BS 7750. Considerable compromise is required for the setting of such standards, especially in the European and international context (see: ENDS Report 240, January 1995, pp. 25–7). Standard setting will inevitably be influenced by the sensitivity of monitoring equipment, but should more properly be based on a scientific assessment of the risk and hazard to ecosystems and organisms.

The techniques of predicting outcomes and consequences from existing data and information remain complex. Risk assessment techniques and mathematical modelling procedures attempt to establish predictive and quantitative assessments of the likely impact of man's activities on the local and global environment. It is on these predictions that future policies and regulations may be developed.

Scientists may have yet another role to perform in environmental monitoring, that is, determining the probable source of a pollutant incident. Evaluating who is responsible for environmental damage may involve a degree of scientific detective work, but may not necessarily provide solutions as to how to clean up the environment or prevent harm in the future. The principle that 'the polluter pays' may simply result in clean-up costs being borne by the end user, who is able to pass costs on to the consumer. Thus a notional environmental 'overhead' may be built into pricing mechanisms. This does not provide long-term benefits for the environment. Scientists must also contribute to environmental management by meeting the challenge inherent in the development of economic remediation and restoration techniques (Steele, 1995).

Environmental management techniques have adapted to accommodating a more problem-focused and policy-driven approach to the environment. Public education and forging interrelations between science and industry, government and law are an intrinsic part of the work of the environmental scientist today. Scientists may be able to determine the extent of 'harm' to the environment and suggest procedures to limit, control or ameliorate the harmful effects. This knowledge is, however, only truly valuable if it is used to inform industry, policy makers and the public realistically and fully. The creation of new agencies, the new Environment Agency and the Scottish Environment Protection Agency under the Environment Act 1995, and the European Environment Agency, is set to reflect public demands for standards setting and auditing of the environment – demands that must ultimately be met by scientists.

▶ Conclusions

Policy makers and politicians must face the important challenges that arise from many of the environmental problems discussed and highlighted in this book. The recent passage into law of the Environment Act 1995 is one illustration of the legal complexity that defines environmental law. Consisting of 24 schedules and 125 sections, the 1995 Act will be supplemented by numerous regulations, codes of guidance and ministerial guidance notes and circulars. It is a classic example of *ad hoc* and piecemeal reform. Under the 1995 Act recent statutes such as the Environmental Protection Act 1990 are amended and new sections inserted into major legislation such as the Water Resources Act 1991 and the Water Industry Act 1991. Environmental lawyers face a formidable challenge in interpreting the complexity of legislation. In the 1995 Act the opportunity was not taken to codify the law or provide coherent and clear principles in an easily readable and understandable form. A further challenge arises when in many instances the 1995 Act provides more powers to the relevant Secretary of State than hitherto, e.g. in the development of future policy for the Environment Agency or in defining the guidance in the definition and identification of contaminated land. Environment policy and law are intertwined, with the likely consequences of increased litigation.

There is also a further dimension to understanding environmental problems. All aspects of human activity, including agriculture, industry and population centres, impinge on the environment in which we live. Environmental problems transcend national, European and international legal systems. The global economy and the use of natural and energy resources must be confronted at every level, both local and global. The implementation of policies for sustainable development must measure the foreseen benefits as well as the detriments of man's activities, and attempt to predict unforeseen effects. Sustainable development must secure the best use of the world's resources measured in long-term as well as short-term strategies. Proactive rather than reactive policy making must be found in economic and scientific instruments that are sanctioned by law. Finally, environmental laws must take account of the consequences of scientific and technological achievements and the unpredictable nature of human endeavour.

▶ References and further reading

Gilpin, A. (1995) *Environmental Impact Assessment.* Cambridge University Press, Cambridge.

Haagsma, A. (1989) 'The European Community's Environmental Policy: a case-study in federalism'. *Fordham International Law Journal,* **12**, 311.

Hester, R.E. and Harrison, R.M. (eds) (1995) *Waste Treatment and Disposal.* The Royal Society of Chemistry, Cambridge.

Kerry Turner, R., Pearce, D. and Bateman, I. (1994) *Environmental Economics.* Harvester, London.

Kiss, A. and Shelton, S. (1993) *Manual of European Environmental Law.* Grotius, Cambridge.

Kramer, L. (1991) 'The implementation of environmental laws by the European Communities'. *German Yearbook of International Law,* **9**.

Kramer, L. (1992) *Focus on EEC Environmental Law* (London, 1992)

Kramer, L. (1993) *European Environmental Law Casebook.* Sweet and Maxwell, London.

Leeson, J.D. (1995) *Environmental Law,* Pitman, London.

Macrory, R. and Hollins, S. (1995) *A Source Book of European Community Environmental Law.* Clarendon Press, Oxford.

Maloney, W. and Jordan, G. (1995) 'Participation and the environment'. In *Contemporary Political Studies.*

Mannion, A.M. and Bowlby, S.R. (1992) *Environmental Issues in the 1990s,* John Wiley, Chichester.

Mungall, C. and McLaren, D. (eds) *Planet Under Stress.* Oxford University Press, Oxford.

O'Riordan, T. (ed). (1995) *Environmental Science for Environmental Management.* Longman, Essex.

Pearce, D.W. (ed.) (1991) *Blueprint 2: Greening the World Economy.* Earthscan, London.

Pearce, D.W. and Warford, J. (1992) *World Without End: Economics, Environment and Sustainable Development.* Oxford University Press, Oxford.

Rehbinder, E. and Stewart, R. (1995) *Environmental Protection Policy.* De Gruyter, New York.

Steele, J. (1995) 'Remedies and remediation: foundational issues in environmental liability'. *Modern Law Review,* **58**, 615.

Tolba, M. *et al.* (1992) *The World Environment 1972–1992.* Chapman & Hall, London.

Tromans, S. (1987) *Best Practicable Environmental Option – A New Jerusalem.* UKELA.

UK Strategy (1994) *Sustainable Development: the United Kingdom Strategy.* HMSO, London.

UK Annual Report (1995) *This Common Inheritance,* Cm 2822. HMSO.

United Nations (1992) *Agenda 21: The United Nation's Programme of Action from Rio.*

UNDP (1992) *Human Development Report 1992.* Oxford University Press, Oxford.

Winter, G. (1990) 'Perspectives for environmental law – entering the fourth phase' *Journal of Environmental Law* 1 (1), 42.

World Bank (1992) World Development Report 1992. Oxford University Press, Oxford.

World Commission on Environment and Development (1987) *Our Common Future.* Oxford University Press, Oxford.

List I and List II substances (EC Groundwater Directive 80/68/EEC)

▶ List I substances

List I contains the indvidual substances which belong to the families and groups of substances specified below, with the exception of those which are considered inappropriate to List I on the basis of a low-risk toxicity, persistence and bioaccumulation.

Such substances which with regard to toxicity, persistence and bio-accumulation are appropriate to List II are to be classed in List II.

1. Organohalogen compounds and substances which may form such compounds in the aquatic environment.
2. Organophosphorus compounds.
3. Organotin compounds.
4. Substances, the carcinogenic activity of which is exhibited in or by the aquatic environment. (Substances which are in List II which are carcinogenic are included here.)
5. Mercury and its compounds.
6. Cadmium and its compounds.
7. Persistent mineral oils and hydrocarbons of petroleum.
8. Persistent synthetic substances.

▶ List II substances

List II contains the individual substances and the categories of substances belonging to the families and groups of substances listed below which could have a harmful effect in groundwater. Where certain substances in List II are carcinogenic, mutagenic or teratogenic they are included in category 4 of List I.

1. The following metalloids and metals and their compounds:
   Zinc; Copper; Nickel; Chromium; Lead; Selenium; Arsenic; Antimony; Molybdenum; Titanium; Tin; Barium; Beryllium; Boron; Uranium; Vanadium; Cobalt; Thallium; Tellurium; Silver.
2. Biocides and their derivatives not appearing in List I.

3. Substances which have a deleterious effect on the taste and/or smell of products for human consumption derived from the aquatic environment compounds liable to give rise to substances in water.
4. Toxic or persistent organic compounds of silicon and substances which give rise to such compounds in water, excluding those which are biologically harmless or are rapidly converted in water to harmless substances.
5. Inorganic compounds of phosphorus and elemental phosphorus.
6. Non-persistent mineral oils and hydrocarbons of petroleum origin.
7. Cyanides, fluorides.
8. Certain substances which may have an adverse effect on the oxygen balance, particularly ammonia and nitrites.

Index

Entries in **bold** relate to definitions given in the main text.